ZIMBABWE'S CINEMATIC ARTS

ZIMBABWE'S
CINEMATIC ARTS

· ·

LANGUAGE, POWER, IDENTITY

KATRINA DALY THOMPSON

Indiana University Press
Bloomington and Indianapolis

This book is a publication of

Indiana University Press
601 North Morton Street
Bloomington, Indiana 47404-3797 USA

iupress.indiana.edu

Telephone orders 800-842-6796
Fax orders 812-855-7931

Library of Congress Cataloging-in-Publication Data

Thompson, Katrina Daly, [date]
Zimbabwe's cinematic arts : language, power, identity /
Katrina Daly Thompson.
p. cm.
Includes bibliographical references and index.
ISBN 978-0-253-00646-2 (cloth : alk. paper) — ISBN 978-0-253-00651-6 (pbk. : alk. paper)
— ISBN 978-0-253-00656-1 (electronic book) 1. Motion pictures and television—Social
aspects—Zimbabwe. 2. Mass media and language—Political aspects—Zimbabwe.
3. Zimbabwe. Broadcasting Services Act. 4. Motion picture industry—Zimbabwe—
Foreign influences. 5. Zimbabwe—Social conditions—1980– I. Title.
PN1993.5.Z55T48   2013
791.43'096891—dc23
2012028173

1 2 3 4 5   18 17 16 15 14 13

For my friends, family, and colleagues in Zimbabwe.

Pamberi nevanhu!

CONTENTS

ACKNOWLEDGMENTS

I owe a great deal to colleagues, students, friends, and members of my family who have helped extend my involvement in African studies, cultural studies, and applied linguistics and who have encouraged and enlightened me. I am grateful for funding from Fulbright-IIE, which enabled me to do research in Zimbabwe, as well as from the Academic Senate and the Dean of Humanities at UCLA, who provided me with time to write. Thanks also to Dee Mortensen, Marvin Keenan, and Sarah Jacobi at Indiana University Press for helping bring this book to fruition.

I would like to thank the professors who nurtured my interest in the verbal arts and in African studies. At Grinnell College, Saadi Simawe encouraged me to be an English major, while Christine Loflin, George Drake, and Roger Vetter introduced me to African literature, history, and music. At the University of Wisconsin–Madison, Magdalena Hauner and Antonia Schleicher nurtured my interest in African languages. Linda Hunter showed me that I need not choose between linguistics, literature, and other verbal arts, encouraged my interest in African popular cultures, and has served as a valuable mentor. Jim Delehanty, Aliko Songolo, Jo Ellen Fair, Dean Makuluni, Hemant Shah, and Shanti Kumar encouraged my research and gave invaluable feedback on drafts of this book. Judith Kaulem of the Scripps-Pitzer Program in Zimbabwe instilled in me a deep interest in Shona language and culture, which was further developed through work with Thompson Tsodzo, Albert Natsa, and Robert Chimedza at Michigan State University.

I owe a great debt to colleagues at the University of Zimbabwe, where I was welcomed into the Department of African Languages and Literature while conducting research. In particular, Pedzisai Mashiri, Rino Zhuwarara, Mickey Musiyiwa, Peniah Mabaso, and Aquilina Mawadza provided invaluable advice and assistance with the project.

At UCLA, my mentors Joseph Nagy and Vilma Ortiz have been incredibly generous with their time, offering very useful feedback on my writing and, more importantly, encouragement. I am also grateful to Susan Plann, Olga Yokoyama, Tom Hinnebusch, Andrew Apter, and Ned Alpers, who have helped me make an academic home at UCLA. Thanks also to students Michelle Oberman, Olga Ivanova, Deborah Dauda, and Nancy Gonzalez, who helped with data analysis and copyediting.

Friends and colleagues elsewhere have also helped with this book. Sally Campbell Galman, Heather Dubois Bourenane, and Jane Zavisca have been wonderful writing partners, as have anonymous members of my writing group on

Academic Ladder. Sarah Cypher at the Threepenny Editor gave me many helpful suggestions on an early version of the manuscript.

I am grateful to my mother, Brenda, my stepmother, Amy, my son, Coltrane, and numerous friends who have never stopped cheering me on. Thank you.

Finally, I would like to thank the families in Zimbabwe with whom I lived in 1996 and 2001, who made me feel at home and helped with my research. This book is dedicated to my Shona brothers, Netmore and Clemence, and to Lisa, Heidi, and Meghan, good friends with whom I explored Zimbabwe for the first time in 1996. Meghan, you are missed. *Ndatenda chaizvo!*

ABBREVIATIONS

AIASVF	An International African Stories Video Fair
BBC	British Broadcasting Corporation
BSA	Broadcasting Services Act
CAFU	Central African Film Unit
CCJP	Catholic Commission for Justice and Peace
CDA	critical discourse analysis
CFL	Central Film Laboratories
CFU	Colonial Film Unit
CGI	computer-generated imagery
CNN	Cable News Network
DSTV	digital satellite television
FBC	Federation Broadcasting Corporation
GALZ	Gays and Lesbians of Zimbabwe
GNU	Government of National Unity
IIFF	International Images Film Festival for Women
MABC	Munhumutapa African Broadcasting Corporation
MDC	Movement for Democratic Change
MFD	Media for Development Trust
MISA	Media Institute of Southern Africa
NBC	National Broadcasting Corporation (of the United States)
NDA	National Development Assembly
NGO	nongovernmental organization
PSI	Population Services International
RBC	Rhodesia Broadcasting Corporation
RTV	Rhodesian Television Limited
SABC	South African Broadcasting Corporation
SADC	Southern African Development Community
SFP	Short Film Project
UDI	Unilateral Declaration of Independence
URTNA	Union of National Radio and Television Organizations of Africa
ZAMPS	Zimbabwe All Media and Products Survey
ZANLA	Zimbabwe African National Liberation Army
ZAPU	Zimbabwe African Peoples Union

ZANU-PF	Zimbabwe African National Union–Patriotic Front
ZFVA	Zimbabwe Film and Video Association
ZBC	Zimbabwe Broadcasting Corporation
ZIFF	Zimbabwe International Film Festival
ZIPRA	Zimbabwe Peoples Revolution Army
ZTV	Zimbabwe Television

ZIMBABWE'S CINEMATIC ARTS

Cultural Identity in Discourse

This book offers a critical discussion about cultural identity in Zimbabwe by analyzing talk and texts about the cinematic arts. Zimbabwe's economic and political crises have been well documented by scholars and the Western media; I argue that a related cultural crisis is also under way. With a dual focus on cinematic texts and on discourse about them, this book shows that a reductive framework of foreign and local identities assigned to cultural products, as well as to those who produce and consume them, not only builds on a history of exclusion from Zimbabwe's national resources but also helps perpetuate current inequalities and consolidate an authoritarian state. Attention to marginalized discourse, however—talk produced by viewers and filmmakers—opens up possibilities for less polarized identities and more democratic futures.

Becoming Zimbabwean:
Understanding Identity as Socially Constructed

When we use talk or writing to communicate with others, we present ourselves in ways that construct our own and others' identities and produce meanings that may come to be shared. Cultural studies theorist Stuart Hall outlines two ways of understanding identity, the first of which focuses on the shared meanings that can develop through talk about national or cultural concerns. "The first position defines 'cultural identity' in terms of one shared culture, a sort of collective 'one true self,' hiding inside the many other, more superficial or artificially imposed 'selves,' which people with a shared history and ancestry hold in common." Hall argues that, although such a position ultimately offers only imagined identities, it remains important because of the critical role it played in struggles against colonialism. Moreover, "it continues to be a very powerful and creative force in emergent forms of representation among hitherto marginalized peoples" such as the cinema of black Caribbean filmmakers that Hall examines.[1]

The second view of cultural identity Hall offers is more complex and is the one on which this book is premised. Among people of shared ancestry or experience, "as well as the many points of similarity, there are also critical points of deep and significant difference which constitute 'what we really are'; or rather—since history has intervened—'what we have become.' . . . Cultural identity, in this second sense, is a matter of 'becoming' as well as of 'being.' It belongs to the future as much as to the past. It is not something which already exists, transcending place, time, history, and culture."[2] The concept of cultural identity as predicated on both similarities and differences is important not only for understanding identity as complex and variable but also for the critical project of exposing the use and misuse of imagined monolithic identities by those in power.

Hall offers a useful framework for understanding cultural identity as variable, but his focus on *becoming* doesn't tell us much about *how* cultural identity becomes what it is. Critical discourse analysis, however, shows how identity is constructed through talk and texts and what material effects it produces. By understanding the complex relationships between discourse, power, and identity, we can also explore resistance. "True" Zimbabweans are constructed through state discourse as black people with rural ties, belonging to a limited number of ethnolinguistic groups, supporters of the ruling party, and as opposed to the West. Can Zimbabweans construct other meanings that incorporate their racial, ethnic, linguistic, and political diversity and their complex relationship with the West? Unlike forms of scholarship that claim to present unbiased accounts, both cultural studies and a critical approach to language use acknowledge that all discourse—including academic analysis—is always biased and rejects "any possibility of critical distance or objectivity."[3] My aim is not to contribute to the accumulation of knowledge for its own sake but rather to critique how dominant discourse on Zimbabwe's cinematic arts and cultural identity maintains the interests of those in power and to explore other possibilities that are present in the marginalized discourse of filmmakers and viewers.

Creating and Questioning Identity:
Identities in Discourse

A conversation with a Zimbabwean filmmaker and a film review published in an English-language newspaper illustrate the contrast between these two ways of conceiving cultural identity, how they play out in discourse about Zimbabwe's cinematic arts, and one way of constructing a Zimbabwean identity, through race. In a 2001 conversation with filmmaker Simon Bright, who advocates a regional definition of "local" cinematic arts among the southern African states, I asked him, "Do you think that film can play any role in fostering a national identity, or will that be subsumed in a regional identity?" He responded with the example of his short film *Riches*, which had just come out:

> It depends on how you create an identity, but already *Riches* has provoked
> a sharp outburst from a film critic in the *Financial Gazette* regarding iden-
> tity. I'm quite happy with that reaction because I think . . . your identity

is strengthened in a number of ways, and one way is to have that identity questioned.

Admittedly, my own use of the word *fostering* unfortunately suggests that a national identity already exists and must simply be nourished. Bright's response, however, constructs identity in a way that differs strikingly from the sense in which early African filmmakers elsewhere used it and in which it continues to be used by the Zimbabwean state. Bright frames identity not as a preexisting, shared culture based on common ancestry that can be rediscovered but rather as something that is *created,* can be *strengthened,* and that benefits from being *questioned.*

The sharp outburst Bright refers to is an article by Grace Mutandwa, arts editor for the *Financial Gazette,* written after *Riches* premiered in Harare, Zimbabwe's capital, at the Vistarama cinema in early April 2001, and published in the 5–11 April 2001 issue. *Riches,* a short fiction film produced by Bright, directed by his wife, Ingrid Sinclair, and distributed by their production company, Zimmedia, is inspired by the life and writings of South African writer Bessie Head. It tells the story of a "coloured" (i.e., mixed race) woman from South Africa who moves to a Zimbabwean village to work as a teacher and struggles against the villagers' inhospitable treatment of her as a foreigner. In Mutandwa's review of *Riches,* titled "Movie a Mockery of Black Zimbabwean Women," she decried the film's depiction of rural black women as scared, weak, poverty-stricken, and ignorant of their rights.

> Any honest black Zimbabwean man or woman will tell you that what makes the flesh of this film is definitely not a true reflection of Zimbabwean life in the rural areas. . . . I wonder how the British High Commission feels about *Riches* considering that they poured 50000 pounds for its production. . . . Maybe Zimmedia should consult the people whose lives they turn into movies to ensure that they give a true representation, unless of course this is meant to be pure fiction.

Mutandwa does not mention Bright and Sinclair's whiteness, but she alludes to it by contrasting their cinematic construction of "Zimbabwean life in the rural areas" with what "any honest black Zimbabwean man or woman will tell you"; she constructs Bright and Sinclair as either dishonest, white, not Zimbabwean, or all three. This wording also constructs her own identity as an *honest black Zimbabwean woman* and functions as category entitlement, suggesting a prima facie truth-value. Working up category entitlement allows Mutandwa to claim the right to speak with authority and credibility on Zimbabwean rural life by virtue of her membership in the group *honest black Zimbabweans* and makes it unnecessary to explain how she knows what life is like in the rural areas. It also suggests consensus among black Zimbabweans, asserting that any one of them would corroborate her claims.

She constructs rural Zimbabwean life as a static and singular phenomenon which can and should be reflected truthfully, and film as a medium which should be used only to represent the truth. Her emphasis on truth and honesty serves to deflect undermining of her claims, since any black Zimbabwean who disagrees can be dismissed as dishonest, much as Mutandwa dismisses "pure fiction." Finally, her inclusion of details about the funding of the film not only constructs her review as factual but also rhetorically associates the film with a foreign country, its former colonizer, raising unspoken questions about the filmmaker's motives.[4]

The contrast between the two views of identity contained in these discourse samples is stark. Mutandwa constructs an imagined Zimbabwean life in line with the shared culture of people with a shared history and ancestry described by Stuart Hall. Although her emphasis on "black Zimbabweans" does leave room for people of other races to consider themselves Zimbabweans, as Bright and Sinclair do, it also suggests that cultural identity is primarily race-based, transcending other differences such as rural and urban experiences. Moreover, it also questions the ability of white Zimbabweans to "give a true representation" of black experi- ence, *the* black experience conceived in monolithic, essentialist terms. Conversely, Bright makes no claims about Zimbabwean identity, despite my somewhat leading question; instead, he focuses on the concept of *identity* itself. When he says that "your identity is strengthened" by being questioned, his impersonal use of the second-person possessive adjective *your* is unclear: does he see the film itself as questioning identity, and if so, what identity? Or does he see Mutandwa's response as questioning his or Sinclair's identity? Or both? This ambiguity adds to his sug- gestion that questions about identity may be more important than answers.

The way in which foreign and local identities are discursively mobilized by the state, filmmakers, critics, and viewers sheds light on how identities are, on the one hand, constructed and policed through legislation and state media and, on the other hand, reconstructed and resisted through independent media and everyday talk. A critical awareness of the powerful ideologies that underlie cultural legisla- tion not only points to the political importance of popular cultural forms such as films and television programs in everyday life, but also reveals resistance to hegemony, and points to avenues for democratic change. Such concerns are not particular to Zimbabwe; rather, the Zimbabwean case focuses our attention on the complex relationships among ideas about national sovereignty, democratic citizenship, and the role of the state in cultural policy. How these ideas are worked out in Zimbabwe will have a great influence on other African countries in the years to come.[5]

Serious Engagement with Processes of Culture and Power

By analyzing various texts—films, television programs, newspapers, legislation, and talk—from Zimbabwe in relation to power, this book responds to Jan Blommaert's call for critical analyses of discourse from countries outside of "the first world" and for a greater sense of history within critical discourse analysis. We cannot assume, he argues, that first-world "societies can usefully serve as a model for understanding discourse in the world today, for the world is far bigger than Europe and the USA, and substantial differences occur between different societies in the world."[6] The particular discourses of cinematic culture in Zimbabwe are shaped by its unique history: its experience of settler rule; the use of the cinematic arts as colonial propaganda; the involvement of whites, expatriates, and Hollywood in post-independence film production; racial, ethnic, linguistic, and geographic differences in access; and a multilingual globalized mediascape in which *Days of Our Lives* is viewed back-to-back with Shona local drama. The labeling of cinematic texts and the people who produce, broadcast, and view them as either foreign or local is part of this history, the analysis of which reveals ways in which power is discursively constructed, maintained, and challenged.

One way that both state discourse about the cinematic arts and the majority of cinematic texts themselves maintain the status quo is through the use of English, the first language of less than one percent of the population. An examination of culture and power would be incomplete without an analysis of the linguistic resources on which Zimbabweans draw as they make sense of their own and others' identities. This study pays attention to the use of both Shona and English in films such as *Yellow Card*, television talk shows such as *Talk to the Nation*, and in viewers' interpretive talk about cinematic texts, as well as through critical analysis of the *absence* of multilingualism as a concern in state discourse. While my own linguistic competence limits the scope of textual analysis to Shona and English talk and texts, these issues are of equal, perhaps greater, importance for Ndebele and the country's minority languages. Wherever possible I try to expand the discussion beyond "the dominant ethnic and racial groups—the Shona, the Ndebele, and the whites" to argue for a more complex approach to Zimbabwean identity that also includes minority groups and immigrant communities.[7]

Not only because of its focus on language use, my approach to cinematic arts in Zimbabwe differs in significant ways from other studies of African cinematic arts. Within film studies, scholars have often imagined an African cinema that spans the continent. Zimbabwe is usually mentioned only in passing in such studies, displaced by those countries with larger and more clearly "African" film industries such as South Africa, Mozambique, and the former French colonies in West Africa, where African film is defined—at least implicitly—as films made by black African directors. On the one hand, this neglect of Zimbabwe within African film studies is symptomatic of the very issue that this book takes as its focus: the involvement of foreign elements in the country's film industry, as Hollywood used the country as its set and expatriate white filmmakers established the local industry. On the other hand, when scholars *have* analyzed individual films from Zimbabwe, they take the localness of such films for granted despite the extensive involvement of foreigners in the country's film industry. In historical studies, scholars typically use as data archival documents produced by colonial filmmakers, invoking African audiences to help account for the perceived effects of colonial films on their viewers but rarely including the perspectives of audiences themselves.[8]

By way of contrast, the present book examines the role of foreign elements *in* the local culture as well as how these two terms are discursively treated by the media, the state, filmmakers, culture workers, and viewers. Rather than restricting analysis to discourse *about* Zimbabwean viewers, the research presented here focuses on conversations with viewers themselves. In addition, I include the perspectives of those in all levels of the film and television industries: actors, producers, screenwriters, cinematographers, directors, broadcasters, and distributors. Including such diverse perspectives provides an opportunity to contrast state policies and rhetoric about what it means to be local with the views of those whose livelihoods, creativity, leisure practices, and access to information are affected by such policies—those living through Zimbabwe's current crisis and its struggle for a cultural identity.

The Approach of This Book

This book investigates a series of connected themes through analyses of particular texts—films, television programs, and legislation—as well as the discourse of those who produce and use these texts. These themes coalesce in four ways. First, I take film and television, in this particular cultural context, as a unified field of inquiry under the label *cinematic arts*. Examining how these media are defined and discussed by Zimbabwean viewers and filmmakers, I look more at the similarities between film and television than I do at their distinctiveness, while recognizing that they have important differences, particularly in terms of access and distribution.

Second, I emphasize culture as a social process rather than a static phenomenon and use analysis of talk and texts as the means to show how culture is constructed through language. Be it through conversations, speeches, narratives, letters to the editor, television and film reviews, or legislation, both those in power and ordinary Zimbabweans are engaged in defining what it means to be Zimbabwean. Examining language use, on the one hand, means tracing the particular terms that are used to define Zimbabwean identity with regard to race, indigeneity, nationalism, patriotism, citizenship, ethnicity, totems, landowner-ship, and political party. On the other hand, it means paying attention to which languages are used in which contexts, who benefits from the use of a powerful language like English or a majority language like Shona, and who is excluded. Understanding how Zimbabweans and their government talk about the foreign and the local and the languages they use to do so is crucial to understanding con-temporary Zimbabwe.

Third, in terms of the time frame I examine, the book coalesces chronologi-cally around a particular piece of legislation enacted in 2001, the year in which I conducted my fieldwork and the majority of my interviews. The Broadcasting Services Bill had been introduced at the end of 2000 when I arrived in Zimbabwe on a Fulbright fellowship, and it quickly overtook my initial focus on Shona media. However, my decision to focus on the bill, later passed into law as the Broadcasting Services Act, was not simply a matter of timing. Rather, it became clear that dis-course about the bill in newspapers and among filmmakers throughout my time in the field was framed as a response to other "problems" in Zimbabwe's history of cinematic arts, such as the dominance of whites both behind and in front of the camera in most film and television that Zimbabweans watch, and these problems echoed other race-based disparities. The state's role in television broadcasting reveals its concern with nationalizing the media through greater representation of the black majority, a project that began at independence and is still necessary today. And yet the need for revenue—whether through advertising, bringing in American dollars via Hollywood crews, or simply saving money by not producing local content—has always been a counterforce that results in more foreign than local films and television programs on Zimbabwe's screens.

Fourth, this book is concerned with power. Historically, film and television have been seen as powerful media, with powers greater than the printed word to influence people's perceptions, opinions, and behaviors. Throughout Africa and elsewhere, during white rule this belief led to the use of film as a means to spread colonial propaganda and to try to mold viewers' identities as colonial sub-jects. Television, introduced around the time of independence in many African countries, also became a means of spreading the viewpoints of those in power. In Zimbabwe, television was introduced during white rule and controlled by the Rhodesian UDI government; its use as a tool of government propaganda did not change when it was taken over by a black government in 1980. Ethnographic studies of film and television viewers all over the world have demonstrated that although the cinematic arts are powerful in the sense that they play an important role in people's lives, they do not have a monolithic influence on viewers, who actively interpret what they watch, and may bring to them different meanings than were intended by filmmakers or expected by government censors. The relation-ship of repressive governments to the cinematic arts demonstrates the importance of what viewers do, or might do, with cinematic texts. Local cinematic texts are censored so that Zimbabwean television viewers see only what the government wants them to see, foreign filmmakers are prevented from working in the country, and local filmmakers can be harassed, arrested, tortured, and even killed for producing images the government doesn't want seen. These facts point not only to the government's power to control the cinematic arts but also to the power of these arts themselves and the potential power of viewers, who, the government seems to fear, would rise up if they had access to uncensored information. The dominant themes in this discourse are the relationship between film and television as powerful texts, the government as a powerful agent with the ability to control people's access to these texts, and viewers as supposed victims of Western cultural imperialism and propaganda from which they must be protected by their government. These themes play out in discourse produced by the state in newspapers and legislation as well as in talk and texts produced by filmmakers and viewers. While Zimbabweans have very little power in the face of a repressive state, their continued use of, production of, and talk about film and television reveal their ability to critique both imported and local texts in ways that undermine state rhetoric about what it means to be a Zimbabwean.

The discourses surrounding film and television not only shed light on how Zimbabweans view motion pictures, but they also have a wider application as fascinating sites for exploring ideological constructions of local and international identities. Chapter 1 introduces dichotomies that are used as major themes in discourse about Zimbabwean identities and its cinematic arts. The terms *foreign* and *local* are constructed through discourse, allowing people to construct their own identities vis-à-vis their claims about what it means to be Shona, black, Zimbabwean, African, or whatever the case may be. Chapter 2 examines Zimbabwe's cinematic arts during the twenty-one years between independence (1980) and the Broadcasting Services Act (2001), showing how both film and television developed in relation to, and sometimes in response to, colonial cinematic history. Chapter 3 offers a deeper look at the post-independence cinematic arts through a focus on film. The examination of viewers' talk and writing about such films demonstrates that Zimbabweans bring their culture to bear on the cinematic texts they watch, effectively "localizing" them as well as using them to author their own meanings of "local" and "Zimbabwean." Chapter 4 examines the immense popularity of imported soap operas and the interpretations that Zimbabwean viewers and critics bring to these programs as they contrast them with local content and with "factual" programming produced by the state. Chapter 5 examines the political implications of discourse about the cinematic arts by analyzing the text of the 2001 Broadcasting Services Act and the response to it in local newspapers and culture workers' talk. Chapter 6 analyzes an event when viewers used television as their medium, and language choice as their means to disrupt state discourse. It shows us a vision of how things could be different in Zimbabwe and the role that ordinary Zimbabweans can play in creating social change through discourse. Finally, in my conclusion, I use news coverage, recent scholarship, and new interviews with culture workers to offer an update on the current political context, a description of how film and television have developed since 2001, and a vision of an "ethically argued preferred future" for Zimbabwe's cinematic arts and national culture.[9] Listening to independent discourse, multiple voices in multiple languages, may be the key to a more democratic construction of ordinary people's identities, a cinematic culture that better represents all Zimbabweans, and an inclusive national identity.

CHAPTER 1

• • • • • • •

A Crisis of Representation

We're in a crisis. Zimbabwe as a nation, as an emerging new nation, needs to find its identity.

—Actor Edgar Langeveldt speaking at the
Book Café in Harare, 8 August 2001

One evening each week in a Shona village in Chiweshe Communal Lands in northeast Zimbabwe, Mrs. Jaunda* gathers up her five children and walks down the dusty road to her neighbor's yard. There they join some thirty adults and children in the *kicheni*, a round kitchen building still smoky from the family's supper. Gathered around the fireplace, instead of participating in their usual conversation and storytelling, the group is fixated on a small black-and-white television powered by a car battery, enjoying *Mvengemvenge*, a program of Zimbabwean music videos. They raucously comment on the latest songs, comparing preferences for one performer over another, laughing, and occasionally imitating a dance move. The shows they watch, and their talk about them, are discourse.

In a high-density suburb of Kadoma, a small city near the center of Zimbabwe, Mrs. Kaseke turns on the television in the living room as soon as she wakes up in the morning, and it stays on all day. She and her daughters catch snippets of *Oprah*, children's cartoons, and music videos while they polish the floors, prepare meals, and fold laundry. When Mr. Kaseke comes home from work, he sits in front of the TV and catches up with his family on the day's events, the children's progress at school, and news brought by visitors who happened by. The television drowns out the sounds of similar conversations in their neighbors' homes. The parents eat their evening meal in front of the TV, having their own quiet conversation while their four children eat at the dining room table. During and after dinner, they watch the evening news. Mrs. Kaseke watches the Ndebele news, Mr. Kaseke watches the Shona news, and the children join them to watch the English news. Later, the whole family watches the American soap *Days of Our Lives* while taking care of other tasks. The children do their homework, Mr. Kaseke reads the newspaper, and Mrs. Kaseke makes doilies that she will later sell. The older children stay up talking and watching TV until the Zimbabwe Broadcasting Corporation shuts down after midnight. The shows they watch, and their talk about them, are discourse.

---

*All names of viewers have been changed.

In Mablereign, a low-density suburb of Harare, Zimbabwe's capital, two teenage boys rent Eddie Murphy's *Coming to America* (1988) on video and watch it on their large color television. They talk with surprise and amusement about the film's representation of Africa as a place where elephants and other wild animals roam the grounds of the palace where Murphy's character grows up, and they are fascinated but somewhat bewildered by the comic representation of African Americans in the film. The family's domestic worker, who does not speak English, watches without paying full attention, and occasionally the boys translate or explain to her a few funny lines. Later that evening, while the boys do their homework in another room, she watches the Shona news and "local drama" while chatting with the boys' mother, both women savoring some relaxation after their work-filled days. The movies and shows they watch, and their talk about them, are discourse.

In 1996 I lived with these three families while studying Shona language and culture and Zimbabwean literature. I developed a strong interest in Zimbabwean written literature, but I realized that the people with whom I lived had almost no experience of it. In contrast, the cinematic arts played an important part in their lives and their conversations, even when the availability of electricity, leisure time, and disposable income limited their access to the programs and films they enjoyed so much. Through cinematic texts, they accessed locally produced and international discourse about the world; in conversation about what they watched, they not only interpreted such discourse but also created their own.

Four years later, in 2000, I returned to conduct fieldwork in Zimbabwe on the cinematic arts. I spent nine months watching television and films with these and other families, working with *Africa Film & TV* magazine and with a mobile cinema project that showed films to audiences in low-income high-density areas, and talking with people about their experiences of the country's cinematic culture. I spoke with filmmakers, producers, broadcasters, actors, festival directors, distributors, writers, government officials, and most importantly, ordinary people who watch films and TV—Shona villagers in Chiweshe, Shona and Ndebele speakers in Kadoma, and (mostly Shona) residents of Chitungwiza, Glen Norah, and Mbare, Harare's largest and poorest suburbs. Put into cultural context, these conversations can help us understand how Zimbabwean identity is being made. In contrast to the public discourse on foreign versus local cultures to be found in government publications, print media, and public debates among scholars and artists, viewers suggest that foreign and local elements are inextricably intertwined. The analysis of texts and talk about local and foreign cinematic arts becomes a lens for addressing questions of identity and belonging, questions that are central not only to Zimbabweans' experience of film and television but also to their representation *in* these media and by their government.

Overwording: A Problematic History

This book examines the many conversations that arise from Zimbabwean cinematic arts, the key people who engage in them, and what they say about what it means to be Zimbabwean. My analysis is based on fieldwork undertaken in 2001, the year a restrictive broadcasting services act was passed that defined and elevated a prejudice against foreignness into law. I offer case studies of viewers talking and writing about various cinematic texts. These texts include imported and locally made TV programming in various genres, films made in Zimbabwe by diverse crews, and films and TV programs in indigenous languages as well as in English. The analysis reveals both continuities and ruptures between government discourse and the talk of viewers who are ordinary Zimbabweans. Government discourse pathologizes foreign images; viewers articulate a much more complex and varied stance toward foreign and local cultures.

A central argument of this book is that the category *local* is not an a priori one into which a person, a cultural object, or practice automatically falls. Imported artifacts pervade Zimbabwe's culture because of its history of British and South African settlers and more recent globalization: British tea-drinking, street names, and educational structure; Chinese restaurants; Hindu temples; and Kentucky Fried Chicken are just a few examples. These elements originated elsewhere, but most Zimbabweans no longer consider them foreign. Instead, they are parts of everyday life, not indigenous but nevertheless local. They demonstrate Arjun Appadurai's claim that "at least as rapidly as forces from various metropolises are brought into new societies they tend to become indigenized in one or another way."[1] Imported cinematic texts such as *Coming to America, Oprah,* or CNN news are often similarly indigenized, simultaneously both foreign and part of a local culture. Particular films or TV programs are not inherently or essentially local or foreign, no matter their sites of production or consumption. Instead, they become local (or don't) through the talk and writing of those who produce, consume, critique, and legislate them.

The indigenization, or local mediation, of foreign media resources by both filmmakers and viewers has been documented in numerous countries where U.S. programming dominates. For example, in Trinidad in the early 1990s, people scheduled their days around viewing *The Young and the Restless* and used the program to construct their identities as global consumers. In the Philippines, filmmakers adopted studio, star, and genre systems, as well as iconography, from Hollywood cinema, but retained local melodramatic traditions and ideological values. In Israel, viewers critically analyzed *Dallas* and used it as a conversational resource across ethnic lines. Despite claims that American programming is imperializing the world, research continues to show that viewers the world over use such programming in unintended and complex ways. Such programming may begin as foreign, but it often becomes local through viewers' discourse.[2]

Similarly, in Zimbabwean public discourse, culture is often framed in terms of a foreign vs. local dichotomy, while in practice most cultural elements are better understood as both foreign and local. Regardless of the definitions of *foreign* and *local* used, both foreign and local films and TV programs are produced, legislated, distributed, viewed, discussed, and enjoyed in the country by both foreign and local people. In fact, viewers are more accepting of foreign elements on television than in any other media. Moreover, an individual film or TV program, and even an individual filmmaker, might be considered foreign by some Zimbabweans and local by others, depending on the criteria used to define these fluid terms.[3]

The categories of foreign and local applied to cinematic texts and other media are part of a broader Zimbabwean discourse marked by dichotomies that divide rural from urban people, blacks from whites, citizens from aliens, and those loyal to the ruling party from those who seek democratic change. These dichotomies are central to discourse in Zimbabwe and yet also extremely slippery.

The centrality of the foreign/local dichotomy to Zimbabwean discourse is reflected in the frequency with which foreign and local cultural elements are discussed in public forums. *Foreign* and *local* have become what critical discourse analyst Norman Fairclough calls "culturally salient 'keywords.'" A diverse vocabulary has developed to encompass these contrasted terms through a process of overwording, "a sign of intense preoccupation with a particular ideology."[4]

Thomas Turino, in a study of the discourse of globalism, shows that through "the highly redundant juxtaposition of a particular set of terms"—in this case foreign/local, colonial/independent, white/black, modern/traditional, urban/rural—"within public discourse across a variety of fields," over time "strong indexical relations are established between the paired terms such that one can come to replace the other,"[5] so that words like *foreign* and *colonial* are used as equivalents. For example, on 13 April 2000, the *Financial Gazette,* a Zimbabwean newspaper, reported that President Robert Mugabe called Movement for Democratic Change leader Morgan Tsvangirai a "puppet of the British." In doing so, he associated his opponent not only with foreign funding but also specifically with the former colonial power. Winning public acceptance for a unilateral definition of the ideal Zimbabwean serves Mugabe's interests. In speech after speech, and through state-owned newspapers and TV programs that endlessly quote him, he decries the West, Britain, foreigners, whites, the opposition, and the independent press. Analysis of how similar labels were used in pre-independence discourse illustrates the extent to which his rhetoric has been ironically "colonized" by these words' histories. Moreover, attention to the ways in which filmmakers and viewers resist the dominant meanings of these words suggests that Mugabe's hegemony is far from complete.

Historically, the dichotomy between foreign and local emerged when the country was still Southern Rhodesia (1901–65). Diana Jeater's work on the politics of translation between English and Shona in the early twentieth century demonstrates how both indigenous people and white settlers referred to one another using variants of these terms. For example, English-language texts for white audiences referred to local people as natives, but in the Shona translations *natives* was rendered as *vatema*, "black people." Whereas Shona speakers at that time referred to themselves simply as *vanhu*, "people," the colonial translation imposed "a skin color–based categorization of peoples that was not found at all in indigenous modes of thought." Similarly, in translations whites named themselves with a Shona term borrowed from Nguni, *varumbi*, which meant "bosses," while Shona speakers referred to whites as *mabvakure*, "those who come from somewhere else," emphasizing their foreignness.[6] Translation and naming are linked with ideologies of class, race, difference, and social context.

The term *alien* offers another example. *Alien* was frequently used both in the realm of politics and in filmmaking to describe other African locales beyond the country's or region's borders. For example, the settler government distinguished between Africans indigenous to the country and "alien natives," Africans coming from neighboring countries, who in fact constituted the majority of the African population until the 1950s in the capital, Salisbury (now Harare). It was not just people who were considered alien, but also film locales and films themselves. For example, when the Central African Film Unit (CAFU) was screening films in Southern Rhodesia, Northern Rhodesia (now Zambia), and Nyasaland (now Malawi) from 1948 to 1963, it labeled those produced outside of the Central African Federation as alien, finding that "films with an alien setting were usually less popular" and "alien to Central African concerns."[7] One can surmise that "Central African concerns" were the concerns of the settler government, not those of the indigenous peoples they governed. In contrast to the term *local*, *alien* suggests not only foreignness but also strangeness, inappropriateness, and even threat.[8]

Uses of the label *alien* in different contexts reveal how the word was applied in contradictory ways. For example, during minority rule, cultural nationalists argued that "the vernaculars were 'alien' and had been appropriated by Europeans," becoming more "colonial" than English. In contrast to the alien vernaculars, English was seen as the language of local economic advancement and even, during the war of liberation, the language of revolution, because "guerrillas came from different linguistic groups and English was the only language that they could use amongst themselves and with those from the organisations that were funding the liberation movement."[9] This example shows that conceptions of alienness led to a language policy that favors English, which impacts the languages used in the cinematic arts.

While *alien* typically referred to foreignness within Southern Rhodesia, the term *overseas* was used for more distant foreign locales. In British English, *overseas* has historically referred to "anywhere unspecifically not in 'U.K.'"[10] In Rhodesian English its meaning was even broader: beyond Africa, usually in Europe or the United States. Louis Nell, a producer for the CAFU in the 1940s, writes proudly about Geoffrey Mangin's color travel promotion documentaries, *Wish You Were Here* and *Fairest Africa,* as "the first Southern Rhodesian films to obtain cinema release in South Africa and overseas."[11] While *overseas* was mostly a neutral term, already overseas film industries were having a negative effect on filmmaking within the country: cinemas in Southern Rhodesia would not show locally made films such as Mangin's because "their agreements with their overseas distributors did not allow them to screen films from any other source."[12] Such agreements continued to impact film distribution in cinemas in 2001.

The foreign/local distinction, closely linked to film, television, and other media, continued during the Unilateral Declaration of Independence (UDI) period (1965–79), when terms associated with foreignness often developed a negative connotation. After declaring Rhodesia's independence from Britain, Ian Smith's Rhodesian Front government became very concerned with its image "overseas," especially in Western Europe, North America, and the former British colonies. It used film and television broadcasts to project a positive image of itself to these audiences. "There might have been visitors and odd amateurs sending over distorted stories" to Europe and America, Rhodesians worried. In order to control how they were represented, the UDI government hired private production houses to produce short newsreels for European and American television news. Mangin recalls: "We felt that if we continued to send accurate progressive ones, these would keep their world viewers correctly informed about the true facts of a peaceful Southern Africa."[13] The idea that the cinematic arts could be used to construct Southern Africa as "peaceful" during both apartheid in South Africa and a violent struggle for independence in Rhodesia highlights how discourse can be used to support those in power.

Overseas concerns were contrasted with "internal services," a division of the Ministry of Information that oversaw the various media intended for black viewers within Rhodesia. The propaganda role of Rhodesian media was perceived as threatened by externally produced media that would undermine its credibility. "Potential listeners had access to broadcasts from overseas or from neighbouring countries where a 'voice of Zimbabwe' could be heard," providing an alternative source of information.[14] For example, during the liberation war, Voice of Mozambique played Zimbabwean music and speeches from Zimbabwe African National Union (ZANU) leaders, which were heard not only in the frontline camps but also inside Zimbabwe along its border with Mozambique. Foreignness clearly depends on one's point of view. For whites who saw themselves as Rhodesians, radio programming by black Zimbabwean "terrorists" (as they often were called) in Mozambique was indeed foreign and fed into the perception of foreign media as a threat. But for blacks and other freedom fighters who saw themselves as Zimbabweans, such media were inextricably "indigenous," no matter where they originated.

Zimbabwe became independent in 1980. The new government, ruled by the Zimbabwe African National Union–Patriotic Front, or ZANU-PF, and led by Robert Mugabe as prime minister and later president, took control of the Rhodesian Broadcasting Corporation, renaming it the Zimbabwe Broadcasting Corporation and effectively inverting the definitions of *foreign* and *local*.

Many of the terms used to denote the foreign by white settlers before independence have been revamped during the current crisis in Zimbabwe. Whereas the settler government referred to "alien natives," the ZANU-PF government now effectively defines aliens as "those constituting a real or imagined political threat to the ruling party."[15] Moreover, many farmworkers from immigrant or other minority ethnic groups have been categorized as alien in order to deny their land claims, even if they have lived in the country for many generations. Labeling certain ethnic groups or other constituencies as alien impacts media policies that are designed to protect the local, by defining local interests as those of the ruling party's supporters.

Unsurprisingly, the term *colonial* has become a descriptor that not only denotes "of, belonging to, or relating to a colony," but also connotes a derogatory meaning. For example, Ndebele was constructed as a "colonial language" by early Shona cultural nationalists who believed it was an "inauthentic" mixture of Zulu and Kalanga created by Europeans, and therefore they saw it "as promoting European values under the guise of so-called indigenous languages."[16] Recently, the word *colonial* has been used to describe the mind-set of anyone who disagrees with the ruling party. For example, during the run-up to the 2000 parliamentary elections, state-owned television news and other media depicted the opposition party, the Movement for Democratic Change, as "a front for white Rhodesian, British colonial, and other Western imperial interests plotting to overthrow the ZANU-PF government."[17] The term *Eurocentric* often stands in for *colonial* in dominant discourse: Pedzisai Mashiri notes that in many Zimbabwean television dramas, "ideological and legal changes that challenge the status quo and facilitate the empowerment of women and gender equality are depicted as Eurocentric and destructive."[18] The use of *Eurocentric* to describe progressive locally made programs amid the large number of imported TV programs featuring white characters in American, British, and Australian settings illustrates how the selective use of dichotomies serves the interest of those in power.

The differences between competing views of what it means to be Zimbabwean are articulated not only in language but also in the organization of state institutions that control the meaning of categories such as foreign, local, white, black, citizen, alien, colonist, and terrorist. Institutions such as the Ministry of Information create laws that define *local* in ways that serve the values and interests of the ruling party, and they use other state-controlled institutions, such as Zimbabwe Television (ZTV), to disseminate their definitions.

Agents of these official organs seek to explain and justify media restrictions in terms of nationalism, tradition, and racial difference, but viewers and culture workers often see broadcasting regulation in radically different terms. It is, for example, repressive of immigrants, supporters of the Movement for Democratic Change, producers of cinematic texts that criticize the ruling party, white filmmakers who have helped establish the local film industry, and viewers who want access to uncensored information. The discourses developed to represent these interests seek, among other things, to redefine what constitutes the local and the foreign by taking into account racism, globalization, and human rights. The redefinition of these terms within the country's cinematic culture has had important implications for those who are rhetorically labeled "enemies of the state" by Mugabe and therefore for questions of national identity and belonging.

Redefining Citizenship: Who Belongs in Zimbabwe?

Citizenship—both literal and figurative—was an important signifier for localness before independence, and it is even more important today. Before and during the UDI period, black Zimbabweans were treated as second-class citizens despite early attempts by the British to prepare them for "citizenship of the Empire."[19]

Eight years after independence, in a report titled "The Democratization of the Media in Independent Zimbabwe," the new government prided itself on having made "great strides in making the mass media responsive to the needs of the majority of its citizens."[20] The phrase *the majority of its citizens* is used interchangeably with *the black majority*, but defining the majority solely in terms of race ignores the ways in which Zimbabweans' interests may not be served by the mass media. For example, most news stories on television cover events in Harare, the country's capital, which is in Mashonaland, and therefore Ndebele speakers and other ethnolinguistic minorities are unlikely to appear. In contrast to actors and politicians of Shona background, Ndebele people—let alone people from smaller ethnic groups—are seldom found in film or television, and their languages are rarely used. Similarly, the majority of Zimbabweans are rural people, whose access to the mass media is often limited by technology, money, leisure time, and language.

Citizenship has recently been redefined both rhetorically and through legislation to further restrict definitions of who qualifies as Zimbabwean and who as alien. Horace Campbell writes of alien farm workers: "After UDI in 1965, more than 54 percent of rural workers were from neighboring countries. Their children, who were born in Zimbabwe, have no real legal status. Even second- and third-generation workers carry identification cards bearing the designation 'alien.'"[21] Moreover, in preparation for the 2002 presidential elections, the government passed the 2001 Citizenship Amendment Act, which revoked the Zimbabwean citizenship of anyone who failed to formally renounce dual citizenship held else-where, effectively denying between 5,000 and 100,000 people—both whites with British citizenship and the farmworkers that Campbell describes—the right to vote, own land, or apply for a broadcasting license. Amanda Hammar writes that, for Mugabe and his spokesmen, "only the deeply rural, that is those who adhere to their 'traditional roots in the village' and who are still in possession of their totems, can be considered 'true' citizens of Zimbabwe."[22]

In 2001 I attended a public discussion of the new Broadcasting Services Act (BSA) at Harare's Book Café, a popular spot for culture workers and students, where novelist and poet Chenjerai Hove connected the issue of citizenship to the government's attempt to legislate local film and television. "There is a way in which people want to believe that those who have no totems are not Zimbabweans," he said, referring to the belief that Shona and Ndebele people have a patrilineal asso-ciation with an animal whose meat they are forbidden to eat and which symbolizes the unity of a group that shares the same ancestor. A focus on totems denies a Zimbabwean identity to both whites and migrants. Hove continued,

> People want to have the fiction of thinking that Malawians and Zambians are a very small percentage of our country. But I know they are at least thirty percent of the population of this country. Now if they want to do a film in this country about their experiences—since they have been here for generations—it would probably not have a chance to be shown on television, because our local content is . . . only those who have a totem must be on television.[23]

Hove spoke of an unofficial policy of exclusion based on long-held cultural tradi-tions, further evidence of the current government's equation of "totemic identity with national citizenship," an equation "carefully crafted in the politics of exclu-sion to turn whites and non-indigenous blacks into disposable residents of the state."[24]

Hove's comments offer an example of how citizenship—whether based on totemic identity or otherwise—has also become a legal criterion for participation in the production of documentary films and other news coverage. The Access to Information and Protection of Privacy Act of 2002 requires all journalists to register with the Ministry of Information, and one must be a citizen to register. News agencies based outside of Zimbabwe have been excluded from access to the country through such legislation, which effectively hinders not only report-ing on Zimbabwe beyond its borders but also Zimbabweans' access to news not produced by their government.

It is telling that African Americans have escaped the anti-foreign sentiment that Mugabe has attempted to foster in Zimbabwe. This was clear, for example, in Vinette Pryce's article in the *New York Amsterdam News* on 14 September 2000 titled, "Harlem Hails Harare, Havana," in which she quotes from Mugabe's address to a group of African Americans in Harlem. He told them, "Come home. Come home to render service, or in intellectual and emotional terms, come home. Their [Black Zimbabweans'] destiny is your destiny. We are a perfectly united family now. Those who separated us have been vanquished. There is oneness between us." Mugabe's welcoming approach to African Americans is based solely on race, the inverse of his attempts to render whites as foreigners and colonialists. Moreover, he ignores the literal foreignness of African Americans and therefore demonstrates how the labels *foreign* and *local* have more to do with allegiance and affiliation than with national identity or cultural affinity. This stance has led to a major inconsistency in the country's film and television culture: Western productions are criticized by the government for culturally dominating Zimbabwean viewers, but productions starring African American actors are sought out by the government broadcaster. This practice ignores major differences between African American and black Zimbabwean cultures as well as the role of white American television executives in such productions.[25]

What Is "Local Culture"?

Questions of who belongs in Zimbabwe illustrate what media studies scholar Kedmon Hungwe has called the "problematic" of identifying what the term *local culture* means in Zimbabwe. However, in his own study of media use in the country's primary schools, Hungwe sidesteps this problem by fixing local culture as "African culture," where *African* is used exclusively to mean black. "If attention is confined to the needs of rural areas, where the vast majority of the people live, and which are the main target of educational expansion, it becomes possible to restrict the definition of culture, within the context of this study, to African culture."[26]

The foreign/local dichotomy in this example overlaps with an urban/rural one. Rural people are perceived and constructed as less tainted by colonial culture, more clearly indigenous, and with moral rights to Zimbabwe's land; therefore, they epitomize the "authentic" local. Rural Zimbabweans are constructed as the ideal viewers of Zimbabwean cinematic texts and their relative lack of access to them as evidence that Zimbabwe has no cinematic culture. In contrast, urban people are perceived as multicultural, contaminated by "colonial culture" and proximity to whiteness, and as having greater access to imported goods and media; therefore, they epitomize the foreign.

Although many Zimbabweans use the word *African* to mean "black African," there are also those who deliberately use the words *African* and *Zimbabwean* to include all Zimbabwean citizens, including whites. For example, in 1982 white filmmaker Simon Bright convened a workshop at Audiovisual Services that resulted in the founding of the Zimbabwe Film and Video Association, the goal of which was "to try to increase the number of African films shown in Zimbabwe on TV and in cinemas,"[27] no doubt including Bright's own productions. Whites who want to live in Zimbabwe have a stake in defining African and Zimbabwean identities without reference to racial categories.

Such examples of whites discursively constructed as "African" are, however, relatively rare. As with other terms, the meaning of the word *white* and its relation to the idea of *foreign* is variously broadened or narrowed to meet the biases of the speaker. In government discourse, whiteness is evoked by terms such as *settler, expatriate,* or *commercial farmer.* For example, the supposed foreignness of Zimbabwean whites is extended to others associated with them, both within Zimbabwe—such as the "alien" farmworkers discussed above—or beyond, as when Mugabe added South African Jews to his list of enemies in 2001. In the same year, the *Scotsman* of 20 November quoted Mugabe describing the murder of ruling party leader Cain Nkala as "the brutal outcome of a much wider terrorist plot by internal and external terrorist forces with plenty of funding from some commercial farmers and organizations . . . like the Westminster Foundation, which we have established beyond doubt gets its dirty money from dirty tricks, from the British Labour Party, the Conservative Party and Liberal Party and also of course from the government of Tony Blair." Here Mugabe links whites not only to Britain but also to terrorism, murder, and brutality. This speech marked Mugabe's turn toward frequent talk about a "war on terror," ironically capitalizing on a discourse imported from President George W. Bush's post-9/11 rhetoric. Eric Worby has documented the increase in the use of the words *terror* and *terrorist* by Mugabe and the ZANU-PF government to foreignize those perceived as threats to the ruling party, much as the term was used by Rhodesians during the UDI period to describe black soldiers in the war of liberation.[28]

Legislating Dichotomies

Examples of the various terms used to express the foreign/local dichotomy reveal its roots in the history of Southern Rhodesia and Rhodesia, its stronghold in post-independent Zimbabwean discourse, and the political uses to which it is being put during the current crisis. They also demonstrate the extent to which it is linked to the circulation of media images both in and concerning Zimbabwe. In 2001, the ruling party capitalized on this linkage by passing the BSA. This created a 75 percent local content quota for television and radio broadcasters, restricted ownership of broadcasting to Zimbabwean citizens, and established a committee known as the Broadcasting Authority of Zimbabwe charged with reviewing applications for broadcasting licenses. As Zimbabwean media studies scholar Dumisani Moyo observes, on the surface the BSA's various provisions and "its emphasis on the promotion of national culture, national languages, local ownership, and local production industry are a remarkable improvement from the previous colonial legislation."[29] However, the act has been used primarily to prevent alternative (both internally and externally produced) perspectives from reaching Zimbabweans.

The effects of the act were not yet known during my fieldwork in 2001, but it was a major topic for discussion among Zimbabweans that year; my conversations with both filmmakers and viewers reveal the hopes and concerns about foreign and local film and television that the act raised for them.

Approaches to Listening In

Locating moments when the government's dichotomies are disrupted through alternative discourse offers a productive way of understanding them and their sociopolitical implications. For example, Thomas Turino's study of Zimbabwean cosmopolitanism offers a necessary corrective to simplistic concepts of the category *local,* recognizing that Zimbabweans do not simply embody preexisting national and "African" identities but rather actively and continuously construct them. He suggests that a considerable number of Zimbabweans have incorporated various elements of the "foreign" into their identities and everyday practices through the cultural capital they gain from study abroad and contact with the "outside world."[30] In this way local and foreign aspects of their identities are intertwined.

However, it is not only among cosmopolitans like those Turino studied that such binary conceptions are slippery and in need of refinement. We can learn not only from Zimbabwean cosmopolitans like the musicians Turino studied and the filmmakers and government officials whose voices are analyzed in this book, but also from ordinary people whose main access to the "outside world" is through watching film and television.

Analysts of Zimbabwean media have, with good reason, heavily criticized the ruling party's increasingly authoritarian use of the cinematic arts and other media to restrict people's access to information. Sarah Chiumbu notes with frustration and some exaggeration that with the banning of public meetings via the Public Order and Security Act, "the only 'spaces' for Zimbabweans to discuss issues freely without fear are weddings and funerals!"[31] However, in searching for some hope in otherwise bleak times, it has become commonplace to point out that Zimbabweans have not been fully silenced by their government nor completely cut off from contact with the outside world. Those Turino calls "cosmopolitan" still have opportunities to travel as well as to access the Internet, fax machines, and direct broadcast by satellite, while even the least cosmopolitan of Zimbabweans may benefit from continued scrutiny by independent filmmakers and the international media.

Wilf Mbanga, editor of the independent newspaper *The Zimbabwean,* wrote in a 2 March 2011 *Business Day* editorial titled "We Need to Keep Telling Zimbabwe's Stories," that Zimbabweans today are "desperate for information," seeking it out wherever they can find it, "watching satellite television and reading whatever independent news they can get hold of," a claim supported by filmmakers with whom I conducted follow-up interviews in 2011. Even in rural areas, Mbanga suggests, "week-old newspapers are passed on and read avidly," making circulation figures obsolete. The majority of Zimbabweans now own cell phones, and communication via text message has become an important way to stay abreast of local, national, and even international news. Zimbabweans are also engaged in writing letters to the editors of national and international newspapers, publishing and reading underground newspapers, producing and listening to clandestine radio programs beamed from other countries, blogging, connecting on Facebook (the most frequently accessed site in the country), and simply having conversations. All of these activities point to the agency of ordinary Zimbabweans, not only critiquing repressive discourse but also seeking out and creating alternatives to it.

While Turino, Chiumbu, Mbanga, and others hint at the remaining spaces for counternarratives to the dominant discourse of belonging and nationhood in Zimbabwe, we don't know much about what those counternarratives actually are. Informal conversations about a topic as seemingly banal as film and television are one of the "spaces" still available.

In analyzing cinematic history, cultural legislation, particular cinematic texts, and language use, I draw on a variety of approaches. An overview of research frameworks adopted here provides context for the analysis by situating current interest in Zimbabwe within broader theoretical trends. These frameworks include cultural studies, critical discourse analysis, and postcolonial theory.

From cultural studies, I am drawing on the work of David Morley to move away from the text-centric approach of literary and film studies as well as to reject the theory of media effects. The cinematic arts, Morley suggests, cannot be "reduced to a textual phenomenon," nor do their "messages automatically have an effect on us as their audience."[32] Instead, a cultural studies approach requires a fourfold examination of (1) the cinematic arts in relation to (2) their production, (3) their interpretation by active audiences, and (4) sociohistorical context. Morley's concept of active audiences is linked to Stuart Hall's concept of identity. Hall writes that identity "is not something which already exists, transcending place, time, history, and culture." Nor is the meaning of a cinematic text. People, influenced by their culture and history, actively construct both texts and identities. In this light, media legislation, the film and television industries, and specific

cinematic texts are part of the cultural context I examine, with *culture* used to sig-
nify not only cultural artifacts (such as cinematic texts) but also discourses about
them. The latter—texts and talk *about* the cinematic arts—are my main focus.

Critical discourse analysis (CDA) is similar to the fourfold cultural studies
approach. CDA takes a discursive event as its focus and analyzes it in relation to
its production, interpretations, and sociohistorical context in order to reveal the
ideologies it promotes as well as those it challenges. A discursive event might be
a speech, a conversation, a newspaper article, or a law—any form of text or talk.
What makes my approach to text and talk "critical" is the negative view I take
toward ideology "as a means through which social relations of power are repro-
duced,"[33] in this case the means through which Zimbabwe's ruling party controls
its image in order to stay in power. Norman Fairclough's theory of the relationship
between discourse, ideology, and context is a fruitful one for understanding how
and why the foreign/local dichotomy is mobilized at this moment in Zimbabwe.

For a study of Zimbabwean cultural identity, cinematic arts, and discourse,
the centrality of sociohistorical context to both cultural studies and CDA calls for
an understanding of the country's colonial history. Historian Luise White reminds
us that Southern Rhodesia was not a British colony in the sense of being governed by the metropole; rather, it was a site for mineral exploitation, followed by
white settlement, and was later granted self-governing dominion status. I follow
White in departing from other scholars' tendency to refer to Southern Rhodesia
as colonial Zimbabwe, English as a colonial language, and the Rhodesian Front
as the colonial government. As White argues, the overuse of *colonial* and related
words in reference to Zimbabwe's history not only obscures continuities between
Southern Rhodesia, Rhodesia under UDI, and post-independence Zimbabwe,
but also divides Zimbabweans along that problematic line between so-called foreign and local: local patriots who support the ruling party versus foreign-backed
troublemakers who aim to recolonize the country.

With these cautions in mind, White nevertheless suggests that *colonial* "is a
fair enough shorthand that allows for some important generalizations regarding
social processes and how rule over Africans was instituted."[34] In this shorthand
fashion, *colonialism* can be understood in Ania Loomba's sense as "the conquest
and control of other people's land and goods," more or less synonymous with
imperialism.[35] Recognizing the similarities between minority rule in Southern
Rhodesia and British colonialism in other African countries allows a postcolonial
critique of Rhodesian and Zimbabwean discourses, both engaged in exploitation
and oppression.

In this critique I draw on Simon Gikandi's concept of postcolonialism, used
"as a code for the state of undecidability in which the culture of colonialism continues to resonate in what was supposed to be its negation." He writes, "The
argument that colonialism has been transcended is patently false; but so is the

insistence that, in the former colonies, the culture of colonialism continues to have the same power and presence it had before decolonization."[36] Gikandi's concept of postcolonialism is useful for studying both Zimbabwe's cinematic culture and its larger struggle for a cultural identity that is independent of its colonial history. Colonial culture here can be understood not only as white Rhodesian culture but also the imported elements of British and American cultures, including the cinematic arts. Attention to reception, resistance, and localization addresses both appropriation and critique. Zimbabwe's ruling party insists that colonial culture still exists and must be resisted. Viewers of the cinematic arts have not transcended colonialism, but they do offer important critiques of it. Moreover, their critiques address not only foreign colonialism but also local oppression.

Why "Cinematic Arts"?

Television has been a prime concern for media studies scholars since the 1970s, but the medium has been largely ignored in African studies.[37] I argue that there are good reasons to examine film and TV together under the collective label *cinematic arts*. By doing so I treat film and television as Zimbabwean viewers and producers do: as closely related cultural products involving moving images and words. Both film and TV exist in complex relationships to foreign and local cultures.

One reason that television has been overlooked in studies of African media is a widespread assumption that radio is a more important medium. For example, in an analysis of the state of Zimbabwean media in 2004, Dumisani Moyo wrote:

> Television, which has become the "defining medium of the age" in the West, is yet to make a wider impact in Africa, where radio remains domi- nant for a number of reasons. With its capacity to overcome problems of illiteracy, distance, linguistic diversity, and press scarcity, radio plays a far more significant role than both television and the press in reaching the majority of Africa's populations, which reside in the rural areas. In Zimbabwe, for example, while television signals can be accessed by 56% of the population, radio signals are received by 75% of the population.[38]

The statistics Moyo cites are from a 1996 report, and he indicates in a foot- note that signal strength has improved since then. Nevertheless, it remains true that radio is a relatively inexpensive medium both to produce and receive, and Zimbabweans own more radios than televisions.

Yet numbers that address reception are not the best means to assess the nebu- lous concept of "impact." Indeed, such statistics obscure the fact that the cin- ematic arts, both foreign and local, have been an important source of information for Zimbabweans as well as significant pleasures in their lives, and they often watch these on television. Like the family I lived with in Chiweshe who watched TV in their neighbor's kitchen, many Zimbabweans watch television communally. In this excerpt from our 2001 conversation at her home in Harare, ZTV talk show host Rebecca Chisamba describes communal viewership:

> Our people are used to sharing. In the high-density area, you might have one person with a television set amongst seven homes or so. People are free to come and watch television. If they have a program they want to watch, they will just come and say, "Can we watch *Mabhuku neVanyori* [Books and Readers]? Can we watch *Zvakanangana naMadzimai* [Concerning Women]?" And a lot of people share ideas. Out there in high density, a lot of things are communal. They have a shopping center where all the people go. Maybe they have a recreation hall where all the people go. They talk about the program. They actually phone, looking for me or my producer, or the head of productions. "Why was that program like that? What does it mean?" And at times they help us with the topics—"Why don't you discuss 1, 2, 3?" So, even out now in the rural areas, some people have electricity or there is solar. And in most growth points there is electricity; some use [car] batteries. So the television goes a long way. And even those who don't have batteries can watch TV in other people's homes.

In this excerpt, Chisamba constructs Shona society as one in which sharing and communal living is traditional (people are *used to sharing*). Yet she presents this tradition as one with modern uses with regard to television (as well as shopping centers, recreation halls, and telephones). This mix of tradition and modernity seems especially resonant for viewers of programs in the Shona language—many of which Chisamba hosts, including the two she names here. She depicts Shona viewers as engaged in what they watch, not only talking about the program with one another but also asking questions of Chisamba and other television workers, even making suggestions. Chisamba's comments suggest that the impact of the cinematic arts cannot be judged by access or ownership alone, but must take into account how and why viewers use it.

Statistics about access and ownership are also changing. The 2006 Zimbabwe All Media and Products Survey found that both radio listenership and newspaper readership were declining, while television viewership was increasing. In the early 1980s, Tirivafi Kangai, who worked for the Zimbabwe Broadcasting Corporation, claimed that for a newly independent African nation, "Television is the most effective means of mass communication compared to radio and the press," arguing that its use of both images and sounds makes it "closer to reality than any other means of mass communication."[39] The viewers I spoke with would agree.

Film and video also have the advantage of combining images and sound and can therefore be grouped with television under the broader category of the cinematic arts. Scholars in other contexts have analyzed TV and film as distinct media, each with its own body of literature. Yet in the practice of producing, distributing, viewing, and discussing the cinematic arts in Zimbabwe, TV and film constantly converge.

Some viewers do make distinctions between TV programs (zvirongwa in Shona) and videos (mavhideyo in Shona), and they call projected films cinema or movies (mabhaisikopu in Shona, from the British English term bioscope). However, they also use these terms interchangeably, often referring to the technological medium used to view them rather than the production format, so that anything broadcast on TV may be considered a TV program. For example, when I asked viewers about their favorite TV programs, many listed movies, because they watched them on TV. But when I asked viewers about their favorite movies, many listed TV programs, an indication that the word movie does not mean the same thing in Zimbabwean English as it does in British or American English.

The overlap among personnel involved in the production of film and television suggests another reason for considering these media together. For example, two of the actors in the feature film Yellow Card (2000) had previously appeared in local TV dramas, bringing instant recognition to the film. Others began in film and went on to television, like Ben Mahaka. He was working primarily as a director and producer of documentary videos for Zimmedia when I met him in 2001, but a small role in Yellow Card landed him a starring role in Zimbabwe's first soap opera, Studio 263, in 2002.

Filmmakers also refer to these media as unified. In 2001, Yellow Card's director, John Riber, told me, "When I talk about film I mean motion picture media—certainly I mean television; I certainly mean video." Riber has worked primarily in film, but his films have also been shown on state-owned television and in cinemas and are available on video. Local nongovernmental organizations (NGOs) also use VCRs to screen his movies in the rural areas, where they are projected at makeshift outdoor cinemas. While Riber refers to Yellow Card as a film, many Zimbabweans know it as a TV program, drama, or video.

The distinctions Zimbabweans do and do not make among films, TV programs, bioscopes, and videos point to the need to consider these media together, whereas in another cultural context they might be considered individually. This choice allows the inclusion of both movies and TV programs in the scope of analysis, combining them as Zimbabwean viewers do. When referring to Zimbabweans' use of these media, I therefore either group them together as the cinematic arts, quote the terms used by individuals with whom I spoke, or refer to them as film and television.

How important are the cinematic arts to Zimbabweans? Questionnaires give a sense of the scope of film and television viewing, while conversations and letters allow Zimbabweans to explain their viewing choices and interpretations in depth.

Among the seventy-two people who responded to my questionnaires, more than half had been to the cinema at least once; 20 percent listed "going to the movies" as an activity they enjoy. Most had been to a cinema ten or more times, and many had been more than fifty times. It is likely that most cinemagoers attend the cinema more than twenty times. More people have access to video than to cinemas, and most people who responded had watched a video at least once. Among those, the majority had watched at least twenty videos, and many had watched more than fifty. Unsurprisingly, those who have watched the most videos are those with a VCR at home, many of them watching videos three or more times each week. In all, almost one-third counted "watching movies at home" among their favorite activities. Television is much more widely available than is cinema: everyone who responded had watched television, and the majority had watched more than fifty times. Even more striking is that three-quarters of television viewers watched every day, and less than 8 percent watched less than once a week.[40]

Conversations give deeper meaning to these statistics. Consider the following excerpt, from a conversation recorded with my host mother, Mrs. Jaunda, and host sister, Kanyadzo, in the smoky kitchen outside their village home in Chiweshe:

> KDT: *Unoona terevhizheni zvakadini?*
>
> Jaunda: *Kuona terevhizheni? Ndinenge ndichida kuiona mazuva ose. Zvino handina asi kana iripo ndoda kuona mazuva ese.*
>
> KDT: *Asi kune vanhu mu[Chiweshe] vane terevhizheni here?*
>
> Jaunda: *Ehe.*
>
> KDT: *Saka muchida munongona kuenda kunoona?*
>
> Jaunda: *Ehe tinoenda. Tinoenda kana pane chirongwa chinotifadza. Zvedrama neMvengemvenge. Ndizvo zvinonyanyondifadza. Kana taendawo kunoona maT.V., meterevhizheni evamwe, tinoenda Monday.*
>
> *Handiti ndipo parinoitwa ka?*
>
> Kanyadzo: *Ehe.*
>
> Jaunda: *Monday! Iye zvino izvi wrestling yave kuitwa Chitatu. Tinoda kuiona. Tinoenda Monday yoga yoga. Pamwe tinochirika zvinoenderana nem-uridzi weTerevhizheni. Pamwe anovhura pamwe haavhure.*

> KDT: How often do you watch television?
>
> Jaunda: Watch television? I would love to watch it every day. Now I do not have one, but if it were here, I would love to watch it every day.
>
> KDT: But are there people in Chiweshe who have televisions?
>
> Jaunda: Yes.
>
> KDT: So if you all want to, can you go and watch?

Jaunda: Yes, we do go. We go when there is a program that pleases us. Dramas and *Mvengemvenge*. Those are the ones that please me the most. If we go there to watch TVs, others' televisions, we normally go on Mondays. *(Addressing her daughter)* Isn't that when it is shown?

Kanyadzo: Yes.

Jaunda: Monday! Now we have wrestling on Wednesdays. We love to watch it. We go each and every Monday. Sometimes we skip days depending on the owner of the television. Sometimes he turns it on, and sometimes he doesn't.

Mrs. Jaunda constructs an identity for herself and her family as TV viewers even though their access to television is limited, dependent on the whim of their neighbor. She accomplishes this by describing their viewing as a regular activity, "each and every Monday." In contrast, I observed that while her family owned a radio, they listened to it only haphazardly, rarely intentionally seeking out a favorite program. Even Zimbabweans who have never been to a cinema and do not own a television still have some access to the cinematic arts, present them as a source of entertainment, and express the desire to make the cinematic arts a regular part of their lives.

Examples like my conversation with Mrs. Jaunda illustrate the divide between statistics and lived experience. Scholars know a great deal about the structures of media production and distribution, but very little about reception and interpretation by audiences, especially in Africa. Critical ethnography, such as analysis of the conversations I took part in and observations I made while living with Mrs. Jaunda in Chiweshe, reveals a more complex picture than quantitative data offers. Analysis of such talk enables us to see "what people are doing or not doing, how they are doing it, and how it is connected to other things they are doing, rather than . . . how often they are doing it, how much they are doing it, and so on."[41] The cinematic arts don't just reach people in a way that can be assessed by counting the number of television sets and cinemas. They are not just accessed and received, but also viewed, discussed, laughed over, interpreted, and critiqued as people make meaning from them through talk.

The cinematic arts take various forms: government propaganda presented as local news, imported (and censored) CNN and BBC world news, feature films made by American and British expatriates and exported as Zimbabwean films, and American soap operas whose representations of capitalist excess allow some to criticize the West and others to relate to it. Whether local or foreign, fact or fiction, these texts offer opportunities for Zimbabwean filmmakers and viewers to discuss their cultures, their representations, and their relationships to the nation.

Film and television share common features and are discursively treated as the same media by many Zimbabwean viewers, but they do have different histories

with regard to the state's project of constructing a national identity and opposing colonial influences. Black African filmmaking emerged in many countries
"out of the excitement of nation-building and a quest for the revivification of
Africa's lost cultural heritage and identity."[42] However, in Zimbabwe, early post-
independence filmmaking was not the work of black Africans but rather white
Americans—Hollywood producers who used Zimbabwe as the set for feature
films, particularly those meant to take place in apartheid South Africa, which was
closed off to them. Black Zimbabweans were collaborators in the production of
a number of Hollywood films, but they took control of television production in a
more meaningful way. It was in TV programming that a national cultural identity
was constructed, under the watchful eye—if not complete control—of the state
broadcaster.

CHAPTER 2

• • • • • • • •

Cinematic Arts before the
2001 Broadcasting Services Act:
Two Decades of Trying to Build a Nation

In 1980 a newly independent Zimbabwe found itself with an inherited cinematic culture dominated by white producers and mostly aimed at white viewers. Only a handful of domestically produced films and some imported Westerns had been directed to black viewers, and these were often thematized by racism and paternalism. Both film and television were transmitted predominantly through the English language. In the first two decades of independence, Zimbabwe struggled to adapt this inheritance to meet the needs of a multiracial, multicultural, and multilingual society, while balancing the imported and domestic resources available to its cinematic industries. A number of scholars have criticized Zimbabwe's cinematic arts, and TV broadcasting in particular, for their failure to transform after independence.[1] A detailed examination of the goals that the newly independent government set for the cinematic arts in the early 1980s reveals that by 2001 some changes *had* occurred, but they were extremely uneven. Analysis of archival materials, conversations with filmmakers, and critical commentary by viewers allow us to see how anxiety about Zimbabwe's colonial history and present-day "cultural imperialism" has structured debates about what it means to represent Zimbabwe.

It was ironic that within a few months of independence, then prime minister Robert Mugabe called in a study group from Britain to advise the new government on how the country should reform broadcasting. In 1980 the BBC published its *Report by the Study Group on the Future of Broadcasting in Zimbabwe*, which assessed the broadcasting system Zimbabwe inherited from Rhodesia and made suggestions on how to improve it. A critical analysis of the BBC report—what it emphasized and what it ignored—provides a useful framework for assessing Zimbabwe's accomplishments in TV broadcasting and film. By focusing on three goals emphasized in the BBC report—privatization, democratization, and nation-building—we can understand the attempts made to restructure television broadcasting and develop the cinematic arts from independence in 1980 to the period just before the 2001 Broadcasting Services Act was introduced.

Each of these three goals relied on a binary opposition to the cinematic arts that had been established during white minority rule. If the cinematic arts had divided blacks and whites, rural and urban people, Shona and Ndebele speakers before 1980, afterward they would ideally unite them. If broadcasting and film were state propaganda tools before 1980, afterward they would ideally be privatized and unbiased. If access to the cinematic arts and self-representation favored the white minority before 1980, afterward it would ideally favor the black majority. Zimbabwe did make some progress toward these goals, most notably in increased production of its domestic films and TV programs and greater distribution networks. But such binary oppositions did not allow for the development of a cinematic culture that represents the diversity of ethnicities, languages, and political opinions of Zimbabwe's filmmakers and viewers.

Privatization: Limiting State Control of Television

Television arrived in Southern Rhodesia in 1960, overseen by Rhodesian Television Limited. RTV was only the second television service in sub-Saharan Africa (after Nigeria in 1959), and it operated as a branch of the newly formed Federation Broadcasting Corporation. Both the FBC and RTV were private companies, commercially driven and entirely funded by advertisers. In the 1960s, the FBC underwent a series of transformations that finally created the Rhodesia Broadcasting Corporation (RBC). Soon after Rhodesia's Unilateral Declaration of Independence (UDI) from Britain in 1965, the Rhodesian government withdrew the private corporation's license to televise and turned the RBC over to the state. A final name change came in 1980, when the letter R was removed from the RBC sign outside of the state broadcasting corporation and replaced with the letter Z.[2] Changing the name was easy, but massive reforms were needed to make the Zimbabwe Broadcasting Corporation truly different from its predecessor.

The BBC report commissioned by Mugabe challenged the ZBC to gain the trust of the people. Since the RBC had owned the television transmitting stations, there had been almost no limit on the manipulation of television by the state during UDI, and this unlimited power stood in the way of public trust. The BBC report remarked, "The fact of broadcasting having been used as an arm of the government and as an instrument of political, ideological, and psychological propaganda for so long has evolved in the population at large a degree of mistrust and, for the great majority, a stronger sense of alienation."[3] Zimbabweans needed to know that they could trust their new government with broadcasting.

Propaganda had been the main function of film and television before independence. Colonial administrators believed that film had great potential for disseminating not only more "accurate" and favorable portrayals of whites than the negative ones they perceived in imported commercial American productions but also information about "development." As J. Merle Davis, founder of the Bantu Educational Kinema Experiment, explained in 1934, development was conceived of as helping uneducated and illiterate Africans adjust to Western capitalist society. Geoffrey Mangin, a cinematographer for the Southern Rhodesian government, recalls using film to teach Africans to abandon practices conceived of as "witchcraft"; to acquaint them with public health, agriculture, and literacy; and to encourage "foreign skills [like] boat-building and commercial fishing." Various experiments using cinema to educate, develop, and modernize black Africans took place throughout the late 1920s and early 1930s, but it was with the establishment of the Colonial Film Unit (CFU) in 1939 that imperial ideology and cinema became inextricably linked. In 1936 colonial administrator S. A. Hammond actually said that film was a means of preparing Africans for "citizenship of the Empire"; not long afterward, the CFU began producing propaganda films to explain World War II to "African and other unsophisticated colonial audiences in order to enlist their co-operation in the war effort." After the war, the institution found funds to produce instructional films as well.[4]

The BBC report constructs Zimbabweans as highly distrustful of film and television. The first step to regaining their trust, the report argued, was to detach the broadcaster from the government, something both Mugabe and Nathan Shamuyarira (then minister of information) had already indicated they planned to do. In theory this meant that broadcasting would have been "properly insulated from governmental, party, commercial, or any other pressure,"[5] with ZBC operating as neither a private nor a state entity, but rather as a public broadcaster, along the lines of the BBC in Britain or the Corporation for Public Broadcasting in the United States.

ZBC's structure retained a high degree of involvement from the state despite the government's stated intention to create such insulation. Tirivafi Kangai, director-general of the ZBC, explained in 1983:

> The ZBC is a parastatal body created by the [1957] Broadcasting Act, under which the constitution and operation of the Corporation are controlled by a Board of Governors appointed by the President of Zimbabwe. They are charged with outlining the policy of the Corporation and are responsible for its financial affairs. Then comes a Board of Management led by the Director-General, whose appointment is controlled by the President. This Board has the responsibility of executing the policies as laid down by the Board of Governors and for the day-to-day running of the Corporation.[6]

Kangai's description of the ZBC illustrates the president's power over broadcasting. It also makes clear how little had changed, with the state still operating under a colonial broadcasting act that had been passed in 1957 and amended in 1974.

Continued state involvement in broadcasting led many to see the changes from RBC and RTV to ZBC and ZTV as merely nominal transformations. The government continues to call the ZBC a public service broadcaster (although it is not), just as its predecessor did with the FBC. By using this label, the ZBC draws on positive connotations associated with the term. These connotations include not only the insulation from pressure mentioned in the BBC report but also public accessibility, concern for national identity and culture, and revenues generated through viewer licenses rather than relying solely on advertising.

ZBC failed to fully adopt a public service mandate. For this reason, its structure and leadership are widely perceived by viewers to be controlled by the state to achieve its own political ends. In the late 1990s, the Media Institute of Southern Africa (MISA), a nongovernmental organization (NGO) that monitors media freedoms, accused the minister of information, posts, and telecommunications of not only selecting board members "because of their relationship with the ruling party" rather than because of their "competency or commitment to Press freedom," but also forcing them to resign when their actions ran counter to the minister's wishes.[7] Such abuses became even more commonplace in the period surrounding the 2001 Broadcasting Services Act.

Rather than truly give up control over the cinematic arts, the state reworded its practices, avoiding the term *propaganda* in favor of *news, information,* and *education.* Grey Tichatonga, ZBC director in the early 1980s, wrote, "The ZBC's obligations to the Zimbabwe community include among other things to disseminate news, information, educative programmes as well as providing entertainment. The content and direction which these programmes take should reflect national goals, and fully mobilise the masses for the achievement of those objectives."[8] Here Tichatonga disingenuously constructs ZBC as an agent not of the state but of the Zimbabwe community. News, information, and education flow in one direction, from the ZBC to a monolithic group defined by nationality, lumped together as "the masses." While the final phrase suggests some minimal agency for the masses, they are still grammatically passive, the object of mobilization. Moreover, they are mobilized to achieve not their own objectives but undefined national goals. Independence saw state television reframe propaganda rather than reject it.

Viewers interviewed by Christine Lamb noted that TV had gone "from a propaganda vehicle for [Rhodesian President Ian] Smith to one for Comrade Bob," as Mugabe is derisively called by some of his critics. James Zaffiro writes, "In the early months following independence, [white] callers flooded the switchboard at Pockets Hill [ZBC headquarters] every night after the main news program, with a series of complaints about 'Marxist content,' continuous praise of ZANU (PF) liberation efforts, references to white racism, and oppression under previous regimes." These complaints faded over the years, but the content has not changed much. According to Michael Bruun Andersen, "The president and the ministers can and do order ZBC news to cover their activities."[9]

Viewpoints that contradict those of the ruling party are likewise often excluded from ZTV. For example, after Mugabe banned Gays and Lesbians of Zimbabwe (GALZ) from the Zimbabwe International Book Fair in 1995 and began attacking "homosexuality as a decadent Western import," ZBC "refused to broadcast a panel discussion on violence against women after it learned that one of the panelists was a GALZ member."[10] Rather than presenting the diverse perspectives of its citizens and their organizations, ZBC has tended to stifle oppositional voices.

Government control of broadcasting does not always take the form of heavy-handed censorship, however. Self-censorship among news production staff is also quite common. Alexander Kanengoni, head of research at ZBC in 2001, told me:

> We are told, in no uncertain terms, that we belong to government. We should never forget that. So ultimately, what I'm saying is that there is so much self-censorship. It's so heavy. You wouldn't want to be the person whose story is discussed at the level of Jonathon Moyo [minister of information]. So in the end you do your own censorship inside your head and you look for stories that will not get to that point.

Even in entertainment programming, government influence is evident. For example, "local dramas" emphasize simple domestic themes and fail to address social issues that might upset the government. According to Pedzisai Mashiri, "Corruption, betrayal, poverty, unemployment, retrenchments, regionalism, poor governance, political opportunism, party politics, and land and housing problems" are off-limits. "It would be suicidal" for the broadcaster "to encourage plays that expose the government's shortcomings."[11]

Until 1997, ZBC operated two channels, ZTV1 and ZTV2, and several radio stations. Viewers variously refer to ZTV as ZBC, ZTV, ZTV1, and ZBC TV1. Initially, ZTV1 broadcast primarily imported entertainment punctuated with domestically produced advertisements and was transmitted nationally, while ZTV2 was operated as a noncommercial educational channel airing informational programs and documentaries to only Harare viewers at a cost of $17 million per year. The first small steps toward privatization came seventeen years after independence, when ZBC began to seek revenue by leasing out ZTV2 to three commercial broadcasters: Joy TV, Munhumutapa African Broadcasting Corporation (MABC), and LDM. At the same time the government drafted the Communications Bill, which was expected to both privatize and deregulate the broadcasting and telecommunication sectors.[12]

Privatization, such as it was, did not last long. Both MABC and LDM were short-lived operations, on the air for just over a year. Filmmaker Willie Memper told me that MABC broadcast low-quality programming, featuring mostly music and dancing, what he disparagingly called "African-type" shows. The corporation was dedicated to "African content" and aired a number of films made in Zimbabwe, including Ingrid Sinclair's feature film *Flame* (1996), about the role and treatment of women during and after the liberation struggle, and Edwina Spicer's documentaries. MABC's attempts to broadcast primarily Zimbabwean and other African content stood in stark contrast to ZTV, which had never aired more than 50 percent domestically produced content.

Neither MABC nor LDM had its own transmitter, instead paying ZBC for a license to use the one owned by the state. MABC was on the air daily from 10:30 PM to 2 PM, and LDM from 2 to 5 PM. Because LDM was on the air for such a short time, and at a time of day when few viewers were at home, no viewers I spoke with even remembered it. Both stations had bad time slots that failed to attract advertisers, so it was no surprise that license costs exceeded their revenues. In March 1998 ZBC revoked the licenses of both corporations for failing to pay what MISA has called "exorbitant rental fees."[13] A year later, the government announced that liberalizing broadcasting had failed and that it no longer intended to proceed with liberalization. The Communications Bill was reworked into the Postal and Telecommunication Bill and passed into a law that focused on cell phones rather than broadcasting.

Joy TV remained the only independent broadcaster from 1998 to 2001. In contrast to MABC and LDM, Joy TV was on the air during prime time (from 5 to 10:30 PM), attracting advertising revenues that helped pay for its license to transmit, and it broadcast very little locally produced content. As late as April 2000, Erica Fungai Ndewere, a lawyer for ZBC, cited Joy TV's existence as evidence that the state was committed to providing "alternative news bulletins and programming." Alternate views on Joy TV, however, were minimal. ZBC forbade Joy TV to broadcast local news, so when Joy TV rebroadcast BBC news, it was forced to edit out BBC reports on Zimbabwe, violating an agreement with BBC that its bulletins would be aired in full.[14]

The example of Joy TV and the other short-lived broadcasters speaks to the relationship between privatization and debates about foreign and local content. Even though ZTV broadcasts a great deal of imported programming, by maintaining control over the airwaves the state determines which "local" images reach nationwide audiences. Public mistrust of broadcasting therefore continues.

"Why You Should Film in Zimbabwe!"
State Involvement in Film

The state's relationship to film has been more distant. Only a few films were made by the newly independent government. These included educational 16mm films such as the Ministry of Information's *Zimbabwe* (c. 1981) and Production Services' *Know Your Snakes* (1982), *Traditional Dancing* (c. 1984), and *Oliver Mtukudzi* (c. 1984). Video, however, was used extensively. Just four years after independence, international donors had given video equipment to at least eighteen government departments or parastatals, which they used to create training videos for agricultural workers and other civil servants.[15]

The government's greatest involvement with film came in the mid-1980s, when it began to recruit international filmmakers to use Zimbabwe as a location. The Ministry of Information even went so far as to establish the Division of Foreign Filmmaking. In 1985, the Ministry published a brochure, "Why You Should Film in Zimbabwe!" It promoted not only the temperate climate, varied terrain, and beautiful flora and fauna, but also a well-built infrastructure, government assistance, safety, technicians, and above all, the Central Film Laboratories (CFL).

The CFL had been opened in 1960 by a group of entrepreneurs in what was then Salisbury (now Harare). The labs were initially a part of the Central African Film Unit (CAFU), a joint enterprise between Southern Rhodesia and the British colonial government of Northern Rhodesia and Nyasaland to make educational films for African audiences, but they became a commercial enterprise after 1963. With the lab's establishment, film could be processed within the country, rather than being shipped to South Africa or overseas. The CFL remained "one of the most sophisticated film labs on the continent" and was used by a number of international productions until it was closed in the late 1990s.[16] Many of the filmmakers I spoke with remembered it nostalgically.

Zimbabwe's attempts to attract foreign filmmakers were highly successful. Ben Zulu, then director of the African Script Development Fund, comments on the reasons for this success in an excerpt from our interview.

> We have beautiful locations. We also, in terms of crew, have enough people who have worked on big productions and have very good skills. And then we have a very good banking infrastructure. People can bring in money here and know that they are not going to be dealing with weak or corrupt institutions that you see in other countries. They know that they can transfer their money here to a reputable bank. They can withdraw their money. And there are services as well. They can go and contact somebody who can feed their crew and cast. That's what makes the industry. There are people who have worked in big productions here, who can supply those services. So there is potential. There is a base on which we can create something.

Zulu's echoing of the government's brochure sixteen years later illustrates how effectively the state constructed an identity for Zimbabwe as a place where international films are made. Filmmakers have a stake in maintaining this image, though it has become much more difficult to argue that Zimbabwe is an economically viable place to make films.

Only a year after "Why You Should Film in Zimbabwe!" was published, twelve international feature films were scheduled to be shot in Zimbabwe. Among the first were *King Solomon's Mines* (1985) and its sequel, *Allan Quatermain and the Lost City of Gold* (1987), both based on H. Rider Haggard novels of imperialism. In his book *Black African Cinema,* N. Frank Ukadike observed, "There is such a large breakthrough in the film industry in Zimbabwe that people are calling it the African Hollywood," though he understandably questioned the extent to which the industry at that time could be called "African."[17]

The government's interest in filmmaking had more to do with profit than it did with encouraging the country's own film industry. Interested in the potential money to be made, Zimbabwe involved itself in producing an American film set in South Africa, *Cry Freedom* (1987). The film tells the story of South African activist Steve Biko and his friendship with white journalist Donald Woods, played by American actors Denzel Washington and Kevin Kline. According to media studies scholar Kedmon Hungwe, the government invested US$5.5 million in the project, but did not receive a return on its investment, and it has not invested in international film production since then.[18]

The upshot of the government's brief experience courting foreign filmmakers was a large financial loss that resolved it against supporting the domestic film industry. Its success in attracting foreign filmmakers, however, did help provide a basis for development by affording local film workers the opportunity to participate in foreign productions, as well as by creating an infrastructure that would serve domestic as well as foreign filmmakers.

Zimbabwe dabbled in the international film industry, but the state undermined this by refusing to let its own film industry blossom. Unlike Ghana and Nigeria, Zimbabwe did not "attempt to integrate film into their cultural policy, either as an essential element of development or as entertainment." Zimbabwean critics have noted that Zimbabwe has neither a national film policy nor a broad cultural policy. Leaving filmmakers to their own devices might be lauded as privatization, but it has left the domestic film industry struggling. For example, film distribution, as in most other parts of the continent, "has faced a ruthless and monopolistic exploitation by American, European, and Indian distribution companies," a situation many blame on the lack of government protection for national cinema in the form of import quotas or freezing of box office receipts to create a film fund.[19]

Filmmakers in Zimbabwe pressed the government for assistance in developing a domestic film industry throughout the 1980s and 1990s. For example, a group came together in 1982 to form the Zimbabwe Film and Video Association (ZFVA), chaired by producer Simon Bright. ZFVA's members argued that Zimbabwean workers in the foreign film industry "were often hired at extremely cheap rates compared with their Western counterparts"; the separate Zimbabwe Film Television and Allied Workers Union was formed in the mid-1980s to handle these concerns. ZFVA did little more than organize training courses for projectionists in the 1980s, but in 1991 it was revived and became an NGO. The group "had ongoing dialogue with the Zimbabwean government with regard to policy promoting the interest of local filmmakers" and urged the government to subsidize the revival of the Central Film Laboratory, but their calls went unheeded.[20]

Even without state involvement, post-independence cinema has not escaped the propaganda role of its colonial predecessor. International NGOs have stepped in where the government has not, playing a prominent role in funding the production of films with "social messages." Like the state broadcaster, NGOs and independent filmmakers recognize the propaganda value of cinematic texts. In a 2001 conversation with me in his Zimmedia office, Bright recalled his early goals in making documentary films:

> If you look at it from Reagan's point of view and you see the [Afrikaner] nationalist party in power successfully torturing the majority of the population, keeping them under control, and you see a good rate of return in investment terms coming out of South Africa, then the idea is: "Keep your money in South Africa." So what we needed was a series of documentaries and films which would show them that, on the contrary, apartheid was actually falling apart. Because the will of the Front Line States and the will of the South African population [were] actually stronger than apartheid. That needed to be documented and represented in order to hasten the end of apartheid. And in fact that's what happened. Apartheid crumbled and fell. Our small role in that was to produce a series of films. One was *Corridors of Freedom*. There was another film which also focused on the transport corridor [the rail line used for transporting goods between Zimbabwe and Maputo, allowing the landlocked countries of Zimbabwe and Botswana to avoid dependence on South Africa]; it's called *Limpopo Line*. And there was one called *The Sanctions Debate*. And so, during the period 1985 to 1990, we focused on redressing the information distortion that we perceived was key in the way that the West, or the North World, saw Southern Africa. So that's how I got involved in making films.

Even feature films can be considered propaganda, although filmmakers generally don't call them that. An excerpt from my email exchange with filmmaker Rory Kilalea illustrates how the term *propaganda* is narrowed in a way that protects the interests of independent filmmakers.

> KDT: You mentioned the "social messages" of film but also wrote, "Art is not propaganda." How do you balance these two?
>
> Kilalea: Propaganda is a forced message from government. Without the freedom to be able to reject it. Social message (while often paternalistic, admittedly) is more didactic—with more choice allowed to be able to decide what is truth. Of course propaganda superbly

produced can be close to this—but finally, it is the freedom of thought which I think differentiates them.

Whereas ZBC television reworded its propaganda as information and news, filmmakers like Kilalea and John Riber call theirs social message films. Social message films, development or development-oriented films, didactic films, educational or education-oriented films, edutainment, infotainment: the proliferation of labels to describe this work suggests an avoidance of the term *propaganda.*

By 2001, seven feature films had been produced: *Jit* (1990), *Neria* (1992), *More Time* (1993), *I Am the Future* (1993), *Everyone's Child* (1996), *Flame* (1996), and *Yellow Card* (2000). All but *Jit* and *Flame* are so-called social message films, and four were produced by Media for Development Trust (MFD), a domestically based NGO and production company run by expatriate Americans.

Who's Got the Money?
"Foreign" Agendas

The dominance of social message films has arisen precisely because of the availability of donor funding and the lack of government support for a domestic film industry. Independent filmmaker Albert Chimedza told me: "Basically what's happened is that people are desperate to make films. So the money available is for donor projects." With the exception of *I Am the Future,* which was domestically funded, all of Zimbabwe's feature films and the majority of its shorts have been funded by international NGOs or development agencies. For example, Olley Maruma's *After the Hunger and Drought* (1985) was funded by the French Foreign Ministry, and *Consequences* (1988) was financed by Pathfinder International, a nonprofit international family planning and reproductive health organization based in the United States. In our 2001 interview, Maruma described the latter as "a didactic donor film" whose message is "Teenage pregnancy can fuck up your life." Other MFD projects have been funded by UNICEF, Pathfinder International, the United Kingdom Department for International Development, the U.S. Agency for International Development, and the Ford Foundation. Edwina Spicer's documentaries have been funded by both international donors and the Zimbabwe branch of the Catholic Commission for Justice and Peace.

Because all of MFD's films address development issues—women's and children's rights, teenage pregnancy, premarital sex, and HIV—their films have been extremely popular with international donors during preproduction and with local NGOs after the films are released. As Riber told me, his decision to make development films was motivated by the money available from international donors: "I came into the situation and said, 'How am I going to make films in this part of the world where it's not a commercially viable activity? Who's got the money?'"

With foreign funding have come threats—perceived or real—to the intellectual freedom of filmmakers. Novelist Chenjerai Hove comments: "Our filmmakers mostly—local filmmakers—depend on donor money. No donor will sponsor a biological film of fish under the Kariba, in the waters. No donor will do that. A donor will say, 'I can only give you money to do a film, a documentary film, on rape. Or AIDS. Or inheritance. Or human rights.'"[21] The litany of fund-worthy topics Hove rattles off is not hypothetical; these are the themes of Zimbabwe's films. Rape is treated in *Flame* and *Everyone's Child,* respectively the rape of female combatants during the liberation struggle and the sexual exploitation of young women by powerful older men. The main character in the latter is an orphan because of AIDS, which also plays a role in *Yellow Card. Neria* concerns women's inheritance rights. All of these topics can be considered aspects of the broad theme of "human rights," the discourse of which has been the main theme in many of Edwina Spicer's documentaries.

Debates about the effects of donor agendas on Zimbabwean filmmaking follow a pattern: those who have been most successful in attracting donor money deny that it influences their own work, while less successful filmmakers tend to blame donors. Riber and Bright represent the former. When I spoke with Riber at his MFD office in 2001, he described donors as affecting film agendas only in the loosest sense, funding broad themes like AIDS, infrastructure, environment, women's issues, and gender.

> KDT: Could you talk a bit more about how donor funding works?
>
> Riber: We keep our finger on the pulse of what's going on in the donor community and we say, "All right, let's know that [there are] resources out in this field." If we're not creative enough to come up with something that's really interesting and fun and can capture audiences in the realm of gender, for example, I mean, my God, come on!

Similarly, Bright denied that donors influenced his films, but he made this claim by differentiating his own "art films" from Riber's social message films. In 2001 he told me:

> If you have a message couched in terms which are designed not to antagonize a wide range of commissioning people who are empowered to censor, effectively, or define, or determine the script, you cut out a large possibility of controversy, creativity, and various other things that give films impact. If you have a bunch of do-gooder NGOs defining the message and saying, "Don't tread onto that ground; it's too politically delicate, too socially delicate," you're not going to get the impact.

Bright was careful, however, not to criticize donor funding itself, which he can't afford to lose. He argued that donor funding does not constrain his own brand of films:

> There is a large attack on donor money, and I don't think that what I've
> said previously is an attack on the donor funding per se. It's just trying to
> explore a mechanism that can neutralize the creativity of a film. But you
> can also use that money to make very creative films. One of the key ele-
> ments of that is not to have one single donor—is to have multiple donors,
> because none of them has a controlling position in relation to your work.

With limited donor funding available, Riber's and Bright's contradictory claims
about donor agendas must be understood in the context of competition for scarce
resources. Riber argued that the critique of donor agendas in social message films
is simply misguided. At the same time his claim that "we are getting away with
more and more now as we learn how to make films better" suggests that his complete disavowal of donor influence is disingenuous.

In contrast to Riber and Bright, a number of less successful filmmakers did
report unwanted influence from donors. Hove's example of a local filmmaker
wanting to make a documentary about fish may be facetious, but it reflects a
discourse among filmmakers who can't make the films they want to because of
the clash between their own agendas and those of donors. For example, Arthur
Chikuhwa, director of the Capricorn Video Unit, told me:

> Most of the time, if you're donor funded, there is always an influence. "I
> give my money, so what about my influence?" Yeah, sometimes you will
> hear things like, "What will be our influence on this project?" They come
> up with their ideas, but sometimes you are doing the thing the way you
> didn't want to do it—one or two things in the film—because you want
> to accommodate someone who is giving you money.

Similarly, filmmaker Olley Maruma described donors as pushing didacticism into
the films they fund, sapping directors of creativity and preventing their work from
becoming art. He told me:

> The first movie that I tried to do with donor money was trying to expose
> corruption in the donor community, where they give money. You know
> they talk about transparency and accountability; they are not even pre-
> pared to be accountable themselves. I wanted to make a movie about that
> to show that there is corruption in the way donor money is used. I didn't
> do it with malice or wanting to destroy donor funding, but to make it
> more transparent and more efficient. They are not interested in that. I've
> tried other films; they are not interested.

It is difficult to know why a film is not funded, but it is common for directors
whose work has gone unfunded to blame donor agendas.

To what extent do donor agendas differ from colonial propaganda? Is a social
message concept of development different from that utilized by colonial filmmak-

ers? Filmmakers and critics alike have lauded the potential of both film and television to aid in economic, social, and cultural development. Often, their statements echo those of colonial film administrators. While avoiding the word *propaganda,* Shingai Gwarinda writes of cinema's potential as an informational and educational tool: "The fact that film entertains while it informs and educates makes it a generally more attractive medium for development with a wider reach (especially in rural Zimbabwe where the problem of illiteracy still exists) as one does not have to be literate to watch a film!"[22] Are *information* and *education* different from *propaganda* or simply a rewording?

In Gwarinda's interview with television scriptwriter Steve Chigorimbo, former deputy regional secretary for the Pan African Filmmakers Federation, Chigorimbo insists on the balance of education with entertainment, seeing the role of film in Africa as edutainment. He argues that entertainment is a neglected tool of development that can be used to bring issues to people who would otherwise lack access. MFD followed a similar line of thinking, particularly with *Yellow Card,* which combined highly entertaining soccer scenes—intended to be especially appealing to young men—with its educational messages.

MFD arguably moved beyond the colonial attitude toward development, which was simply to instill propaganda and effect change in the behavior of African audiences. MFD acknowledged the ability of film viewers to negotiate with what they watch and with the effect, if any, it will have on their behavior or attitudes. Riber told me, "We see filmmaking as an intervention. It isn't just a description of a successful project. It's a tool, and it can be used directly in the process of development. It's a broad term, but I mean empowering people with information in a way that helps them rather than just shows them the possibilities." His comments make clear that, while still conceptualizing its films through the social messages supplied by international donor agencies, MFD had increasingly moved toward open-ended messages that left room for audiences to engage with their films on multiple levels and through dialogue.

The impact of donor funding on the themes of Zimbabwe's film industry raises questions about "foreign" perspectives in "local" films. But the absence of state funding for a domestic industry has meant that filmmakers must rely on foreign donors. With television, the state can exert great control over its image because it produces most of the local content. Ironically, by failing to support the domestic film industry, the state drives filmmakers to donors who undoubtedly have agendas very different from its own. Unlike television, donor-funded film has remained "privatized," but it is still mistrusted by those who fear a foreign agenda is embedded within films that are labeled "local." The economic crisis in Zimbabwe has led many NGOs to pull out of the country, with devastating effects on local filmmakers; this may be an opportunity for the state to revisit its relationship to film. Given the control the state exerts over television, though, state involvement in independent filmmaking might do more harm than good.

Serving All Zimbabweans: Democratization

Film and television's relationship to the state during minority rule meant that the cinematic arts were inherently undemocratic, serving the interests of the white minority. Not only did they exclude blacks from the production process but they also privileged white audiences with greater access to a variety of cinematic texts and censored those available to black audiences. The BBC report recognized these disparities, recommending that the second step necessary to regain the people's trust was to democratize the media, making it "at the same time both reflect and serve the totality of the Zimbabwean people, Shona and Ndebele, black and white, rural and urban." This list is, of course, a simplification of what comprises "the totality of the Zimbabwean people," which also includes at least thirteen other ethnic and linguistic groups (the Tonga, Nambya/Dombe, Venda, Kalanga, Shangaan, Lilima, Shangwe, Birwa, Tswana, Lozi, Barwe-Tonga, Hlegwe, and Chikunda), as well as migrant workers from neighboring countries, Asians and "coloureds" (people of mixed race), men and women, people in various socioeconomic classes, and so on. Zimbabwe, though often depicted in the simple dichotomies used in the BBC report, is in fact a multicultural society, as well as one in which rural/urban divides have been exaggerated. Reaching every subsection of this society through a democratic broadcasting system was a challenging goal for the newly independent country. Oversimplifying the complexity of Zimbabwean society did nothing to make the goal more attainable.[23]

The BBC report suggested that democratizing Zimbabwe's cinematic culture required two elements: reflecting Zimbabwe's diversity and serving all Zimbabweans. Reflecting diversity meant not only redistributing access to the means of film and TV production but also representing black faces on-screen. Moreover, serving all Zimbabweans meant extending broadcasting range, access to televisions, and cinema distribution networks. One might expect that both reflecting and serving diverse Zimbabweans would mean democratizing language use in the cinematic arts to reflect the country's multilingualism, but the issue of language was ignored in the report and has been largely ignored by filmmakers and the government.

Removing the Old Management Apparatus: Democratizing Production

Austen Kark, who headed the BBC study group, observed that before independence, Zimbabwe's broadcasting system had been "dominated by the white hierarchy. We're talking about an organisation of about 500 people including ancillary staff. Of those 500 it breaks down to about half white and half black. But if you broke that down further and looked at the first twenty posts at the top, they are predominantly white." Soon after Mugabe came to power in April 1980, most of the filmmakers who had worked for the UDI government were fired, and many white employees of the sole television broadcaster left. Some former TV workers imply that whites left because they did not want to remain at a broadcaster run by blacks; others, such as Grey Tichatonga, suggest that "removal of the old management apparatus" was a deliberate strategy of the independent government. While there is probably some truth to both claims, by depicting ZBC as acting strategically, Tichatonga constructs the broadcaster as actively pursuing a democratizing policy. Some white television workers initially remained but claimed that they were not being given credit for their work and soon left. James Neill, ZBC director-general, stayed on until late 1982 or early 1983, when he was replaced by Tirivafi Kangai. With such a massive change in personnel, the country began to develop a new television culture.[24]

ZBC benefited early on from a core staff who had trained or worked in other countries during the UDI period and returned to the country after independence. Some, like Temba C. Bassoppo-Moyo, senior controller of programs at ZTV in the 1980s, had worked in the United States during the UDI period. Some staff received overseas training in donor countries, chiefly France and Britain. Others had trained while serving as combatants in the armed struggle for liberation and working for the Liberation Forces Network in Mozambique, where many camps were based. Bassoppo-Moyo notes that for such ex-combatants, returning to work at ZTV meant transitioning from "shooting with a gun to shooting with a camera."[25] A cultural shift was under way.

Like television, film production was also in the hands of a white hierarchy at the time of independence. The government-owned Southern Rhodesian Film Unit had been operated by white scriptwriters, producers, and directors. Roles for blacks were limited to acting and narrating or translating. A handful of white independent filmmakers had also begun to work outside the government in the 1950s, mostly producing commercials.[26]

Television became a black-run operation very quickly after 1980, but independent film producers during the first twenty years remained disproportionately white. The country's first feature film, *Jit*, was written, directed, and produced by white Zimbabweans: Michael Raeburn, Neil Dunn, and Rory Kilalea. Media for Development Trust, a production house responsible for the majority of Zimbabwe's feature films as well as several shorts, was run by two American expatriates, John and Louise Riber. Similarly, Zimmedia was run by Simon Bright and his wife, Ingrid Sinclair, who is originally from England but now holds Zimbabwean citizenship. All of these filmmakers worked with black Zimbabweans in various capacities—actors, writers, even directors—but it remained the case in 2001 that the most successful filmmakers in Zimbabwe were whites, whether raised in Zimbabwe or expatriates. As late as 1998, some filmmakers were complaining that "stories were told through the eyes of white producers simply because they had the finances,"[27] complaints that no doubt factor into the critiques of donor funding discussed earlier. Although many other films could be labeled this way, *Flame* (1996) was a prime example of a Zimbabwean story told through white eyes because many thought the first fiction film about Zimbabwe's liberation struggle should be told by a black Zimbabwean. Ingrid Sinclair and I spoke about this in 2001 in the studio behind her home in Harare.

KDT: You mentioned that with *Flame* you had gotten help from the actors at making it realistic. Could you talk more about working here as a foreigner?

Sinclair: It's got some advantages actually. With *Flame,* certainly in the research stages, it was one of the questions that I asked—pretty much the first question that I asked people when I was researching. "What do you think about a white woman who wasn't here making such a film?" And they all—all the people that I talked to—said, "Great! Nobody else has shown the slightest bit of interest. It's easier for us to talk to you because you don't have any particular political attachment or background. We're not worried that maybe you have a relative in government where if we say the wrong thing we'll get into trouble. You've got the means, and we don't have the means. You can't change the world all in a day. Go ahead and do it." I know that it means I'm a target for certain kinds of criticism, and increasingly so as race becomes more and more of an issue here—although it's always been in a way. It's always been an issue, although it hasn't always been used against people. There's an incredibly high awareness of racial difference in Zimbabwe, probably more than [there is] anywhere else I know. With all the subgroups, that to outsiders would probably not seem to be different. Here [it is] very, very clear. And very noted. These days, that is becoming something to try and hit people with if you feel like hitting people. But I haven't found, and I don't find, within my work, any opposition as a result of that. Obviously there are people who are annoyed or jealous or feel that I haven't got the right, that people like us are taking all the available money. There is some truth to what they've said, but it's not the whole truth. There are other reasons, I believe, that we get money as well as because we're white or educated in a particular way. We work incredibly hard. We are very skilled. I am older than a lot of film workers here, so I would expect to have more experience and more respect from people like funders. We've been at it for a very long time. I've been at it for twenty-two years—that's older than some of the people who are complaining about me! I don't feel guilty or that I'm doing the wrong thing, but I know that other people do.

Sinclair's comments address race in the cinematic arts as a salient and complex issue, heightened by the widespread perception that whites have easy access to NGO money from the West.

The biggest names in film may belong to white producers and directors, but Zimbabwe has a large pool of talented black filmmakers. Many began by working on international films made in Zimbabwe. Some went on to become directors of domestic films, including Olley Maruma, who directed *The Assegai* (1982), worked as assistant director on *Allan Quatermain and the City of Lost Gold* (1987), and then went on to write and direct the short feature *Consequences* (1988). Although a financial disaster, *Cry Freedom* set in motion the careers of a number of Zimbabweans who went on to work on at least seventeen international feature films in various roles ranging from grips, location managers, special effects technicians, unit production managers, actors, and casting directors, all the way up to first and second assistant directors. Like Maruma, many also worked on domestic films. David Guwaza, for example, who played a bit part in *Cry Freedom*, later worked as art director for *More Time* (1993) and *Yellow Card* (2000) and as production designer for *Everyone's Child* (1996). Dominic Kanaventi, a stage actor who had appeared in Clive Harding's *Shamwari* (1980) and played a small role in *Cry Freedom*, went on to play the leading role in *Neria* (1992) and by 2001 had acted in at least fourteen other productions. Walter Maparutsa, who also played a small role in *Cry Freedom*, later became one of Zimbabwe's most famous actors, playing important roles in *Everyone's Child* (1996), *The Last Picture* (1997), and *Yellow Card* (2000).

The list of movies shot in Zimbabwe, found in the filmography, gives a sense of the large number of domestic filmmakers who got their start in international productions. None of this would have been possible without the experience they gained on the sets of Hollywood films. In this way, state encouragement of Hollywood productions in Zimbabwe did contribute to cinematic democratization by involving blacks in the production process and leading to more black actors on Zimbabwean screens.

The relative successes of these individuals notwithstanding, black Zimbabweans who make it to the top echelons of filmmaking are few and far between. The majority were treated merely as cheap labor, as Fiona Lloyd wrote in 1990: "The makers of feature films have brought in most of their resources, human and technical, from outside. Zimbabweans have had to be content with minor roles and responsibilities. Although some skills have been gained, many would-be actors and technicians have felt frustrated and exploited." Echoing these complaints, filmmaker Rory Kilalea told me in an email, "Foreign films made us aware that the heads of depts came in from abroad, and that the workers came from the location country." Both white and black Zimbabweans were marginalized within international productions. Linda Mvusi, coordinator of the First Frontline Film Festival in 1990, complained that "cooperation between filmmakers in the region was weakened by interference of foreign filmmakers who came to Southern Africa under the pretext of helping talented Africans. Local people had no input." Though uneven, black input was far greater on Zimbabwean productions in 2001 than on the early international productions that used Zimbabwe as a location.[28]

While working under the prominent white directors and producers discussed above, blacks played major roles in producing the country's first seven feature films. These films featured actors of color and employed filmmakers from various racial and ethnic backgrounds, with many black Zimbabweans working close to the top ranks. For example, in my interview with John Riber, who produced four of these films, he discussed MFD's employment of Zimbabwean filmmakers as part of the NGO's training mission.

> KDT: Could you talk about the training aspect of MFD?
>
> Riber: I see all of our work as done in the context of training. All of our films until *Yellow Card* were directed by first-time African film directors. I've worked with a dozen first-time directors. We also take people who've usually been second assistant runners on Hollywood films, and we put them as heads of department. I really think, from my experience, that that is where filmmaking is learned. I studied film production at the University of Iowa. It was great, theoretical, kind of fun, but when I went out to India to make a film—that's where you really learn. The greatest classroom is really on set and working with people—give them the budget, the responsibility, and just get on with it.

Zimbabweans who have worked for Riber include Godwin Mawuru, who directed *Neria* and *I Am the Future;* Isaac Mabhikwa, who directed *More Time* and went on to run the Southern African Film Festival; and Tsitsi Dangarembga, who wrote the story of *Neria,* directed *Everyone's Child,* and went on to work independently, directing and producing shorts and documentaries. In many cases local filmmakers have made names for themselves while working on MFD films and then led their own projects.

Promoting "the Black Identity": Putting Black Faces on the Screen

After increasing the number of black Zimbabweans involved in cinematic production, the second change needed to represent Zimbabwe's diversity was by putting black faces on the screen. From the beginning of broadcasting in Southern Rhodesia, most of the news, music, and entertainment programs had been produced by the British Broadcasting Corporation. After Rhodesia declared its unilateral independence from Britain in 1965, according to Munashe Furusa, it no longer had access to BBC materials, and therefore the RBC began producing its own television and radio programs, as well as importing U.S. series. Austen Kark, the lead author of the BBC report, noted that the RBC under UDI was "buying whatever they could, largely on the black market because of sanctions, and they were taking whatever they could."[29]

Rhodesian nostalgia for American TV shows is widespread on the Internet. White viewers reminisce about watching *Bonanza*, *I Love Lucy*, *I Dream of Jeannie*, *Hawaii Five–O*, and *The Ed Sullivan Show*, and cartoons such as *Clutch Cargo* and *The Flintstones*. British programming was also popular, such as the children's show *Supercar*, comedy act *Morecamb and Wise*, and sketch show *The Two Ronnies*. Geoffrey Mangin recalled that RTV relied heavily on American soap operas, which even today mostly cast white actors.[30]

Contrary to official reports that emphasize imported programming, Rhodesian viewers also remember various domestic entertainment programs. Music shows like *Teen Time*, *Sound Out*, and *Juke Box Jury* featured "go-go dancers and live local bands—and eventually music videos, too," John Roberts, a Rhodesian TV and film producer, recalls. Other genres included drama series such as *Armchair Safari and Battles* and *Crime Check*, sports programs, and talk shows like *Bric-a-Brac*, *In Studio Minor*, *Forum*, *Frankly Partridge*, *The Kwhizz Kids*, and *Message to the Nation*.[31] None of these, however, included black cast members or on-screen participants, and the majority of them therefore ceased to be produced after independence.

One way in which ZBC increased black cinematic representation was through the importation of programs from other African countries. ZBC became a member of the Union of National Radio and Television Organizations of Africa (URTNA) in 1983. According to the organization's own promotional materials, URTNA is "a professional body with more than 48 active member organizations committed to the development of all aspects of broadcasting in Africa"; one of its purposes is to encourage "the exchange of indigenous programming via satellite and videocassette." Through the URTNA Programme Exchange Center in Nairobi, ZBC receives programs produced throughout the continent, thereby increasing its screening of African programs.[32] In 2001, the majority of these programs filled the "African Movie of the Week" slot and were made in Ghana.

Cannes is another source for television programming with black actors. During a 2001 conversation in his ZTV office, Alexander Kanengoni told me how such programming is purchased by a ZBC buyer:

> At the beginning that task of purchasing programs was done by one person. And obviously there were lots of problems with that, because in the end we were subjecting an entire nation to what one person likes, an individual who doesn't consult anyone, she just buys and comes back. So we recommended setting up a committee that would draw up guidelines

for programs to be bought. We understood that she didn't have time to look through all those programs, so we said, "Point number one: you go out there and buy things that promote the African culture. If there are any African programs there, buy them as a priority. Any produced by any African, buy them." Secondly, we said, "There are a lot of programs out there that try to promote the black identity. Buy the American programs with blacks." That was the second guideline. The third guideline was comedies. But the most important ones were, "If there are African programs, buy them. And when you are buying international programs, as much as possible, try to buy something like this Naomi Campbell."

He pointed to an issue of ZBC's *Look and Listen* magazine with a photo of Campbell, the black British model, on the cover, and concluded: "So at least here we are promoting our African identity, the black identity." The slippage between "African culture" and a black diaspora identity belies ZBC's claims to "promote the African culture" in the face of Western influences. In democratizing representation on-screen, race is more important to the government than is national origin.

In addition to importing African and African American programming, the station also committed itself to increasing production of its own programs. At independence, the 1980 BBC report criticized the conditions and practices inherited by the newly independent broadcaster: "Especially in television, [it] does not originate enough programmes of its own." In an effort to increase production, ZBC planned to undertake on-site television production in the rural areas using two outside broadcast vans donated by Britain. In 1983, Tiravafi Kangai, then director-general of the ZBC, wrote of the broadcaster's intention "to bring the people to the people. There is a wealth of talent latent in the outlying parts of Zimbabwe which has hitherto not featured on Zimbabwean television." Whether or not this goal was ever achieved remains unclear; during my fieldwork in 2001, the outside broadcast vans were parked in a garage at ZBC and being used for postproduction of local dramas.[33]

In 1982, the station added a weekly Shona-language "local drama," *Mhuri yavaMukadota* (Mukadota's Family), adapted from a popular radio program that had aired from 1970 to 1982. Similar slapstick comedies followed in the form of *Parafini* and *Gringo*, two of the most popular programs on TV during my fieldwork. By 1988, domestically produced programming included not only *Mukadota* but also news, documentaries, a "face-the-press" style program called *The Nation*, sports, and a music program, *Mvengemvenge* (Mixture), which showcased "traditional Zimbabwean music as well as more popular artists like Thomas Mapfumo or The Bhundu Boys."[34] In 2001, the most popular domestic programming included *Gringo Ndiani?* (Who is Gringo?) and other local dramas; news; *Mutinhimira weMimhanzi* (Musical Sounds), a new name for *Mvengemvenge*; *Madzinza eZimbabwe*

(Clans of Zimbabwe), a talk show on which issues of "traditional" Shona culture were discussed; *Coke on the Beat,* a music video show with Shona- and Ndebele-speaking announcers who played music videos made in Zimbabwe and elsewhere; and *Psalmody,* a Sunday morning gospel music program.

ZBC steadily increased the percentage of local content after independence through such efforts. The BBC report noted that 30 percent of content was local in 1980, but a 1988 government report called *The Democratization of the Media in Independent Zimbabwe* announced, "The ZBC has increased the number of local programmes on television from 16 percent to about 45 percent, . . . a departure from the pre-independence tradition where most of the TV programmes came from Britain and the United States of America." Why is there a difference between the BBC's and the government's estimates for domestic programming at independence? One possibility is that "local content" remains undefined. Another is that the government sought to show significant improvement, perhaps more than actually occurred. Even independent sources, however, do acknowledge increase. In 1990, UNESCO found that about 35 percent of TV programming was domestically produced. Media studies scholar Michael Bruun Andersen analyzed ZTV's published television listings in the late 1990s and found that 20–25 percent of programming was Zimbabwean. However, my own experience suggests that television listings are not an accurate indication of what is shown on TV, something viewers love to complain about. Actually observing what is on TV is a much more accurate way of determining how much is local and how much imported. Furusa used this method to study one week's broadcast in 1999 and found that 37 percent was local, which he defined as "made by ZTV1 or in Africa."[35] Furusa's definition of local points to a difficulty in ascertaining percentages of domestic and imported programming, since the definitions of these terms can vary, and most references do not define them or indicate how they were determined.

By importing film and TV programs from other African countries and the diaspora, and increasing domestic production, Zimbabwe has certainly achieved its goal of increasing black representation on-screen. However, other elements of the country's diversity remain underrepresented in its cinematic culture, including multilingualism and the rural majority.

"We Don't Have Any Local Language Films": Democratizing Language

Language issues were ignored by the BBC study group, and this oversight has continued to plague Zimbabwe's cinematic arts. The absence of a concern for multilingualism in the BBC report may have been a result of its foreign perspective, but domestic support for multilingualism has also remained low. Domestic film and TV production increased from 1980 to 2001, but the majority of it still used English, as do most imported films and TV programs.

Prior to my fieldwork, only one director, Albert Chimedza, had tried to make a feature film in Shona. We spoke at the National Gallery in Harare in April 2001 about his film project *Itai Tione* (Do It, Let's See).

> We wanted to do a film in Shona because we don't have any local language films at the moment. I don't think people think it's as important as it actually is. To have cinema in a local language done at a level where everybody can go to see it because they want to, not because they have to.

Chimedza makes a distinction between Shona films people would "want to" see and those "they have to"; the latter critiques the lack of choice that viewers experience when only one African-language weekly drama series, either in Shona or in Ndebele, is shown on television in any given thirteen-week period. Chimedza began *Itai Tione* in the 1990s but never completed it. All of the feature films produced in Zimbabwe in the twentieth century were made in English. If Shona and other African languages were used at all, it was typically through dubbing or subtitling.

Why do filmmakers in a multilingual country want to work in English? When I asked producer Simon Bright in 2001, he responded at length, in terms similar to those I heard from many other filmmakers:

> Basically it's for distribution, because I don't think that there is a large enough audience within any particular language group, apart from possibly Zulu and Swahili, certainly not Shona, to justify making a relatively high budget—in African terms—fiction film in what amounts to a minority language. There are issues around authenticity and representation, which could argue, for example, that *Flame* should have been done in Shona and the performances would have been better in Shona; the film would have been stronger. Which may have been the case. But we researched it quite widely. The black co-producer was one of the ones who insisted on English, for reasons of distribution. And we discussed it with people like Idrissa Ouedraogo from Burkina Faso, and he said, "If you've got the possibility of making an English language medium film, then do it for marketing and distribution reasons." The representation issue covers quite a wide spectrum. As I've said, there's the spectrum of the representation of Africa, within wider Africa—within the continental mass—and internationally. Those are as important as the issue of representation and identity within the country. So, essentially, we're working on that local, national, and international arena, and we believe that we can create films for all of those audiences. We have done that, and the films have worked for all the audiences. There are other people for whom the issue of authentic representation in indigenous languages is a key issue. I wouldn't argue against that. I don't think you can prioritize the one over the other. What I can say is that for the time being, people

haven't found a commercial, or a market, way of getting a return on minority language production.

Here Bright considers the financial implications of language choice and raises important questions about what "representation" means in cinematic texts. But he also performs several discursive strategies to justify the decision to work in English. First, he devalues Shona—the first language of 85 percent of Zimbabweans and one of the top eleven languages on the continent by number of first-language speakers—by calling it "a minority language." Second, he authenticates his decisions by claiming support based on race and African identity. By attributing the insistence on English to *Flame*'s "black co-producer," categorized by race rather than identified by name (Joel Phiri), Bright does not take responsibility for the language decision he and his wife made as producer and as director. He also depicts one of Africa's most famous filmmakers, Idrissa Ouedraogo, as instructing him to make the film in English. By identifying Ouedraogo by his nationality rather than by his films (most relevant of which here is *Kini and Adams,* which Ouedraogo shot in Zimbabwe), Bright absolves himself of responsibility for his language choice and also suggests that language choice is authentic if made by black Africans like Phiri and Ouedraogo rather than a white African such as himself, regardless of which language is ultimately chosen. His comments suggest a certain degree of defensiveness, uncertainty, or, at the very least, awareness of a potentially unpopular stance, especially for a white film producer already accused by some critics of imposing a foreign perspective through donor-funded films. By justifying the use of English as a commercial consideration (reworded as "distribution") rather than a cultural one, Bright also unwittingly plays into the argument for continued government control over broadcasting, which claims that "commercial broadcasters would be driven by profit and ignore the needs of the poor majority."[36]

Another reason that Zimbabwean film and television workers—including perhaps Bright's "black co-producer"—choose to work in English is that they do not value other African languages. Rebecca Chisamba, a former schoolteacher who hosted several Shona talk shows for ZTV, suggested this in a conversation at her home in March 2001:

> KDT: Why do you think there are so few programs in Shona? It seems like most of them are yours, and there are just a few others.
>
> Chisamba: When I spoke to you in Shona, you were speaking better Shona than my daughter. You see? I think most of our people are still colonized—whether it's still psychological or what have you— most people look down on Shona.

Chisamba's concern about the devaluation of African languages is shared by many Zimbabweans, including monolingual English speakers. Film and TV producer

Rory Kilalea, who speaks neither Shona nor Ndebele, participated in an email exchange with me about this issue in 2001.

> KDT: Do you think there is any room for films made in indigenous Zimbabwean languages?
>
> Kilalea: Colonialism destroyed the essential dignity of the people—by implanting a "superior" language, a culture, a lifestyle—and thus the traditions—be it with the Amandebele or with the Manyika or the Shona or Karanga—have been denigrated. This has resulted in the narrative traditions being eroded—and I personally believe that this lack of self-worth—of self-confidence—has actually reduced the effort, the means for the Zimbabwe people to wish to step into the medium of narrative television or filmmaking. Zimbabwe has largely become separated by the middle class, and the rural has also been segmented by this language barrier. Young girls—friends of my daughter—have laughed when they hear the accented English spoken by the rural folk—(they come from the gwasha's [*sic; gwasha* is Shona for ravines], they say)—and they do not speak Shona unless they have to. English has become the preferred means of class distinction.

Kilalea uses a reference to younger generations to construct Zimbabweans as mentally colonized. Chisamba presents a more positive view, arguing that the use of Shona on television, while minimal, has begun to change people's attitudes toward the language, even her own. She told me how often she is approached by fans.

> KDT: When you run into people on the street, do they usually speak to you in Shona?
>
> Chisamba: A lot of people say, "Mai Chisamba, where did you learn this Shona? Did you grow up in the rural areas?" or what have you. I made an effort to study the Shona with the help of my sister-in-law. When I speak in Shona, I just speak Shona. And I speak deep Shona; I speak Shona like an *ambuya*. A lot of people want to know how I came to speak this Shona. A lot of my ex-pupils say, "When did you start this? You used to speak to us in English!" and so forth. Now when I want to talk in English, I have to make an effort, and yet a few years back it used to just flow. Now I'm so used to speaking in Shona and in good Shona. And I quite like it. Maybe it's the approach. I try and make sure that everyone is entertained, despite their age. I try to make sure there is something for the toddler, something for the teenager, and something for the *ambuya*.

Here Chisamba refers to herself as Mai Chisamba, using a Shona honorific that can be translated as "Mrs." but literally means "mother"; Zimbabwean viewers construct her as motherly. In our conversation she takes up this identity alongside that of *ambuya* (grandmother), commonly figured as both protectors of tradition and the instructors of future generations. The "deep Shona" Chisamba mentions is a classical register analogous to Shakespearean English. Even native speakers of Shona who are not used to this "deep" variety describe it as difficult to understand, formal, and "old-fashioned," consisting of archaic words that are "long gone" in everyday registers.[37] The meanings of deep Shona expressions are rooted in the past and thus associated with mystery and even mysticism. Its use encourages people to actively engage with a text, to speculate about and thereby self-consciously construct its meanings. Deep Shona functions as a marker of tradition, mythologically connecting Shona speakers to their ancestors. Furthermore, it is not just a register of Shona but also marks discourse that is normally private, the language of people's emotional lives. Chisamba's use of it marks her as traditional and as emotionally connected to her viewers. At the same time, her use of it on television brings it into a modern, public setting, giving new value to the Shona language, to Shona traditions, and to the private emotions of her viewers.

In the past, Chisamba continues, secondary school students (whom she refers to as "scholars") were not interested in Shona, but this is starting to change.

> I tell you, from *Mabhuku neVanyori* ["Books and Authors," one of her programs], a lot of scholars doing Form 6 and above or O level, they are writing a lot of good Shona novels, poetry. . . . I get a good response, very good response, especially from the scholars. Because when I started the program it was just the budding writers and the other seasoned writers [who] used to give me their books, and I would call them for [a] book review. But now about 60 percent are scholars. And they write good Shona, and I can tell you they do research.

Through examples of her impact on young people, Chisamba constructs Shona as a language with both traditional and modern uses. Moreover, she constructs viewers not as passive recipients of her Shona discourse but as actively engaged, even producing their own texts in Shona.

The use of Zimbabweans' first languages in the cinematic arts does not concern only "issues around authenticity and representation," which Bright brushes aside, or the cultural value of hearing one's language used for high functions such as in the media, which Chisamba addresses. The use of Zimbabwean languages in film and television is also a matter of providing Zimbabwean viewers, particularly in the rural areas, with linguistic access to information and entertainment.

> KDT: Do you think that your programs would be just as effective if they were in English?
>
> Chisamba: Yes, they would be. But for Shona, you see, the majority of our people speak the home language; Shona TV programs are

more popular. Our sense of humor is different. If you say something in English, maybe the English don't take it as a joke. And
if you say something in Shona, if you are not Shona, the Shona
don't even laugh. But if you are talking in your own language, you
know the sense of humor; you know what to say and what time
to do it. It has an impact on our people. If you listen to people on
[English-language] television, you hear a lot of laughing. But a lot
of viewers are just looking into the air; they do not even get the
joke. If you speak in Shona, everyone gets the joke, everyone gets
whatever you want to do. So I think Shona or Ndebele has a bigger impact on our people because it gets to rural folk. Most of the
townies speak English, but in the farms, in the mines, in the rural
areas, they speak the home language—either Shona or Ndebele.
Now they have televisions, they have radios.

Chisamba initially claims that her programs would be equally effective in English;
she has a stake in her programs' popularity that she does not want to attribute
entirely to her use of Shona. But the lengthy explanation she gives to differences
in how viewers engage with Shona programming suggests otherwise. African
languages allow greater emotional engagement, and they do so for "everyone."

Television still does not accurately represent the country's language profile,
but it uses Shona and Ndebele far more than film does. This is not saying much,
however, given the minimal time allocated to languages other than English. Table
2.1 summarizes my findings from videotaping one week's worth of ZTV1 (the
national channel) broadcast in 2001; I did not study ZTV2 (leased by Joy TV)
because it broadcast mostly imported programming and only in English.

These numbers, which reflect advertisements as well as regular programming, both domestic and imported, represent a stark reversal of the country's
ethnolinguistic demographics: while 85 percent of Zimbabweans speak Shona as
a first language, almost 87 percent of television broadcasting is in English.

ZBC had no official language policy prior to the 2001 Broadcasting Services
Act. Language choice was not only left in the hands of individual producers, who
tend to reproduce a dominant ideology favoring English, but it was also not subsequently monitored. Consequently, some ZBC staff may have believed the percentage of Shona and Ndebele programming was higher than it really was, and
others believed it to be lower than it really was. ZBC's head of TV production,
Remias Msasa, for example, estimated that 60 percent of domestic programming
was in either Shona or Ndebele, whereas my own study found that 31 percent of
domestic productions used languages other than English during a typical week.
Many of these were advertisements and funeral coverage, programming that
serves corporate and state interests rather than viewers.

TABLE 2.1. Percentage of programming in various languages
aired on ZTV1, 25–31 May 2001

Day of the week	Shona (%)	Ndebele (%)	Mixing Shona and Ndebele (%)	Mixing Shona and English (%)	English (%)	Other Languages (%)
Monday	6.56	4.47	5.33	0	83.87	0
Tuesday	15.44	3.76	0	2.48	80.81	0.13
Wednesday	8.67	1.59	0	0	89.89	0.51
Thursday	6.76	1.94	4.36	0	86.94	0
Friday	0.29	1.43	0	0	95.98	2.12
Saturday	6.06	1.21	0	0	92.22	0.51
Sunday	9.53	11.44	0	0	79.03	0
Average	7.61	3.69	1.38	0.35	86.96	0.47

If Shona, Ndebele, and other African languages are underrepresented on television, the realities of multilingualism are even less audible. Critiquing local dramas, Pedzisai Mashiri writes, "The scripts show evidence of codeswitching from Shona to English and from Ndebele to English, but none between the indigenous languages themselves. . . . The plays also show no interaction between Ndebele and Shona speakers as if to suggest the existence of two separate and distinct tribal communities." In reality, Mashiri says, there is a high mutual intelligibility between Shona and Ndebele, and many urban Ndebele speakers are also highly proficient in Shona. Both Mashiri and Lunga argue that hybrid language use would better reflect Zimbabwe's multilingualism, with urbanites in particular "inhabiting several identities and languages" that cannot be reduced to simple ethnic or linguistic labels.[38] The separation of Shona and Ndebele programming contributes to an ideology of ethnic difference and ignores Zimbabwe's multilingualism.

The extensive use of monolingualism, usually English, in the cinematic arts is directly related to the kinds of audiences it reaches, as Chisamba suggested in the excerpt above. Kanengoni makes a similar argument:

KDT: What kind of audiences do you think ZTV is trying to reach?

Kanengoni: Television addresses the urban people, people in towns. If you were to proceed and look at it from what you said—that it's

only 15 minutes Shona and 15 minutes Ndebele news [compared
to an hour of English news]—you can actually see that even if
we intended to reach the rural people, they would not be able to
understand it because most of them don't understand English.

Excerpts from my conversation with Kanengoni illustrate how television actively
excludes rural viewers through the use of English. In the same vein, Chisamba's
experience with Shona TV shows how things could be different, could engage
audiences more, and could be more democratic.

"The Zimbabwean Nation Resides Mainly in the Rural Areas": Democratizing Access

Democratization is needed not only with regard to representation of black
Zimbabweans and their languages but also in increased access to the cinematic
arts through extended broadcasting range, more televisions, and more effective
cinema distribution networks. Under minority rule, white viewers had access to
both domestic and imported films, with distribution structures favoring imports,
while black viewers' access to imported films was severely limited, subject to strict
censorship laws. Films were sometimes distributed to rural areas via mobile cinemas, but television was limited to urban audiences. When television was first
established in 1960, the federal government determined that it would only reach
Salisbury and Bulawayo, because they did not have enough funds to broadcast to
the entire country. Because RTV was commercial, it could only operate where
it was economically viable, which meant the two urban centers. And it could
only be watched by those who could afford receivers, privileging white audiences
over black. "The politics, culture, and interests of the black majority were totally
ignored" both in and by the Rhodesian media, the government of Zimbabwe
noted in a report on the first eight years of media progress.[39]

Scholars have found that media of most types are not reaching or representing the views of the rural majority throughout Africa, and the cinematic arts in
Zimbabwe face this charge as well. For example, Shingai Gwarinda wrote: "To
this day, there is very little participation and representation of the majority of the
Zimbabwean nation, which mainly resides in the rural areas. Access and participation are limited to the urban elite who own and control the media."[40] Kanengoni
described television similarly in our conversation.

KDT: What kind of audiences do you think ZTV is trying to reach?

Kanengoni: Television is for the urban dwellers. Even the programming
is focused on that target group. Unconsciously, perhaps, but that is
how it is. There is no program on television that tries to address
exclusively people in the rural areas as radio does. There is nothing

> like that. For instance, on radio you get a program on agriculture. Obviously that is addressing people out there. We don't have such kinds of programs on television; there's nothing like that. So actually television is focused on the people who live in towns, and radio is for outside the towns.

Radio is used more than television and film to represent rural audiences because it is less expensive to produce. Limited access to electricity in rural areas makes shooting film or video there technologically difficult and expensive.

Where rural Zimbabweans *are* represented, one must ask how and to what purpose that representation is put. A number of films have depicted rural Zimbabwe, including the feature films *Neria, Everyone's Child,* and *Flame,* as well as shorts such as *Mwanasikana* and *Riches,* although one could argue that all of them treat rural life as harsh and in need of major cultural changes. Rural people's access to, participation in, and representation on television are rare. Harare dominates the television news most of the time, but rural areas are shown more during election periods—the government's attempt to encourage rural people to vote, since they are more likely than urban voters to support the ruling party, ZANU-PF. More specifically, Andersen noted that in the 1995 parliamentary elections, the ZANU-PF audience at Mugabe's rallies was "depicted by ZBC as a mass (outdoor) audience of ordinary people in the rural districts while the audience of the opposition parties is depicted as a handful of in-door Harare elite people."[41] Visual representation is open to ideological misuse.

Cinematic distribution in the rural areas continued to be a major problem after independence. Not only did ZBC's broadcast radius not extend far beyond Harare and Bulawayo, but also few rural residents had access to electricity or to televisions. Austen Kark wrote:

> Do they have a significant black audience for television? That is very difficult to determine. The last official figure for paid-up television licenses in black households was 12,000. Now let's say that was an under-estimate because quite a lot of people didn't pay their licenses; let's increase it even by 50 per cent, let's call it 18,000. Let's then take the maximum figure that researchers tend to use in an African environment and say that maybe ten people watch each set, so we have a figure of 180,000.[42]

By Kark's estimate, television was reaching only 2.5 percent of the black population.

The BBC report included suggestions for increasing access. Although it advocated government withdrawal from direct oversight of the ZBC, it promoted government provision of "television sets in some central places in rural areas, so that the adults as well as children could attend at these places for communal viewing."[43] Concern for rural black audiences was a significant departure from the cinematic arts during minority rule, when even efforts to bring the cinematic arts to rural areas were geared toward white viewers in rural centers. After 1980, the Ministry of Information, Posts, and Telecommunications set out to tackle television's distribution problems, following the BBC's suggestion of setting up centralized televisions for shared use in the rural areas. The director-general of ZBC described the broadcaster's plans in a 1983 report:

> Priority will be given to establishing Communications Centres in each of the growth points, business centres and secondary schools in rural areas. These Communications Centres will have radio listening and television viewing facilities, as the intention is to use radio and television for education and for the dissemination of information and news throughout the country.[44]

Known as growth points, the developing centers where TVs were set up had electricity, shops, and gathering places such as bars, "placed right at the centre of the exchange between modern and traditional ways of life"; today they are well served by modern media.[45]

Bringing these plans to fruition, Rural Information Services, a branch of the Ministry of Information, put televisions and VCRs for public viewing in two to five growth points in each province in 1987. Growth points with televisions in the early 1990s included Murombedzi, Mamina, Magunje, Murehwa, Mutoko, Wedza, Gokwe, Zvishavane, Tongogara, Charandura, Zhombe, Shenje, Guruve, Nzvimbo, Chiweshe, Chivi, Mwenezi, Bikita, Nemamwa, Rusape, Murambinda, Nyanyadzi, Bubi, Lukhosie, Manama, and Maphisa.[46] In 2001, ZBC's head of TV production, Remias Msasa, told me that such growth points typically housed one or two TV sets, often in a shop where people would gather to watch.

In the 1980s, ZBC also extended the broadcast radius of one station and added a second. Viewership had tripled by 1984, and in Harare there were more black than white viewers.[47] By 2001, the signal from ZTV1, a commercial station, could be received nationwide.

A growth in film distribution mechanisms, including cinemas, video rental, mobile cinemas, and festivals, came alongside the increasing broadcast radius for television and the burst of international film production in the 1980s. In 2001, in Harare alone there were at least six movie theaters with at least eighteen screens; other cities, including Bulawayo, Kwekwe, Gweru, and Mutare, had movie theaters as well. John Riber estimated that nationwide there were thirty cinemas at that time. Many of these theaters did make arrangements to show Zimbabwean feature films when available, but films imported from the United States occupied most of their screen time. Domestic films faced a difficult battle for distribution in Zimbabwe's cinema halls, which had had contracts to distribute imported films since the 1940s. These contracts effectively prevented them from running domestic films for as long as their popularity with Zimbabwean audiences might otherwise allow. There were some success stories, however, with *Yellow Card* running more than twenty-five weeks in 2001 and surpassing the country's box office intake for *Mission Impossible 2*, the biggest Hollywood blockbuster of that year.[48]

Short films, which form the majority of Zimbabwe's production, fare less well with cinemas, since costs dictate that most refuse to screen anything but features. Distribution mechanisms for short films mainly take the form of film festivals and are still being developed. These have included the Monte Carlo International Festival, which was run by Ster-Kinekor cinemas for about ten years beginning in the 1980s; the Southern African Film Festival, begun by Simon Bright in 1988; the Frontline Film Festival, which began in July 1990; and the Zimbabwe International Film Festival, which began in 1998. There is also the Documentary Film Forum, which is a venue for practitioners to view each other's films; it is hosted in a different Southern African country each year. Many filmmakers have also been successful in having their work screened at international festivals, including Burkina Faso's Panafrican Film and Television Festival of Ouagadougou (Festival panafricain du cinéma et de la télévision de Ouagadougou or FESPACO), the Zanzibar International Film Festival, the Malaysian Commonwealth Film Festival, the Toronto Film Festival Television, Cinestud, the International Student Film Festival in Amsterdam, Germany's Mannheim Film Festival, and Cannes.[49] Television may well be the most effective mechanism for distributing domestic short films, but by 2001 little progress had been made in getting these broadcast.

The availability of films on video increases Zimbabweans' access considerably. Although exact figures are not available, it is evident that Zimbabweans watch more films on video than in the cinemas. For example, in my own questionnaire of seventy-two viewers split evenly between rural and urban viewers, one-third of those who watched films regularly usually watched them in a cinema, compared with about half who usually watched them at home or at a friend's home. Similarly, one-third reported that they preferred to watch films at home, while one-fifth preferred to go to the cinema. VCRs were owned by more than one-third. It seems likely that at least part of the reason for this preference was the lack of a cinema-going culture prior to independence, when cinemas were segregated and tickets were too expensive for most blacks.[50]

In Harare in 2001, videos were widely available for purchase at outdoor flea markets in the city center as well as in high-income, low-density area shopping centers such as Avondale and Borrowdale and in bookshops and music outlets. Most of the feature films produced by Media for Development Trust, as well as Ingrid Sinclair's *Flame,* were easy to find on video. MFD not only sold and rented its own productions but also rented out development films from other parts of Africa. Video rental was an increasingly popular way for urban Zimbabweans to access films. At least three chains operated more than fifteen video rental outlets in

Harare alone, servicing not only urbanites but also commercial farmers who came into the city for supplies. Since the cost of renting a video was less than watching a film in the cinema, it was an economically attractive option for many people.

Another outlet for cinema viewing exists in the high-density townships such as Mbare, where individuals buy or rent videos and then show them in a beer hall or other public place for a small entrance fee. More research needs to be done in this area, since the majority of urban Zimbabweans live in such townships and little is known about their experiences as film and television viewers. Of particular interest is whether women have access to films when screened in such settings, since women who enter the male domain of a beer hall risk being stigmatized as prostitutes. Film and TV cannot be fully democratic unless everyone truly has equal access.

Mobile cinema units have a greater potential to democratize access. These units were developed during the Federation period. Southern Rhodesia's Public Relations Department, which accrued a library of more than 350 imported 16mm films for schools and group audiences, distributed its films throughout the country via CAFU-owned vans, but predominately for white audiences: "Many were shown by the mobile cinema van which, in one year, reached about 6,000 whites and 5,300 blacks."[51] These are striking figures when one considers that whites never formed more than 2 percent of Southern Rhodesia's population. One white viewer recalled that the films shown by the Film Unit were "propaganda, yes, but also educational. Some Western movies—John Wayne and these types of people." Twenty-one years after independence, remembering mobile cinema caused him to remark nostalgically, "Film in Rhodesia—funny enough there were some things that we did quite well in those days." His comments construct mobile cinemas as an effective means of developing a cinema-going culture, at least for white viewers.

In the late 1950s, the use of mobile cinemas was expanded from CAFU propaganda to commercial uses. CAFU founding member Louis Nell recalls that Solly Benatar, "a highly talented amateur turned professional," who owned Dragon Films, produced 16mm color advertising films for mobile cinemas which were then used by oil, soap, and tobacco companies and Coca-Cola to promote their products.[52]

The Rhodesian Internal Services Department began a new program of what they called "home movies" in 1967. Government information officers were armed with cameras, which they used to make short films of community events. Shown via mobile cinema units within the same rural communities in which they were made, the films were reportedly very popular with black audiences. Their use marked a move away from the minority government's use of cinema chiefly for propaganda. As film shifted to entertainment, mobile cinemas were used merely to draw audiences, often screening imported feature films, especially Westerns.

Government officials could then disseminate propaganda materials in print form, such as the *African Times,* a colonial newspaper for black readers.[53]

Zimbabwe's Ministry of Information continued the traditions of mobile cinemas. According to Kemani Gecau, it operated up to twenty-four mobile cinema units through its Rural Information Services branch after 1980, targeting rural areas with development films and newsreels similar to those used by the Rhodesian government, as well as with entertainment. After independence, Charles Ndlovu became head of production services and began commissioning films "chiefly of an entertainment nature to pep up the usual mobile cinema fare," including comedies and short musicals. The Ministry of Information, Posts, and Telecommunications reported that by 1988 it had produced more than one hundred short films, touting them as "popular vehicles of information, education, cultural activities, and entertainment." Other ministries took part as well. For example, the Ministry of Education collaborated with the Canadian International Development Agency and UNICEF to produce a short social message film, *Mwanasikana* (1995), about the need to educate girls. Rural Information Services was reaching an estimated 45 percent of the rural population with films each year by the early 1990s. However, viewers complained that in some areas the unit visited only once every eight years.[54] The government's mobile cinema units were woefully inadequate.

NGOs also developed mobile cinemas and other mechanisms for distributing films they commissioned from domestic filmmakers. Mike Auret Sr., a former employee of the Catholic Commission for Justice and Peace, told me, "A lot of the rural areas don't have electricity, so we bought generators, and portable TV sets, or VCRs. They've gone out quite widely, and of course all the mission stations—the Catholic ones—have them." CCJP commissioned several films from Edwina Spicer, including *Keeping a Live Voice: Fifteen Years of Democracy in Zimbabwe* (1995), about the lack of fulfillment of people's expectations of independence, and *Never the Same Again* (2000), about political intolerance. It later took on distributing them through its mission stations.

Efforts to bring film and television to rural audiences via growth point televisions and mobile cinema units helped, but high-density urban audiences remained largely overlooked for more than twenty years after independence. This changed in 2001, when Charity Maruta founded An International African Stories Video Fair (AIASVF) as an NGO with the aim of bringing educational and cultural films to both rural and high-density audiences throughout Zimbabwe. AIASVF worked in conjunction with MFD and Group Africa, an experiential marketing company that uses live public performances in Shona and Ndebele to interest consumers in the products they advertise. By mid-2001, AIASVF was reaching more than 60,000 people per month.[55] In doing so, AIASVF modified the system devised by colonial film officers, showing American Westerns first to draw audiences to their screenings of propaganda films. Similarly, AIASVF capitalized on Group Africa's popular performances and giveaways of useful products such as soap to draw huge crowds who then remained to watch MFD's educational films. I attended several AISVF screenings, each with more than five hundred viewers present.

AIASVF is just one example of the forums that developed after independence in hopes of increasing Zimbabweans' access to the cinematic arts. The Zimbabwe Film and Video Association began hosting the First Frontline Film Festival, the first pan-African film festival of the region, in 1990. The festival was launched in Harare and then toured Angola, Botswana, Mozambique, Tanzania, Zambia, and Zimbabwe, screening films in English and Portuguese. In November 1992, they hosted Africa Film Week, a milestone marking the first time feature films by black Africans were screened at a commercial cinema in Harare. The following year this became the Southern African Film Festival. During the festival, films were screened at cinemas throughout Harare and also via mobile cinema units in rural growth points, making African films accessible to diverse Zimbabwean audiences.[56]

"Our Values as a Nation, as a People": Nation-Building

After privatization and democratization, the third and perhaps most important challenge set for Zimbabwe by the BBC study group was the task of nation-building, a typical, if ill-defined, mission for a public broadcaster. Broadcasting, the BBC suggested, should not only serve the needs of each group within Zimbabwe's culturally diverse society but also be a "unifying force" that would bring the nation together.[57] In implying that blacks and whites could and should be brought together through the cinematic arts, the BBC report departed significantly from the policy of the white-run broadcaster that preceded ZBC.

What did nation-building mean to ZBC? The increased availability of television in Zimbabwe had three goals: (1) to "improve the lives of the rural mass[es]"; (2) to "broaden their knowledge of the country, the leadership, and the outside world"; and (3) to educate Zimbabweans about "government policies and projections."[58] These terms strongly link the task of nation-building to development, education, and information, raising the specter of propaganda. The state's goals constructed viewers as passive recipients of government efforts to improve their lives and deliver information to them. We know that viewers watch cinematic texts not just for education and information but also because they enjoy them; is there any room for pleasure in nation-building? How can television improve the lives of rural people if it offers them only the state's interpretation of events? What images of the outside world are allowed in? What does nation-building look like from the perspective of ordinary people? Unfortunately, the state broadcaster failed to address these questions at the outset.

Four tropes have emerged in the cinematic arts and discourse about those arts: the name Zimbabwe, an emphasis on traditional cultures, calls for unity among Zimbabweans of different ethnic and racial—and by implication, linguistic—backgrounds, and an (unmet) expectation that the cinematic arts will both reflect and contribute to a Zimbabwean identity.

Naming Zimbabwe

Although progress in cinema was slow for the first few years of independence, a number of short films and documentaries made by independent filmmakers appeared. Many of these emphasized the new name, Zimbabwe, which is thought to derive from one of two Shona expressions—*dzimba dzamabwe* (houses of stone) or *dzimbahwe* (palace)—a reference to Great Zimbabwe, where the ancestors of contemporary Shona people flourished between four hundred and one thousand years ago. Some applied linguists have argued that changing the name from Rhodesia to Zimbabwe "is significant because it signals an effort to assert the importance and official status of African languages." Since subsequent policies do not indicate that African languages have become important to the state, I would suggest that the choice of an African (Shona) name was more symbolic of an imagined (black) African identity than of indigenous Zimbabwean languages per se. By choosing an indigenous name and rejecting the one imposed by white settler Cecil Rhodes, which connoted colonialism, Zimbabwean nationalists staked a claim to the long history that preceded white settlers.[59]

Zimbabwe's renaming was reflected in post-independence films, including Ron and Ophera Hallis's *I Can Hear Zimbabwe Calling* (1980), the United Nations' *From Rhodesia to Zimbabwe* (1981), Maryknoll Media's *The New Zimbabwe* (1982), Peter Entell's *Moving On: The Hunger for Land in Zimbabwe* (1983), and Olley Maruma's *After the Hunger and Drought* (1986). A number of themes emerge in these titles. Words associated with movement such as *from, to,* and *moving* emphasize progress, while *calling* and *hunger* suggest longing for change. *New, after,* and the repeated use of the name Zimbabwe suggest that change has already occurred. Early post-independence filmmakers were, like the state broadcaster, concerned with the status of the new nation as well as with highlighting differences from its predecessor, Rhodesia.

Tradition

Television tends to invoke tradition to establish a historic authority that is abstract and romanticized. A prominent example is the clip of an African drummer used several times a day to introduce the news on ZTV. In an article on similarly stereotypical uses of "traditional" drumming in Tanzania, Laura Edmonson writes, "The ubiquity of this image could be explained as an inevitable result of urban commodification in which African traditional dances are appropriated and 'de-popularized.'" According to Gaurav Desai, such appropriation of "traditional" arts "entertains the urban elite and reassures the developing nation that it has not ignored its national culture." White and expatriate viewers are especially critical of this image. For example, Christina Lamb sardonically observes that in 1999 "ZBC had turned into 'what the President did today' in between scenes of scantily clad village people dancing and drumming." Aqui, a Shona domestic worker who features in Lamb's book, recalls her white employer referring to ZTV1 as "the drums and bums channel." Through such critiques, white viewers construct state television as actively excluding them from national culture.[60]

Musical and other oral traditions play a prominent role in establishing Zimbabwean cinematic texts as connected to local traditions and thereby national. Giuliana Lund shows that music is not just part of the soundtrack but foregrounded in almost every feature film produced in Zimbabwe.

> These elements of oral culture and performance, including the participation of famous musicians, many of whom are also local heroes associated with the liberation struggle, help the films to attract an audience, particularly amongst rural peoples who, though often illiterate, have vibrant traditions of oral performance. These elements of popular culture make the films more accessible and invite audience participation such as joining in with the recitation of tales, the singing of songs, or the clapping of hands.[61]

Lund argues that the "recognition, identification, and participation" that Shona music creates are crucial for social message filmmakers who aim to change audience behavior. I would add that they also mark these films as Zimbabwean, albeit in a Shona-centric way.

On television, talk shows not only evoke tradition but also explain it to young urbanites who have not grown up taking part in traditional practices. We saw this earlier in Rebecca Chisamba's use of "deep Shona" on the talk shows she hosted. She described one of her programs, *Zvakanangana naMadzimai* (Concerning Women), in more detail.

> We touch a lot of issues. We can even talk about cultural things—like when your husband dies, if you are still a young mother, you are not allowed to get near the grave. They will ask you to stay a few meters away; you should not see your husband's coffin going down. But they don't explain why; they just say, "No, no, it's not allowed." But now it's our chance to tell the people why, so we invite elders to explain why it's taboo, why the young lady is not allowed to say good-bye for the last time to her husband.

Chisamba positions young people and elders as contrasting categories, one ignorant of "cultural things" and the other as their repository. Television, she suggests,
offers a means through which these two groups can come together, enabling traditions to continue.

The recovery of such traditions through the cinematic arts was a response to
the efforts of colonial film producers to use cinema to debunk African traditions.
At the same time, colonial cinema was guilty of romanticizing African traditions,
which continues on television and is used to resist social change. The cinematic
arts have a robust history of fetishizing anything traditional, and the use of "tradition" to facilitate nation-building only repackages the same tendency.

Common Values

One of ZBC's explicit goals is to broadcast an image of the nation united by
common values. Remias Msasa, ZBC's head of TV production, told me that the
purpose of television in Zimbabwe is entertainment, education, and to "talk to
people about our values as a nation, as a people." Moreover, such values are not
merely discussed but also actively promoted in order to "project our people, our
nation, positively." When I asked Msasa what he meant by values, he responded,
"Cultural values," and cited hospitality, collectivity, and the importance of family
as examples.

Nation-building involves the production of national culture, or nationalism, an ideology that constructs the nation as distinctive and natural, emphasizes people's commonalities, and suppresses differences. Attempts to create unity
through the suppression of internal differences are important to ZBC's work in
building a nation and encouraging nationalism. Andersen observes the broadcaster's implicit ideology: "In the name of the unity of the people, no conflict
threatening the unity should be even mentioned." At the same time he notes
that Mugabe frequently criticized whites on television in the 1990s, indicating
that whites were not considered Zimbabweans.[62] By 2001 Mugabe's critiques had
extended to members of the opposition party, Movement for Democratic Change,
regardless of race, indicating a further narrowing definition of "the people" or
"the nation." Not only is the nation Mugabe wants to build a racially homogeneous one; it is also one in which there is no opposition to the ruling party.

In most countries, the dominant language plays a role in promoting common
values and sustaining national unity, and Zimbabwe is no different. Extensive use
of English in film and television is a product of many factors that have already
been discussed, including the dominance of imported cinematic texts, the devaluation of African languages among producers, the lack of indigenous language proficiency among white filmmakers, and attempts to reach external markets through
export. It also plays a role in nation-building by avoiding the use of one indigenous
language more than others.

The English language has been an important element in attempts to create unity through the cinematic arts. In a 2001 interview at his home, Olley Maruma, a filmmaker whose first language was Ndebele, told me: "Once you start using Shona, you've limited your audience to Shona speakers. And there are not many. Even in Zimbabwe, you have cut off the English speakers who don't speak Shona and you've cut off the Ndebele speakers. It's a big problem for the African filmmaker —the issue of language." Ironically, in an attempt to avoid favoritism of Shona or Ndebele speakers, producers use English, a language that even fewer Zimbabweans fully understand. Remias Msasa told me that many of the ZBC producers choose to work in English in order to help everyone understand, "even foreigners." When they do work in Shona or Ndebele for "local dramas," their goal is to alternate between them—for example, filming a ten-week series in Shona followed by one of similar length in Ndebele. This goal is often thwarted by the fact that most of the production equipment is based in Harare, in the heart of Mashonaland.

After English, Shona is the dominant language. Despite Maruma's claim that there are not many Shona speakers, it is the first language spoken by 85 percent of the country. Even the name Zimbabwe, a Shona word, "reflects the extent to which Shona was de facto being made the 'superior' language by some Zimbabwean nationalists," according to applied linguists Makoni, Makoni, and Mashiri. ZANU-PF, the ruling party, is also composed mostly of Shona speakers, leading some to call Shona "the language of the ruling party" and a more powerful language than Ndebele and other minority languages. Many Ndebeles believe that the government promotes Shona people.[63] Using English is presented as building the nation, while using Shona divides it along ethnic lines.

Constructing a Zimbabwean Identity

Like ZBC administrators, many of Zimbabwe's culture workers believe that the cinematic arts should contribute to the goals of developing Zimbabwean society, provide Zimbabweans with relevant knowledge of their own environment and their place within it, make "African culture and values" visible, and give youth a sense of self-worth as Africans. Those more critical of the status quo argue that locally produced cinematic arts should be used as a means of teaching viewers strategies for responding to their own oppression. Most critics of Zimbabwe's cinematic culture argue that it has failed in all of these goals because of its reliance on films and TV programs imported from the West. I would add that its success or failure is difficult to measure because the goals set for it rely on ill-defined concepts. What does it mean to develop Zimbabwean society? Does that society include whites and blacks, rural and urban people, citizens, migrants and expatriates, speakers of all languages? What kind of knowledge is considered relevant? Where are the boundaries of Zimbabweans' environment? What is African culture and what values are distinctly African? Is *African* defined by geography, race, or some other criteria?

Domestically produced feature films have received similar criticisms but for different reasons. There is a culture of competitiveness that stems in part from the greater number of white filmmakers and the perception that their work is driven by the interests of foreign NGOs. Such criticism often speaks to larger issues of cultural identity, seen as inadequately represented in the cinematic arts. Many filmmakers argue that NGO funding affects the identity of the arts, making them less Zimbabwean. For example, novelist and filmmaker Tsitsi Dangarembga told Mai Palmberg in a 2003 interview that for many years "a lot of the cultural funding came from outside and therefore [the arts] reflected the origin of the funding."[64] Similarly, documentary filmmaker Heeten Bhagat, the costume designer for the feature film *Yellow Card,* told me, "The irritating thing about film in Zimbabwe is that it's not really representative of Zimbabwean culture. They're always very Western. *Yellow Card* is a complete sellout. It's interesting that the donors liked it. It's a real compromise."

Not all filmmakers blame donors, but many share concerns about the relationship between the cinematic arts and cultural identity. Ben Zulu, for example, told Kedmon Hungwe in a 2000 interview about the film industry: "It's not creating productions that Zimbabweans can start to look at and say these are stories that are actually telling us about ourselves. That are getting deeper and commenting on us. With characters I can live vicariously through and have insight into my world."[65] Albert Chimedza, in a 2001 conversation with me, echoed Zulu's words with a call for an emotional connection with film.

> KDT: You mentioned that perhaps culturally *Yellow Card* was not successful. What did you mean?
>
> Chimedza: I think it's kind of the Zimbabwe I know, but not the Zimbabwe I feel. Do you know what I mean? But I would really like to see a film that somebody who's not Zimbabwean sees and gets an understanding of really how Zimbabwe is emotionally. I mean, I'm not talking about facts.

I also spoke with director Tawanda Gunda Mupengo, then a student at the UNESCO Film and Video Training Project:

> KDT: Is there something that can be called Zimbabwean film?
>
> Gunda: I think it's still too early. If it's Zimbabwean film just because it was shot in Zimbabwe and by Zimbabweans, maybe yes, there are some Zimbabwean films. But when it comes to something that really reflects a Zimbabwean nationhood in terms of cultural

identity and even the social, political, and economic situation pertaining in Zimbabwe, I think that has yet to be done.

There was an emotional reality that Zimbabweans were aware of in 2001 and that
they believed was a shared experience. But without having seen it in cinematic
texts, they had no way of knowing if it really was a *common* reality, something that
could build a national feeling.

Conclusion

Much remains to be done to improve the state of film distribution in
Zimbabwe, and many see links between television and filmmakers as a potential
answer. "I just think that the real potential for the film industry in Zimbabwe
is going to depend on the ZBC," Ben Zulu suggested, "because, in our kind of
countries, there is no way a film industry can develop without being driven by
television. Television is where you make short productions. This is where your
filmmakers develop into filmmakers of the caliber that you find in countries such
as Australia. When given the opportunity to make your production for television,
that is where you really hone your skills."[66]

Can state-run television provide opportunities for Zimbabwean filmmakers?
Before the 2001 Broadcasting Services Act, filmmakers frequently complained that
ZBC refused to work with them, often rushed into low-quality productions with
undertrained crews, balked at controversial topics, required filmmakers to give up
copyright, and did not pay for the films it aired. Many hoped that the BSA would
create new avenues to build a vibrant cinematic culture in the new millennium.

Given its failure to achieve broadcasting privatization, and its uneven success with respect to democratization of representation and access, to what extent
could Zimbabwe fulfill its goal of uniting the nation and creating a cultural identity through the cinematic arts? N. Frank Ukadike writes in *Black African Cinema*
that in other parts of sub-Saharan Africa, filmmaking emerged "out of the excitement of nation-building and a quest for the revivification of Africa's lost cultural
heritage and identity."[67] In contrast, filmmaking in Zimbabwe emerged out of a
colonial tradition in which white filmmakers controlled the means of production, Western financial interests backed the costs of production and distribution,
and themes centered on development. It is not surprising, then, that those well
versed in other African cinema traditions, including filmmakers, cultural workers,
and critics, would find Zimbabwe's cinematic arts lacking in some hard-to-define
"Zimbabweanness."

CHAPTER 3

Authorship and Identities:
What Makes a Film "Local"?

At the end of the twentieth century, fictional film and television narratives—
dramas as many Zimbabweans call them—became more central to viewers' interaction with cinematic texts as their access to "factual" information decreased.
Two films made in Zimbabwe, *Jit* (1990), the first, and *Yellow Card* (2000), the last
one to appear before the 2001 Broadcasting Services Act went into effect, span
Zimbabwe's first eleven years of feature film production and are largely representative of them. The long history of colonial discourse and later Hollywood
aesthetics in Zimbabwe's cinematic culture is reflected in these films' pairing of
education with entertainment, their depiction of local cultures, and their use
of English. Zimbabwean filmmakers and critics have long debated the extent to
which existing cinematic texts have represented Zimbabwean identity to their
satisfaction, tending to react to films made in Zimbabwe as if such an identity
could be quantified: a film is either completely Zimbabwean or completely not.

What does it mean to viewers for a cinematic text to be Zimbabwean? I
argue that a film's identity cannot be read off of the identity of its author; instead,
identity is constructed through the "authorship" of viewers who write their own
interpretations of a film's story. Moreover, identities are not fixed and therefore
not quantifiable. Cinematic texts, creative and intellectual property, ownership,
and authorship act as proxies in discussions that are really about Zimbabwean
identities.

Decisions about meaning are ultimately ideological, so the question of what
constitutes a Zimbabwean text is open to a range of answers. Looking at film criticism not only by professionals but also by ordinary viewers, we find that what they
say about films is an important kind of discourse—so important that it has the
power to disrupt the binary categories that dominate other conversations about
Zimbabwean identity.

Is a Zimbabwean film one about Zimbabweans? Is it one made by a
Zimbabwean? If so, how do we determine who is a Zimbabwean? Is it one that
expresses a Zimbabwean "vision"? If so, how is that vision defined? In my 2001
conversation with Remias Msasa, the head of TV production at ZBC, he raised
similar questions, asking how local should be defined—Zimbabwean or African?
What if a Zimbabwean makes it with a foreign audience in mind? Or a foreigner
with a Zimbabwean audience in mind? Cinematic texts are produced by a crew

rather than an individual and funded by still others, so we might ask: who counts as a film's maker or author? While race is still a difficult subject, Mugabe's vitriolic discourse about Zimbabwe's white citizens raises questions about whether a white filmmaker is Zimbabwean. The films made in Zimbabwe between 1980 and 2001 may or may not be called Zimbabwean depending on how one answers these questions.

No critic, to my knowledge, has attempted to answer such questions, but the words critics choose to describe a film often implicitly construct Zimbabwean identities. By examining discourse about particular films, we can see how identity has been constructed and contested. I agree with feminist scholar Chris Weedon that "authorship cannot be the source of authority of meaning."[1] The involvement of Zimbabwean people in cinematic production and their viewing of cinematic texts have significant implications for their negotiation of not only a film's identity but also their own identities. Moreover, those identities encompass national identity as well as language, age, stances toward tradition and modernity, socioeconomic class, race, and gender.

What Counts as "Zimbabwean" for Critics?

A concern with "firsts" is often used to delineate the identity of a film. What was the first Zimbabwean film? Who was the first Zimbabwean director? Kedmon Hungwe calls *Jit* (1990), directed by white filmmaker Michael Raeburn, the "first locally produced post-independence feature film," calling attention to the differences between the film and the previous features made by international producers who had used Zimbabwe as a location. On the other hand, William Brown and Arvid Singhal call *Neria* (1992), directed by black filmmaker Godwin Mawuru, "Zimbabwe's first feature film made by a local director."[2] Is Michael Raeborn less local than Mawuru? Does his whiteness make him foreign?

Film critics interested in gender representation in the cinematic arts raise similar questions. Who was Zimbabwe's first female film director? In *Culture and Customs of Zimbabwe*, Oyekan Owomoyela gives this credit to Tsitsi Dangarembga, who directed *Everyone's Child* (1996), the story of a young woman whose parents die of AIDS, leaving her to raise her younger siblings without the help of the community. What about Ingrid Sinclair, the white director who made *Flame* the same year? As a former British citizen who married a white Zimbabwean and took on Zimbabwean citizenship, is she a Zimbabwean director? Are her films Zimbabwean? Does she belong to Zimbabwe?

Like "woman-centered" literary criticism that privileges female authorship and aims to identify a female language and aesthetic, a good deal of film criticism privileges black authorship and aims to identify a black or African aesthetic, with the terms *black* and *African* often used interchangeably. When white filmmakers get involved, this aesthetic is harder to identify. Nigerian film critic N. Frank Ukadike, for example, dismisses many of the films made in Zimbabwe because of the involvement of John and Louise Riber, white American expatriates who ran Media for Development Trust (MFD). Ukadike's repetition of the label *African* in his critique of the MFD film *Consequences* draws attention to Riber's identity as *not* African:

> Directed by John Riber (U.S.) of the Development Through Self-Reliance and independent Zimbabwean filmmaker Olley Maruma, this film, which deals with the problem of teenage pregnancy, is hardly a Zimbabwean film. It is totally financed by American agencies concerned with population control. As other African countries are targets for its distribution, it was wise for Mr. Riber to exploit and utilize the services of African consultants, African actors, and an African codirector.

Riber produced *Consequences,* while Maruma directed, but Ukadike presents Riber as director of the film, exaggerating his role. By labeling him only by his country of birth, Ukadike fails to note that Riber had made Zimbabwe his home and raised his children there. By referring to "other African countries" as Riber's "targets," he suggests that his work is combative and destructive. Ukadike continues, "However, with such exposure one hopes to see Mr. Maruma's own future engagement emerge out of this exploitation, which will be viewed in terms of Zimbabwean and African indigenous production, and more importantly reach the level of self-sufficiency that would create alternatives to the 'white frame.'"[3] Ukadike is right that some filmmakers, including Maruma, have accused MFD of taking advantage of them. However, by simply presenting Riber's work as unexamined exploitation, Ukadike oversimplifies Zimbabwe's cinematic culture. Ukadike and others exaggerate Riber's role in MFD's films in order to criticize the role of expatriates in Zimbabwe's film industry.

At the same time, some critics erase expatriate involvement in films in order to more easily identify them as Zimbabwean. This erasure is illustrated by several critics who have misread *Neria*'s authorship. *Neria* tells the story of a widow who learns to fight for her legal inheritance rights when her husband's family follows Shona customary inheritance practices by taking his belongings. During a conversation at his home in April 2001, Olley Maruma told me how his colleague Mawuru came to direct the film with MFD:

> I know the history of *Neria*. That's Godwin Mawuru's initiative. He initially came to me hoping that I would produce the movie for him, but I was too busy; I was not in a position to do that. But I did help initially with putting some sort of package together. I think initially he approached SIDA [Swedish International Development Cooperation

Agency] for money, and SIDA gave him some money and advised that he
approach John Riber to have the film produced. That's how it happened.
The story was a personal story; it was actually a story that took place and
happened to him [Mawuru] when his mother died.

In contrast to those who would construct Mawuru as exploited, here Maruma
presents him as an active agent in the production process of *Neria*. For Maruma,
Mawuru was unquestionably the film's author.

When MFD agreed to produce Mawuru's project, the Ribers hired
Zimbabwean novelist Tsitsi Dangarembga to write a story based on Mawuru's
experience. Louise Riber then wrote the screenplay, using Dangarembga's story
as a guide. Many commentaries on the film give Dangarembga a much larger role
than the film's production history indicates. For example, in an August 2001 conversation with me, Shona novelist and filmmaker Thompson Tsodzo repeatedly
referred to Dangarembga as *Neria*'s producer and director. Others give her credit
as the writer of the film rather than of the story, implying that she, rather than
Louise Riber, was the screenwriter. Some merely credit Dangarembga with the
entire film, as if it can be read alongside her novels as the work of an individual
author. Jessie Kabwila Kapasula refers repeatedly to *Neria* as Dangarembga's: "In
Neria, Dangarembga reveals the ways in which African women are fighting patriarchal oppression in the public space. Her portrayal of the agency of women in these
spaces shows that patriarchy struggles to establish control in public spaces." This
misreading of Dangarembga's role erases the work of director Godwin Mawuru,
allowing Kapasula to attribute the film's feminist perspective to a woman. But
it also elides the work of white American screenwriter Louise Riber, allowing
Kapasula to read the film as representing an authentic African perspective.[4]

An overt insistence on indigenousness, locality, authenticity, and being an
insider in Zimbabwe's cinematic discourse should be read against the back-
drop of colonial involvement in the country's early films, as well as in the post-
independence use of Zimbabwe as a location for Hollywood films. Both are
practices from which filmmakers who identify themselves as Zimbabwean distance themselves through texts and talk about their work. For example, in our
email exchange, Rory Kilalea hailed *Jit* as the first truly indigenous feature film
made in Zimbabwe, emphasizing that the films that came before it were foreign.
Critic Isabelle Boni-Claverie similarly contrasts *Jit* with international films shot in
Zimbabwe that brought in lead actors and equipment from abroad: "The cast of
Jit is 100% Zimbabwean. So is the crew (with the exception of the lighting cameraman from Maputo). Most of the equipment has been found locally, and the rushes
have been developed and printed at Harare's Central Film Laboratories."[5] Boni-
Claverie fails to mention John Riber, who served as cameraman. Her inclusion of
the Mozambican lighting cameraman, but erasure of the American cameraman, is

used to justify her claim that the film is "100% Zimbabwean." A cameraman from a neighboring African country, it appears, is less foreign than one from the United States. Using the cast, crew, and equipment as measures of the film's identity, and ignoring exceptions such as Riber, most critics have accepted *Jit* as Zimbabwean.

"What Right Have You to Make a Film about Our Country?" The Problem of Nationality

The nationality of a film is often attributed based on the nationality of its director. Filmmakers' comments on their films therefore contribute to discourses surrounding the identity of films and construct their own identities. *Jit*'s director, Michael Raeburn, for example, writes of himself in the third person on his website: "Born and bred in Africa, his best work emanates from there, and is appreciated for an authentic insider's understanding and vision." In a 2001 interview with Kedmon Hungwe, he says, "My roots are African broadly," citing his birth in Egypt, his "partly Egyptian" mother, and his arrival in Zimbabwe via Kenya in the early 1950s as evidence of these roots. Yet when he says, "There was not much contact with African people except through people one would meet almost accidentally through the servants," it becomes clear that the word *African* has more than one meaning for him, both a geographic one and a racialized one.[6] In one sense he is African, and in another he is not.

Isabelle Boni-Claverie argues that Michael Raeburn's films can be read as attempts to assert his Zimbabwean identity. I would slightly modify that claim, drawing on Joseph Bruner's work on narrative self-construction, to suggest that Raeburn constructs his identity through the stories he tells about his life as a filmmaker. His previous films include a satire on Ian Smith's regime called *Rhodesian Countdown* (1969). After making it, he was declared a prohibited immigrant, and he spent twelve years in exile. Outside of Zimbabwe, Raeburn also directed the film version of Doris Lessing's *The Grass Is Singing* (1982) and *Under African Skies,* a television series for the BBC. He told Hungwe he often feels that critics, from the United States in particular, are asking, "What right have you to make a film about our country, our continent?" Yet Raeburn's use of *our* in this rhetorical question suggests a slippage from the United States into Zimbabwe. Who is it that challenges his right to make a film about Zimbabwe, about Africa?[7]

Like Raeburn, American citizens John and Louise Riber have a contested relationship to Zimbabwe and its cinematic arts. The Ribers founded MFD in 1987 and lived in Zimbabwe for seventeen years. What does it mean to be white Americans playing major roles in the production of Zimbabwean films? Michael Raeburn drew on his childhood to establish his identity as culturally "African." In this excerpt from our 2001 interview, John Riber performs a similar move to establish his and his wife's identities as "third world groupies."

> Louise and I grew up in rural India. Our parents were working for various churches. They weren't evangelicals or anything—my father was actually managing a tea estate in Assam, whereas Louise's father was a water engineer. I had quite a colonial upbringing in fact. But I'm a third world groupie kind of person. I grew up in India, and I loved it, and I came to the United States, and I had to get out as quickly as possible. I did my university studies, and I left and went straight back to India. I just want to live in developing countries.

Beginning his narrative with references to his childhood allows Riber to construct an identity in which he identifies with Zimbabwe based on its shared experience with other third world countries, while not claiming Zimbabwe per se as part of his identity.

The Ribers began making films about reproductive health in India and Bangladesh. John Riber recalls,

> I've always been interested in the entertainment side of films, but I thought reproductive health is just a great subject for making entertaining films, because that's what Hollywood does—it's basically sex, love, and then, of course, HIV is the hidden danger. It's got all these elements for great drama. So we sort of became known as "those family-planning filmmakers." And sure enough what brought us to Africa is a film called *Consequences,* on teenage pregnancy—that was the first film we made here.

After *Consequences,* John Riber began to concentrate on producing feature films in Zimbabwe with local black directors. The 1990s saw MFD produce *Neria,* directed by Godwin Mawuru, *More Time,* directed by Isaac Mabhikwa, and *Everyone's Child,* directed by novelist Tsitsi Dangarembga. Riber emphasizes that MFD stayed in Zimbabwe primarily for financial and logistical reasons:

> Zimbabwe is the best place in the world to be making films. You can't beat the climate, the infrastructure, the ease in getting around, getting things done—okay, mind you, in the last couple of years things are falling apart. We're getting our funding, for example, for script development [of a TV series based on *Yellow Card*] from a foundation in Kenya [the Ford Foundation], and they don't care where we make it. We might make it in Kenya.

Because Riber is an expatriate filmmaker, Zimbabwe served primarily as a location rather than a source of cultural inspiration for his work; he can just as easily make a film in Kenya as in Zimbabwe. In fact, in 2004 John and Louise Riber moved to Dar es Salaam, Tanzania, where they now work in social message radio.

The Problem of Profits

MFD proved a mixed blessing for the Zimbabweans involved in its films. On the one hand, the NGO helped develop the filmmaking community by providing employment to local directors, scriptwriters, actors, and technicians. On the other hand, a number of filmmakers complained about bad experiences working with MFD. Some complained that MFD monopolized the available funding for filmmaking. Others claim that MFD controlled the profits of its films rather than sharing them with the African directors with whom it worked, as Olley Maruma told me.

> Maruma: I made *Consequences*, and I was looking at how much money the movie had made—last time I looked we had made the equivalent of 15 or 16 million Zim dollars. And I only got 50,000 out of it. So you don't enjoy your intellectual property. You're working as a writer or director for somebody, which is okay if you're working in the States where there's lots of work. I've tried to own the copyright for most of my films, except *Consequences*.
>
> KDT: Who owns the copyright for that? MFD?
>
> Maruma: Media for Development Trust, who incidentally owns a company in the States; it's called Development for Self-Help.
>
> KDT: Self-reliance.
>
> Maruma: Yeah, self-reliance. I wasn't the one who was getting self-reliance; it was somebody else.

Still others criticized MFD for its promotion of donor agendas. Dangarembga, for example, says she felt "restricted in the MFD concept" of donor-driven social message films while making *Everyone's Child*, and she subsequently refused to work with the NGO.[8]

Already a controversial player in Zimbabwe's film industry, in 2001 MFD made a surprising move. After producing three feature films and achieving great success in attracting donor funding for their social message films, in 2001 MFD released its latest feature, *Yellow Card*, this time directed not by a Zimbabwean but by John Riber himself, who also co-wrote the script. Moreover, MFD brought over white American Sandi Sissel, a director of photography who works primarily on Hollywood films, to shoot *Yellow Card*. According to some technicians who worked on the film, Riber was the film's director in name only, and Sissel played a larger role in determining how the film was made. But Sissel left the production before it was completed. Riber told me, "She didn't like me because I wasn't screaming at people and acting like a Hollywood whatever," although others who worked on the films told me that she was demanding more money because she saw the "lavish lifestyle" that the Ribers led. Both claims may be dismissed as mere gossip, but they reflect Riber's attempt to differentiate himself from other expatriate filmmakers and his local colleagues' views that the Ribers make more money from MFD films than do the Zimbabwean filmmakers they employ.

"A True Version of What Zimbabwe Is All about": The Problem of Authenticity

Filmmakers construct their identities in relation to Zimbabwe through talk about their work in "Zimbabwean films." How do the films themselves, and their viewers, construct notions of authenticity, identification, and interpretation?

Jit tells the story of U.K., a young man so called because his friends say, "He'll go far." A reference to the United Kingdom is an ironic name for the first Zimbabwean character to appear on the big screen. Nephew to the famous Zimbabwean musician Oliver "Tuku" Mtukudzi, who plays himself in the film, U.K. has come to the city with uncertain goals, and he makes only a small living from helping his uncle during concerts at local bars. As the film begins, he falls in love with Sofi, a glamorous young urban woman with a good job, a wealthy boyfriend, and the latest clothes and hairstyles. The same day that he meets Sofi, U.K. begins to be visited by a *jukwa* (spirit) visible only to him and to viewers. The jukwa speaks to him, demanding two things: first, that he take economic responsibility for the rural extended family he has left behind and, second, that he keep her supplied with beer. U.K. is torn between trying to save money to pay the *roora* (bride wealth) he has arranged with Sofi's father and sending money home to his parents. Whenever he fails to do the latter, his jukwa appears to remind him of his obligation and to collect her beer. Only when he begins to bottle his own beer for the jukwa so that he is able to keep her in a perpetual drunken state is he able to concentrate his efforts on paying Sofi's *roora*, dishonoring his rival, and winning Sofi's heart.

Jit borrows heavily from and significantly departs from the urban/rural and modern/traditional dichotomies that played such a prominent role in colonial development films. According to Raeburn, the film "explores the conflict between rural and urban life and it celebrates determination." Yet the two lifestyles are not presented in total conflict; in many ways U.K. moves seamlessly between them. Unlike the "country bumpkin" character of colonial films, U.K. is presented as an extremely clever character who adapts easily to life in the city and develops ingenious ways to earn money—including delivering bread on his bicycle, vacuuming white people's carpets, and transporting his neighbors in a sidecar-equipped scooter. Those characters who are more firmly implanted in the city are not presented in such a positive light, especially Sofi's boyfriend, who is depicted as an overconfident but jealous rival to U.K. and doesn't know the value of money. Likewise, Sofi's father is presented as a corrupter of tradition. While negotiating *roora* payments with U.K., he demands not cattle, the traditional form of payment, but $500 in cash (about US$50 in 1990), an expensive stereo, and a refrigerator—all markers of wealth as well as modernity and sophistication. In contrast to the Central African Film Unit (CAFU) films which, according to historian James Burns, promoted "a crude capitalism in which Western-manufactured consumer goods such as radios, steel plows, and cloth . . . are the rewards of thrift and diligence," *Jit* complicates African desire for such goods. While the film does not actively promote the acquisition of commodities, it does present them as a goal worth attaining, insofar as U.K. spends much of the film trying to find the money to acquire them for his future father-in-law.[9]

The jukwa character, who early on seems a symbol of tradition, is perhaps the most complex component of this otherwise straightforward and lighthearted comedy. The jukwa appears in clothing typical of foreign depictions of traditional healers—grass skirt, beads, and feathers—in striking contrast to the jeans, suit jackets, tight skirts, and other Westernized clothing worn by the film's other characters. Sound effects are used to heighten the audience's association of her with the supernatural; each time she appears, we hear the sound of a snake's rattle and the jukwa's loud, cackling laughter or screams, a treatment that recalls the CAFU films that "depicted 'witch doctors' as both comic and sinister," a "time-honored theme of colonial cinema."[10] Despite the problematic visual inscription of "tradition" in the jukwa character, she departs significantly from the traditional Shona jukwa, a dancing *shave* spirit. A *shave*, or *shavi*, is a patron spirit that takes possession of its human host. In the context of the film, the jukwa does not possess U.K. but appears to him and the viewer in human form as his ancestor. Likewise, her dancing is not a prominent feature of the film, although she does comment on the dancing of young people around her while she observes U.K. at a local bar.

The word *shavi* is also used in the Korekore and Zezuru dialects of Shona to describe someone who shows no interest in his own relatives, a linguistic association that adds another layer of meaning to the jukwa's harassment of U.K. for abandoning his rural family. The jukwa's heavy consumption of beer not only draws on traditional Shona religion, in which beer is often brewed for ancestors and used in spiritual ceremonies, but also pokes fun at it, since the jukwa becomes more interested in her beer than in encouraging U.K. to fulfill his traditional obligations. The film closes with the jukwa sitting atop a hill overlooking Harare, drinking champagne: at first she represents the rural and traditional, but by the end of the film she has become urban and modern. Like U.K., she moves seamlessly between the two lifestyles and draws laughter from the viewer at the humorous juxtaposition of tradition and modernity.

In using the jukwa as a complex symbol of both urban and rural, modern and traditional lifestyles, Raeburn opened himself up to criticism for appropriating and distorting Shona culture. Raeburn told critic Fiona Lloyd, "I try to bridge the gap between being parochial and being authentic by having themes that are internationally recognisable."[11] No doubt the theme of conflict between tradition and modernity is internationally recognizable, but it remains unclear how the use of such a theme bridges any gap.

Raeburn asserts that the responsibility for *Jit*'s authenticity lies with its black cast members, who he believes "would soon tell him if anything were inappropriate or distorted." His reliance on them to authenticate his directorial choices recalls Simon Bright's use of his black co-producer, Joel Phiri, and his colleague, Idrissa Ouedraogo, to validate his choice to film in English. Raeburn also sees himself as symbolically taking on blackness through his work. "In a sense I have been like a few other whites like Athol Fugard," he told Kedmon Hungwe, comparing himself to the famous South African playwright. "Fugard very successfully put himself into a black skin, and I did that to a certain extent in *Jit*." Raeburn narrates a self that is an ally to black Zimbabweans, in contrast to Mugabe's depictions of whites as Zimbabweans' "true enemy."[12]

Raeburn's black cast conveniently endorses his vision of Zimbabwean traditions. Dominic Makuvachuma, who portrays U.K., "laughs at the suggestion that some people might possibly be offended by the film's treatment of traditional beliefs." He told Lloyd, "The film reflects a true version of what Zimbabwe is all about in the 1990s," alluding to the mixture of indigenous and Western traditions that form most Zimbabweans' daily lives.[13] Through his assessment of the film and its other viewers, he constructs himself as authentically Zimbabwean and modern as well as more sophisticated than those who might take offense at the film.

Some viewers disagree with Raeburn and Makuvachuma about the meaning of the film as well as about how Zimbabwe might be depicted "authentically." Thompson Tsodzo is a Shona novelist turned dramatist and filmmaker with strong opinions about *Jit*. In 2001 we spoke in his government office, where he was serving in the Ministry for Youth and Employment.

> The producer knows that, in *Jit*, Zimbabweans are very traditional. They will listen to their traditional spirits a lot. So he takes that idea and he thinks he is doing justice to it, but he is mocking us. He is mocking us with that, because he was told that when a young man in town is looking for a job and he can't get a job, he usually goes back home to brew beer, which he gives to his ancestors by pouring it on the ground, and he asks the other ancestors to help him. And when he does this, he does it through a family spirit medium that assists him. Now these people who produced *Jit* take this and they make a mockery out of everything; the

beer that they give to the ancestor is gin. But this should be traditional beer. And the spirit medium—the woman through whom this young man is appealing to the ancestors—is a crook. You see? Raeburn is laughing throughout; he is saying, "Look at what these people believe in!"

Tsodzo's comments are not only criticism of the film but also a means of authoring his own identity as Zimbabwean, traditional, and an arbiter of authenticity. As the gap between Tsodzo's and Makuvachuma's interpretations reveals, any claim to authenticity or truthfulness is an inherently problematic one, since even Shona speakers of different age groups or life experiences will not agree on how a jukwa—or any aspect of their culture—should be represented. There are differing and even conflicting elements within the Shona interpretive community, and there is no homogeneous notion of what the "indigenous" or "traditional" might be, but certainly not an "authentic" one.

Tsodzo's view of Shona culture is no more or less authentic than Makuvachuma's, but his comments draw attention to the distrust among some black Zimbabweans for depictions of their culture by white filmmakers. His words echo those of a black mobile cinema operator in the mid-1950s who commented on audience objections to a negative depiction of a traditional healer in the CAFU film *Mangwiro and Mudzimu* (Mangwiro and the Ancestral Spirit): "Old, old people do not like it for the reason that white people want to discourage us to carry on our old customs."[14] James Burns shows that black audiences under white minority rule were quick to criticize films that portrayed their cultures as "primitive." It is likely that age is an important factor in Shona ideas about customs, tradition, and authenticity. A critique of customs and tradition, or a failure to depict them "authentically," is more likely to disturb an older Shona viewer such as Tsodzo, who was born in 1943, than Makuvachuma, who was born in 1966.

Jit departs from the clear division between urban and rural in many colonial films. Another important way it differs from both its colonial predecessors and the Zimbabwean feature films that followed it is that it was primarily a commercial endeavor, an entertainment film rather than one with an educational or development agenda. A number of critics have nevertheless interpreted it as participating in the colonial development tradition. Tsodzo, for example, reads the film as a critique of "primitive" elements of African cultures and of Shona culture in particular. The film's message, in his interpretation, is "that we need to change from these ways." Likewise, Shingai Gwarinda lists *Neria, Jit,* and *Consequences* as films that "are intended to elicit a response from the audiences. The audiences are expected to adopt the values that are depicted as good in these films."[15] In *Jit*, positive values are hard work, judicial use of money, resourcefulness, and respect for one's elders and for traditional ways. As one would expect, since U.K. possesses these values, the film rewards him with Sofi as his bride.

My own reading of the film is more equivocal. I do not see it as encouraging Zimbabweans to change their traditional, supposedly primitive ways; rather, geared toward urban audiences who have already done so, it both reminds them not to forget their ancestors and—by placing the jukwa as overseer of the city in the film's final shot—suggests that tradition is "always already" a part of urban life.[16]

Furthermore, while the film may encourage a certain set of values in its audience, these are not foreign or unusual. They are values that are already central to many Zimbabweans. In fact, it seems that Raeburn's intent was not so much to teach his audiences particular values but to teach Zimbabwean filmmakers a lesson: "that it is possible to make a low-budget film of African sensitivity in Zimbabwe, using a Zimbabwean film crew and actors, that Zimbabwean audiences will enjoy."[17] It is one of the few films made for Zimbabwean audiences that does not have a strong "social message" to impart.

Reflecting the "True African Flavor": The Problem of Identification

In contrast to *Jit*, *Yellow Card* epitomizes the social message films made in Zimbabwe. Like *Jit*, it is a love story whose main character is a poor young Shona man in Harare. Tiyane even echoes U.K.'s goal of ending up in the United Kingdom, telling a friend, "I'm gonna go places! Watch me—United!" bragging of his plans to play for Manchester United, a British soccer team. Unlike U.K., however, who ekes out a living, Tiyane's future seems bright. Despite his lower-class upbringing, he is a talented soccer player and a good student. His future is threatened, though, when he succumbs to peer pressure and sleeps with Linda, a classmate and longtime friend. The very next day, Tiyane meets and falls for Juliet, a "coloured" (mixed-race) daughter of wealthy parents. When he learns that Linda is pregnant with his child, he keeps this hidden from Juliet, until Linda drops the baby on his doorstep and leaves town to pursue her education. He and Juliet have already been accepted by each other's parents and declared their love for one another, but their relationship is threatened by the revelation of Tiyane's past indiscretion. The film ends ambiguously, with Tiyane being cheered on in an important soccer match while his parents care for his infant son and both Juliet and Linda listen to the match on the radio. The title refers to the yellow card that a referee gives a player during a soccer match if he commits a foul. The card serves as a warning, in this case a metaphor for the "warning" Tiyane receives when he learns that Linda is pregnant; presumably a red card would have been HIV.

Yellow Card moves away from the "clash between tradition and modernity" theme that is common not only to *Jit* but also to previous MFD films like *Neria* and *Everyone's Child*. Nevertheless, it continues the colonial tradition of using film for development and education. *Yellow Card* is a high-concept film with multiple story lines and themes, most of them driven by the desire to educate African audiences. Fitting into the overall framework of reproductive health issues that are common to MFD's films, it incorporates many themes: peer pressure, sexually transmitted diseases, premarital sex, abortion, rape, and gender bias. These social messages are an important part of viewers' understanding of what a "Zimbabwean film" is.

Gwarinda, in her examination of Zimbabwean development films, asks "whether film in Zimbabwe celebrates Zimbabwean culture."[18] *Yellow Card's* reproductive health messages could take place anywhere in Africa; in that sense the film does not celebrate Zimbabwean culture. Nevertheless, in *Yellow Card's* movement beyond reproductive health issues to include other themes—such as romance across racial and socioeconomic lines, respect for tradition, love, and honesty—MFD has created the space for Zimbabwean audiences to engage with their culture through film.

Most viewers were able to easily identify the film's development messages in an audience study conducted in Chitungwiza in June 2001. Chitungwiza was once Harare's largest high-density suburb, and today it is Zimbabwe's third-largest city. Stephen Mueller and Dambudzo Mariti administered a questionnaire for MFD there, asking more than six hundred young viewers, "What did you learn from the film?" Typical responses reflected that viewers did learn that premarital and unprotected sex has long-term risks that include pregnancy as well as school expulsion, STDs, HIV, and AIDS. For example, for a 19-year-old female, the film's main lesson was that "a few minutes can spoil the rest of your life if you are not careful about the way you behave." A 17-year-old male summarized the film's lesson as "no sex before marriage, 'cause it may ruin your future or you have to protect yourself when having sex, 'cause you may die of AIDS or STDs." And an 18-year-old male learned that "we have to concentrate on schooling not jumping into things like girlfriends." A multinational survey conducted by Population Communication Africa on behalf of MFD found that youth and adults in Kenya, Uganda, Tanzania, Zambia, and Zimbabwe learned similar lessons.[19] The purpose of *Yellow Card* speaks as well to other Africans as to Zimbabweans.

Some Chitungwiza viewers, however, compared the film's messages to their day-to-day reality and found the film lacking. A 17-year-old who had seen the film twice wrote that he learned "really nothing[;] as far as I can see it's not educational because youngsters of today experiment too much." A 17-year-old female who had seen the film more than four times commented: "As an adult I learnt nothing."[20] Both viewers construct themselves as older and more mature than the film's target audience. Yet their repeated viewing of *Yellow Card* suggests that the film may have held pleasures for them other than education.

Some viewers learned different lessons than the reproductive health messages intended by MFD and its international funders. A 17-year-old female learned that "black women/girls are still being viewed as low and they are still under every-one else and also they are used." A 17-year-old male wrote, "I learned that love at first sight is common." And another 17-year-old male learned that "guys from the ghetto can go out with girls from suburbs, which is possible." A 17-year-old female who had seen the film more than four times learned that "if one works toward something or if you really love someone you don't have to tire becoz you will always get it in the end." Her reading of the film suggests a stereotypical Hollywood ending, "whereby a solid, reassuring narrative and a fully understand-able order are reinstated," an imagined ending that *Yellow Card* itself does not depict. These comments demonstrate that viewers in Chitungwiza related the film to their own lives, in some cases using them to critique perceived gender ideolo-gies and in others to refract their own romantic desires.[21]

While audiences in Zimbabwe and other sub-Saharan African countries learned from the film's development messages, Zimbabwean viewers were more likely than those in other countries to engage with the film's other themes. In the Population Communication Africa multinational survey mentioned above, participants were asked to categorize *Yellow Card* as entertaining, educational, fun, boring, or provocative. In all five countries, most young people labeled the film "educational" with percentages ranging from 43.5 percent among Zambian girls to 70 percent among Kenyan boys. Significantly, though, Zimbabwean youths were more likely than those of any other country to label the film "entertaining," with 30.2 percent of the boys and 38.5 percent of the girls choosing this label.[22] This statistic speaks to the film's purpose for Zimbabweans in particular—they see past the message and derive something particularly pleasurable from the story or characters. It is important, therefore, to examine not only what Zimbabwean viewers learned from the film but also what they found entertaining about it. In the Mueller and Mariti survey, Chitungwiza youths were asked this very question. Their responses suggest that what makes the film appealing to young Zimbabweans is its use of actors and themes they recognize as "local."

Those interested in using film to reach African audiences during minority rule believed that most audiences preferred local images, with "local" conceived of as "national" or even "sub-national" rather than regional or continental. Audiences in Northern Rhodesia (colonial Zambia) reportedly found South African or Nigerian films foreign and laughable.[23] Cinematic production has increased throughout Africa, but it is still a rare treat for Zimbabweans to see images they recognize on their screens because of the surplus of imported films and television programs and limited access to cinemas, televisions, and VCRs. When Zimbabwean actors appear on their screens, it is a noteworthy event.

Chitungwiza viewers were asked, "Did you identify with any character(s) in the film? If so, which ones?" Many named Zimbabwean actors by name. For example, Lazarus Boora played only a small part in the film as a gardener, but he was instantly recognized because of his renowned comic role as the title character in the Shona-language local drama series *Gringo*. John Banda, who played Tiyane's best friend, Skido, in *Yellow Card,* was also frequently mentioned, also having made a name for himself as a TV actor. Likewise, many respondents commented on the use of black actors when they were asked, "What did you like about the film?" A 19-year-old female liked that "it was performed by black people, mostly." Indeed, most of the film's characters were black, with the exception of Juliet and her mother, who are "coloured," and a few of Juliet's white classmates, who are minor characters. Although the lead actor, Leroy Gopal, is part Indian, his character, Tiyane, was meant to be black and was perceived as such by viewers. One 15-year-old said he liked that *Yellow Card* promoted "local actors like Lazarus Boora and Tiani." Speaking more broadly about Zimbabwean actors, another male liked that "our people were given an opportunity to star in the film." Similarly, an 18-year-old who had seen the film twice wrote, "It was performed by Zimbabweans" as the element he liked about *Yellow Card*.[24] These viewers construct being Zimbabwean and black as important, identify with characters and actors who share these identities, and find value in this identification. They recognize something Zimbabwean about certain media, most typically if they have something important in common with the actors or characters in terms of language, ethnicity, race, class, or gender. Even though the specifics of what makes a film Zimbabwean remain out of reach, viewers' comments indicate there are aspects of identity that intuitively hinge on recognition and identification.

Some related responses concerned not the actors of the film but the overall portrayal of Shona, Zimbabwean, or even African culture, supporting the view that authenticity and cultural accuracy are very important to Zimbabwean audiences. Still responding to the question "What did you like about the film?" a 17-year-old male wrote, "It really proves our culture or shows our tradition." A 16-year-old female who had seen the film twice liked "the portrayal of different cultures as reflected by Tiyane's family and Juliet's family." Such comments refer to Tiyane's high-density, lower-socioeconomic-status Shona family, which is depicted as urban and modern and yet still practicing traditional Shona gender roles, contrasted with Juliet's low-density, higher-socioeconomic-status mixed-race family, which is depicted as Westernized, wealthy, and without any visible markers of traditional cultures. In one scene Juliet visits Tiyane's home and is socialized into Shona domesticity by Tiyane's mother, learning to kneel while serving dinner to his father. A 21-year-old who had seen the film twice commented on this scene, writing that she liked "when the coloured girl was practising traditional culture. Giving Tiyani's father food."[25]

Chitungwiza viewers, themselves residents of a high-density suburb like the one where Tiyane's family and friends live, enjoyed seeing characters in a similar environment. For example, a 17-year-old female wrote, "I liked that they put an almost exact portrayal of the poor Zimbabwean." Similarly, another 17-year-old female commented, "I like the way they showed life in the high-density areas."[26]

Other viewers enjoyed the film's representation of a local culture, but without giving specific examples of what marked the film as local. A 22-year-old male, for example, liked that "it's a home produced/based movie." An 18-year-old female who had seen the film three times responded, "They showed us clearly African romance." An 18-year-old male who had seen the film more than four times liked "the setting" and added: "It reflects the true African flavour." A 17-year-old female who had seen the film more than four times wrote, "It really is one of the best Zim films." In responses such as these, Chitungwiza viewers indicated their awareness and appreciation of the film's portrayal of their environment and cultures, even while leaving aside definitions of what might be "truly African," Zimbabwean, or "home."[27] To them, there was no question that it is a Zimbabwean film.

Not all responses to *Yellow Card* were positive, however. The Mueller and Mariti survey also asked Chitungwiza youth, "What did you not like about the film? How can the film be improved?" Responses varied considerably but again often related to the representation of Zimbabwean cultures. Some criticized the film for its perceived lack of realism, such as a 17-year-old female who had seen the film more than four times and disliked the film's depiction of easy access to abortion services: "The doctor's part was fiction in the sense that when we focus our Zim life and in Linda's situation she was poor and could not afford to call a doctor and pay him."[28]

Others believed that the film should have portrayed a positive view of life in Zimbabwe rather than a realistic one, echoing Tsodzo's view of *Jit* and those of earlier black viewers who complained that CAFU films "are not able to depict the modern life of the African. When they want to depict African life, they show the worst that is in it, and they do not show that the African is advancing."[29] For example, a male viewer criticized the film's depiction of Cedric, a black gardener played by Lazarus Boora, who acts as a literal and metaphorical gatekeeper in the film, treating Tiyane rudely when he comes to Juliet's posh home; the viewer criticizes the character of Cedric because he "looked down on his fellow kinsmen, our people. The black people." A 17-year-old male complained that *Yellow Card* "made us to look like we're very poor. It can be improved by using better grounds for our soccer." His request for better soccer grounds is similar to those of other viewers who thought the film's responsibility was to correct real societal problems. A 17-year-old female, for example, wrote, "I did not like Juliet's mother's attitude towards black people." The film could have been improved, she added, "by making white people accept blacks as they are and by improving the living standards." Like many viewers, this one mistakes Juliet's mother, who is "coloured," for a white woman, leading to an interpretation of her protectiveness of Juliet as racism toward her black suitor, Tiyane.[30] Viewers suggest that the film's responsibility is not just to portray improved environments, living standards, or relations between races but to actually improve them.

The statements of viewers both pleased with and critical of the film indicate that many were particularly attuned to the cultural indicators of socioeconomic status. This is clear from references to "the poor Zimbabwean," low-income areas known as "high-density areas" on the outskirts of most Zimbabwean cities, "living standards," and so on. Similar results were found in the Population Communication Africa survey, which noted that Zimbabwean and Zambian viewers were more likely than those in other countries to comment on material goods in the film and the difference in class status between Juliet and Tiyane.[31] The comparison of Zimbabwean audiences to those in other sub-Saharan African countries suggests that the former's attention to material culture stems from their own day-to-day experiences in urban Zimbabwe, where such possessions are important markers of one's socioeconomic standing. Zimbabwe's white population, although small, is larger than that of the other countries that Population Communication Africa studied, so it makes sense, too, that many viewers linked socioeconomic status to race, leading them to mistake the characters of Juliet and her mother for white.

Viewers as Authors: The Problem of Interpretation

In addition to examining what viewers liked and did not like about *Yellow Card*, an examination of how they would complete the story's ambiguous ending further demonstrates the degree to which Zimbabweans incorporate their cultural backgrounds into their interpretations of the film, thereby claiming authorship of the story and sidestepping the question of authorial identity as an indicator of a film's identity. The Mueller and Mariti survey offered Chitungwiza youth the opportunity to "tell how you would continue the story." The responses indicate the extent to which viewers, most of whom were Shona, incorporate common Shona or Zimbabwean cultural values as well as Shona literary techniques and themes into their readings—and writings—of the film.

One common theme among viewers' imagined endings to the film is the stereotyping of female characters. Like the women of early Shona novels who are "beautiful and are constant companions to their men," Juliet is depicted by many viewers as the ideal Zimbabwean woman—a forgiving wife, mother, and friend.[32] In authoring a new ending for the story, a young man who had seen the movie three times wrote, "Juliet comes back to Tiyani. . . . The baby will grow up well. Tiyane and Juliet will marry and Juliet will help look after Ronaldo. Became a very happy family." A 17-year-old female wrote: "I would want to see Juliet's final forgiveness for Tiyane for hiding the secret from her and also would want to see Tiyane marrying Juliet." Male viewers also composed romantic Hollywood endings for the film, such as a 17-year-old who wrote: "Tiani will fall in love with his girl [Linda] which had Tiani's baby. His second girlfriend [Juliet] will become Tiani's best friend, and she will help Tiani in whatever problems he was going to face."[33]

Linda was rated as Zimbabwean viewers' least favorite character, and in contrast to Juliet, she is portrayed by many viewers as a deserving victim, criticized for seducing Tiyane and abandoning her baby.[34] This is in keeping with the second stereotypical woman character of Shona literature, the Jezebel figure—the "whore, or sexually aggressive woman" who, Patricia Hill Collins demonstrates, is also common to stereotypes of African American women.[35] Many viewers mete out drastic punishments to Linda for her transgression of cultural mores. In a 21-year-old's version of the story, "Linda becomes a professional whore. . . . Linda becomes an aids victim." In a 17-year-old's version, "Linda will start to admire her son and tries to get him back but she cannot have him at all." A 16-year-old male who had watched the film twice wrote, "Linda must be raped [by] that guy who said he wants to help her and finally she won't succeed in life."[36]

Female viewers, in particular, wrote endings that punished Linda for her culturally transgressive role. A 17-year-old female wrote, "Linda is harassed by [her] second boyfriend." Another 17-year-old female responded, "Linda will not get married, she will be dumped and in this case with [an]other baby." A third 17-year-old female who had watched the film twice wrote, "Linda would get married to Obert [her friend and possibly her boyfriend] and regard [regret?] it becoz he will not be treating [her] like his wife but a servant."[37] Viewers draw on local meanings of the word *prostitute* as "a marker to denote any supposedly 'unrespectable' woman, particularly those who move into space that is considered to be male territory."[38] For example, a 15-year-old female wrote, "I want Linda to die with Aids because she is a prostitute. She get in love and [in] school and she become pregnant." A 22-year-old female who had seen *Yellow Card* three times wrote, "Linda should at least suffer wherever she went." A 16-year-old female articulated the purpose of punishing Linda as a moral lesson: "I would continue shading [shedding] more light on how Linda led her life and there must be some suffering so as to teach other teenagers out here not to have sex before marriage." Although she constructs this as a moral lesson for "teenagers" generally, her treatment of Linda suggests the lesson is primarily for female viewers.[39]

In a small number of cases, viewers wrote Juliet into the role of Jezebel and punished her rather than Linda, presumably blaming Juliet for breaking up Tiyane's relationship with Linda and preventing her from caring for her son. For example, a 17-year-old female who had seen the film four times wrote that Tiyane and Linda's baby "can be a richman and help his mother . . . and the white girl will die"—another misreading of Juliet as white.[40]

Minor women characters associated with Tiyane's promiscuous friend Skido, who contracts HIV, also fall victim to the punishment imagined by young viewers.

A 16-year-old male who had seen the film twice wrote, "As far as the girl friends of Skido are concerned they must fell seek [fall sick] and finally die."[41]

The punishment of sexually or culturally transgressive women serves as an educational purpose, similar to the "mutilation of unsympathetic characters" typical of Shona novels and oral stories.[42] That it is most often female viewers who punish Linda in their fantasies demonstrates that women who internalize oppressive images become effective conduits for perpetuating gender oppression.

Most viewers treat Tiyane, as a male, differently than Linda and other female characters. He is a hero, and his behavior is therefore rewarded. Typical viewers of *Yellow Card,* both male and female, imagine Tiyane succeeding with both soccer and school, marrying, and raising a happy family. For example, a 21-year-old wrote this new ending: "Tiyani's football team will win 2–0. Tiyani will then qualify for the national team [and] become a professional player liked by many people, & Juliet comes back to Tiyani." Similarly, a 17-year-old who had seen the film three times wrote, "Tiyane will finish his school and become a national soccer player then he gets married to Juliet." A 22-year-old female who had seen the film three times indicated that "Tiyane should . . . be successful and play for a big team. (His dream come true.)" A male viewer wrote, "Tiyane's family and Juliet's family will work things out for their children and provide a future for them, and Tiyane would then play for Manchester United and fulfil his dreams and that of his father. He will take his family with him and live happily ever after," another Hollywood ending.[43] Viewers write their own imagined futures.

In the stories authored by viewers, Tiyane plays the role of the idealized hero common to Shona literature. The exaggerated and implausible success he achieves in these creative utopian endings is in sharp contrast to the failures viewers attribute to female characters. Even Juliet, whom most viewers see in a positive light, is resigned to a passive role as Tiyane's helpmate. George Kahari notes in *The Rise of the Shona Novel* that "heroines are few and far between in Shona literature. This is not without reason for women have rarely been seen taking leading parts in the traditional folktale."[44] Chitungwiza youth writing the story of *Yellow Card* are authors within a literary tradition shaped by their culture, not unlike Shona storytellers, novelists, and filmmakers. Viewers who contribute to discourses about the film construct *Yellow Card* through their own authorial identities—making it Zimbabwean—without regard for the film's "real" authors.

The question remains, however: what effect does this literary tradition, playing itself out in the fantasies of young Shona viewers as they view, discuss, and rewrite a film made locally, have on Zimbabwean society today? For example, the fact that the symbolic mutilation of women is prominent in the fantasies of Shona viewers raises questions about what symbolic and social effect MFD's reproductive health films have on women and girls. Mary Gentile argues in *Film Feminisms,*

"If we question when and why we identify with a particular character, and when and why we do not, and if we compare our answers to these questions with other viewers' answers, we will begin to recognize the lines of contradiction and tension within a film's world view, between that world view and the experiences of its spectators." It appears that Zimbabwean viewers remain largely unaware of such contradictions and tensions, instead finding points of similarity between their own experiences—in this case their knowledge of traditional gender roles and storytelling motifs—and those they see on the screen, and harshly criticizing depictions that are dissimilar. In the case of *Yellow Card*, where the director, producer, and director of photography are not Zimbabweans, it may be in the filmmakers' best interest to elide such lines, purposefully not offering a critique of "traditional" gender roles because such a critique might draw attention to their own status as foreign and make it difficult for Zimbabwean viewers to locate indigenous elements in the film. Yet research on the reception of another MFD film, *Neria*, showed that men had conservative reactions to the film, relating more to the male antagonist than to the film's female protagonist. When a cinematic text does critique traditional gender roles, viewers may effectively resist the film's message. Viewers may author their identities and disrupt binaries about what it means to be traditional and modern, but they do so from within a cultural context, where race and gender stereotypes are often fixed and accepted.[45]

Conclusion

Jit and *Yellow Card* were produced eleven years apart and spanned the course of Zimbabwe's still-youthful feature film industry at the turn of the century. In them one finds the culmination of half a century of film production by whites and foreigners. Zimbabwe stands apart from many other African countries in which cinema came under the control of black filmmakers after independence in the 1960s. African filmmakers in other countries present their own cultural environments, whereas in Zimbabwe the most prominent filmmakers have used film to present black Zimbabwean (typically Shona) cultural environments to which they themselves remain outsiders. International donors are understandably biased toward funding filmmakers who have already proved themselves successful, and they are fearful of investing in Zimbabwe during its ongoing economic and political crisis. Given these constraints, in 2001 the imbalanced proportion of white filmmakers in the top ranks of Zimbabwe's industry seemed unlikely to change.

For urban Zimbabwean viewers, it is not the national or racial identity of filmmakers that is important but rather the extent to which they, as viewers, can engage with Zimbabwean culture through a cinematic text and author their own interpretations. Such engagement takes many forms, from appreciating a film's representation of that culture, to critiquing it for its supposed inaccuracy or pessimism, and even to writing their own versions of a film that draw on cultural knowledge, morals, and storytelling techniques. This is easier to demonstrate with *Yellow Card* than with *Jit*, since more audience research has been done for the former. Yet even in *Jit* the character of the jukwa, the most identifiably indigenous component of the film, suggests a potential site for viewers, particularly Shona viewers, to interrogate both tradition and modernity from within their own cultural context.

CHAPTER 4

Changing the Channel:
Using the Foreign to Critique the Local

Just as filmmakers and viewers construct both their own identities and a film's identity through talk about "local" cinematic texts, they also discuss and interpret "foreign" cinematic texts, relating them to their identities in various ways. Filmmakers, broadcasters, and critics have constructed viewers as victims of the imported cinematic texts that are so prominent on their television screens, in video rental stores, and in cinema houses. However, listening to viewers' interpretations shows that they are not victims; domination and resistance are complex. A political position against the domination of local airwaves with foreign content should not preclude the recognition of the real pleasures people experience in imported programming, nor should their enjoyment of such programming be used as evidence of their mental (neo-)colonization. I argue that Zimbabweans are not victims of cultural imperialism but active agents who enjoy imported programming and use it to interpret their own culture and day-to-day lives in ways its producers never intended. On the one hand, such an argument hardly seems necessary because similar findings have been made in thousands of audience studies all over the world. My goal here is not to add to the plethora of studies that "tak[e] the side of the audience," as Meghan Morris describes ethnographic audience studies, but rather to refute the dominant image within Zimbabwe of viewers as "cultural dupes," an image that was used to justify repressive legislation in the form of the Broadcasting Services Act.[1] While viewers' active use and interpretation of media texts may not enable them to make significant political change, it is important evidence that they are not in need of paternalistic laws designed to save them from their own "misguided" enjoyment of what the West has to offer.

Cinematic Junkyards: The Dominance of the Foreign

Critics may disagree about the effects of imported cinematic arts on viewers, but there is no doubt that such programming overshadows local productions both on television and in cinemas. Zimbabwe is not alone; most countries air large percentages of imported programs, usually produced in the United States, the one country where imported programming is minimal. Scholarship points to the excess of U.S. programming in Nigeria, South Africa, Mexico, Denmark, Finland, Ireland, Canada, and many other countries—not only African and other "third world" nations but also European ones that are themselves exporters of programming. And the rates at which these countries import American programming parallel those of Zimbabwe. For example, in Canada 75 percent of what is shown on television is imported from the States. Even Britain, the United States' leading Anglophone competitor in television exports, imports 44 percent of its programs from the States in order to fill its airtime.[2]

The expansion of United States television into other markets has been compared to colonialism, perpetrated not only against the underdeveloped world but also, ironically, against the former European colonial powers. Many cultural critics in Zimbabwe have suggested that the United States has become the country's most recent colonizer in the realms of theater, music, and cinematic arts.[3] Although *colonialism* in this context is a metaphor, United States capitalism is taking advantage of Zimbabwe's own media market. The resource it extracts, money, is abstract, but it does leave Zimbabwean media at a disadvantage.

A major factor in Zimbabwe's reliance on imported programming is economics. Zimbabwe Television cannot afford to produce enough programs to fill its airtime; neither could Joy TV for the three years it was in operation. When I spoke with Nancy Gondo, head of sales and marketing at Joy TV in 2001, she told me that it costs ten times more to produce a local program than to import one produced elsewhere. Alexander Kanengoni, head of research at ZTV, told me that the decision to import programs is "purely a matter of finance. We can't afford [much], so we look for the cheapest options." After getting as many African and African American programs as it can find, ZTV settles for the most inexpensive programs, often without regard for content.

One reason that African broadcasters can purchase imported programs so cheaply is because of "cultural discount," a practice based on the assumption that imported cultural products will have diminished value for consumers in proportion to the cultural distance between the exporting and the importing cultures. Imported programs "portray nonnative values, behaviors, institutions, and the like" and use a foreign language or dialect, so it is assumed that they will be valued less than local programs that portray familiar values and use local languages and dialects. Imported products are therefore sold at lower prices in order to compete with local products. The greater the linguistic or cultural differences between the exporter and the importer, the greater the discount levied on a TV program. For example, each episode of the 1980s American prime-time soap opera *Dynasty* was sold to the United Kingdom for $20,000, to Norway for $1,500, and to Zambia and Syria for just $50. U.S. producers reach a huge national market with their programs, so they have usually already recouped their costs and do not need to make much money from exports in order to turn a profit. Spreading the costs of making a TV program over a large number of buyers also means that producers in the States can spend significant money making programs with higher production values than those made in a small country like Zimbabwe.[4]

The practice of cultural discount has led to accusations by many cultural critics—both in Zimbabwe and elsewhere—of cultural "dumping," the practice of "selling in a foreign market at a price below that in the domestic market or below production cost."[5] Dumping is, in theory, a neutral description of an economic practice, but the term has taken on extremely negative connotations, particularly when practiced by U.S. distributors in economically disadvantaged countries.

Allegations of dumping are popular among critics, who call ZTV and Joy TV "junkyards of outdated Western movies" and argue that dumping "leads to cultural imperialism."[6] On the one hand, dumping allows financially strapped broadcasters like ZTV to access programs that would otherwise be priced out of their ability to purchase. On the other hand, these low prices encourage such broadcasters to air imported programming rather than produce their own. Imported programs are less expensive than local ones, but they are purchased using the same limited funds, so in practice their purchase prevents the production of local programs.

What proportion of the Zimbabwean airwaves does imported programming take up? In 1997, Michael Bruun Andersen reported that roughly 66 percent of what was broadcast on ZTV was imported. In 1998, he indicated that this number can vary up to as much as 80 percent, basing this estimate on ZTV's printed schedule. Munashe Furusa, in 1999, studied a week's broadcast on both ZTV and Joy TV and found that 62.3 percent of what was aired was foreign on ZTV and 98.4 percent on Joy TV. Since Furusa defines foreign as not produced in Africa, these numbers are actually lower than they would have been had he looked at all imported programming, defining foreign as not produced in Zimbabwe. Using this definition, Fred Zindi estimates that 95 percent of what is shown is foreign.[7]

Like Furusa's, my research on Zimbabwean television is based on actual broadcasts rather than printed schedules, because the latter are notoriously unreliable. I found a lower percentage of foreign programming on Zimbabwean television than other researchers have found. In 2001, I recorded and later viewed ZTV1's broadcast from Monday, May 23, to Sunday, May 29, from station start-up to shutdown each day for a week. By noting the origin and length of each program, including commercials and station filler, I calculated percentages of local and imported material broadcast; table 4.1 summarizes my findings.

This method is more accurate than simply counting the number of programs in each category, which would result in a higher percentage of local content, since many locally made programs are shorter than imported ones. I found that, on average, about 41 percent of what was shown on ZTV1 was locally made, while 59 percent was imported. Significant variation occurred on Friday, however, when much more imported material was broadcast (about 75 percent), and on Sunday, when much less imported material was broadcast (about 37 percent). In both cases the variation can be attributed to soccer; on Friday several international matches were broadcast, while on Sunday a lengthy local match aired.

TABLE 4.1. Percentage of time for local
and imported programming on ZTV1

Day of the week	Local (%)	Imported (%)
Monday	45.28	54.72
Tuesday	49.23	50.77
Wednesday	32.90	67.10
Thursday	37.63	62.37
Friday	24.99	75.01
Saturday	34.58	65.42
Sunday	62.67	37.33
Average	41.04	58.96

My estimate is much closer to that of the Ministry of Information, which controls ZBC and ZTV. It should be clear, however, that the majority of material shown on ZTV *is* imported; on Joy TV these percentages were even higher. In 2001, Joy TV aired only five local programs: a teen talk show, *Who Is Next?*, a music video program, *Tambai*, and three promotional programs produced by local corporations.

These figures show that Zimbabwean television is indeed more foreign than local, but imported programming is not quite as dominant as has been put forth. While the numbers speak for themselves, the relevance of television's origins remains less clear. Does it make a difference to viewers whether the cinematic texts they watch are locally produced or imported? What meanings do they make, and what pleasures do they find, when viewing imported cinematic texts? Despite the fears of erosion of culture or of national identity in "third world" countries, documentation of such erosion has been scarce. Although data regarding the flow of cultural products from Europe and the States into Zimbabwe is readily available, few studies have measured Zimbabweans' exposure to imported media, and no one has examined the impact of such media on their attitudes and values.

"Viewers Might Be Fooled": Constructing Audiences as Victims

Media studies scholars used to assume that audiences were passive recipients of the ideologies inherent in the texts they consume. Nothing could be further from the truth. Audiences have agency, and they have the power to interpret,

negotiate, contest, and resist the messages the media send out. Unfortunately, outdated assumptions about audiences still dominate critics,' filmmakers,' and broadcasters' discourse about viewers in Zimbabwe, with limited empirical evidence to
support them. Cinema producers and government officials in Southern Rhodesia
not only discursively constructed black viewers as passive but also misconstrued
their resistance to propaganda as evidence of their supposed inability to understand cinema as a storytelling medium.[8] Similarly, contemporary commentators
on Zimbabwean audiences tell us more about how audiences are constructed than
about real viewers.

We saw in earlier chapters that social message filmmakers often rely on theories of media effects developed during the colonial era, believing that the cinematic arts have direct, observable influences on people's values or behaviors. Ben
Zulu, director of the African Script Development Fund, explained that through
educational films "you create characters that can actually motivate your audiences
to accept those values."[9] On the flip side, the idea that film can change audiences
leads to a fear of films that might impart foreign values.

Critics, filmmakers, and broadcasters in Zimbabwe continue to rely on theories of "media imperialism," imagining viewers as victims of cinematic ideologies,
in need of protection from the onslaught of imported programming. Television
critic Tazzen Mandizvidza writes, "The clothes, music, language, and general
behaviour of people seen in such programmes constitute a whole Western package
white-washing our minds into accepting anything Western as better than local."
Media studies scholar Munashe Furusa similarly argues that American soap operas
screened in Zimbabwe reinforce viewers' beliefs, including ideas that "riches make
people unhappy and miserable" and "money gives people license to be irrespon-
sible and helps them to get away with the worst evils." But Mandizvidva's and
Furusa's own experiences as viewers undermine their argument, forcing them to
distinguish between sophisticated viewers like themselves and the unsophisticated
masses, arguing that the latter "might be fooled into thinking that the films present models of life they should imitate." "Therefore," Furusa concludes, "African
youths cannot gain a sense of their worth as African people." Such comments
echo those of "urban, educated, self-proclaimed 'emerged' Africans" examined
in James Burns's work on Southern Rhodesian cinema. These viewers "shared
white concerns about the cinema's influence over the African masses" while never
doubting their own abilities to criticize cinematic ideologies.[10]

Very little empirical research exists on Zimbabwean viewers, and what does
exist is minimally useful. In the late 1990s, theater specialist Kimani Gecau found
that rural viewers "are very hungry for entertainment" and would attend a mobile
cinema screening no matter what kind of film was screened. We may know that
certain cinematic texts are "popular"—such as the World Wrestling Federation,
sports, *Mutinhimira weMimhanzi* (Musical Sounds), and local drama on television,

or "action-oriented, crime and violence, kung-fu and karate, and Eddie Murphy" films at video rental stores in the early 1990s—but we don't know why or how viewers watch these particular programs and videos. We know that viewers at mobile cinema screenings in the early 1990s would have liked "more news and current affairs, sports, music, *MacGyver,* action films, Kung-fu and Karate" as well as "films on AIDS and the Economic Structural Adjustment Programme," but we don't know whether they wanted such programs to replace what they had access to or simply more programming overall.[11]

The dearth of empirical research on actual viewers has led commentators to present monolithic views of imagined viewers. Beginning in the colonial era, Africans were constructed as preferring films featuring local elements to those made in other parts of Africa, and films made in Africa over those made in the West. For example, CAFU cinema officer Louis Nell reports that the more local films he brought to villages, the more responsive viewers were. Assumptions about audience preference for local cinematic texts continue. Susan Manhando, then working for ZBC, reported that viewers in the late 1990s "would rather watch repeats of old episodes of local dramas like *Mukadota Family* than the Australian *Neighbors* and the American *Santa Barbara* soap operas that appear three days a week on television and have been running for the past ten years." Claims about imagined viewers tell us very little about real Zimbabwean viewers.[12]

Paradoxically, many believe the opposite, claiming that Zimbabwean viewers prefer imported content to local content. Mike Auret Jr. and Gerry Jackson, for example, opposed the 2001 Broadcasting Services Act on the grounds that increased local content would be bad for viewers, who "would be forced to watch badly produced programming in the vein of ZBC, which is what they have been crying for an alternative to."[13]

How can Manhando, on the one hand, and Auret and Jackson, on the other, present viewers in these starkly different ways? Their comments demonstrate that there is no such thing as a monolithic audience with shared values and tastes. Some Zimbabweans do prefer local content while others prefer imported cinematic arts; many state no preference. But knowing that certain viewers prefer one type of programming to another does not address the reasons behind these preferences. Discourses about audience preferences reflect the attitudes and political motivations of those who create them. For example, inherent in Manhando's claim is an ideology that ranks local cultural products over imported ones. Auret and Jackson had a vested interest in the Broadcasting Services Act's failure, since it was created partly in response to their attempt to open the first independent radio station in the country, which was blocked by the government.

To claim that viewers prefer local cinematic texts to ones with less familiar settings and story lines is to ignore extensive evidence of the long-standing popularity of imported cinematic texts. Both Nell and Burns address the popularity

of silent comedies and Westerns in Southern Rhodesia. Westerns were enthusi-
astically received by black viewers while giving Rhodesians a sense of their own
whiteness. In a study of Zimbabwe's liberation war, Gerald Horne writes, "Seeing
American Westerns on Rhodesian television, which frequently showed the Indians
going down to defeat before the more powerful whites, filled an important psychological need, helping to convince the European minority that they could prevail
just as easily over their own 'colored' opponents." The popularity of action films
continued after independence, with kung fu films replacing Westerns.[14]

Those who anthropomorphize the cinematic arts as "whitewashing" viewers
and reinforcing viewers' conservative beliefs grant more agency to cinematic texts
than to viewers themselves. Scholars are finally recognizing that Zimbabwean
viewers are not the passive recipients of the ideologies inherent in the cinematic
arts. For example, Pedzisai Mashiri critiques various ideologies implicit in ZTV's
"local dramas," but cautions, "This is not to imply that the audience is completely
vulnerable to the images provided." Similarly, Michael Bruun Andersen hypothe-
sizes that "the images, models, and values displayed in entertainment make receivers discuss, think about, or reflect on their own values." Unfortunately, neither
Mashiri nor Andersen includes discussions with viewers in their work. When we
listen to viewers, we find that a particular cinematic text may offer, encourage,
or display certain ideologies, but there is space for viewers to reject or negotiate
them.[15]

Listening to Viewers

Letters to the editors or television critics of local newspapers and to ZBC's
own *Look and Listen* magazine provide ample evidence of viewer engagement with
and critique of the cinematic arts. Viewers complain, for example, about censorship, propaganda, and the ethnic bias of locally produced television:

> The August 10–16 edition of the *Zimbabwe Standard* newspaper reports
> that viewers have asked the Zimbabwe Broadcasting Corporation
> Television (ZBC–TV) to screen war documentaries on Zimbabwe
> Peoples Revolution Army (ZIPRA) war heroes. According to the
> paper, the Ndebele-speaking viewers who supported Joshua Nkomo's
> Zimbabwe African Peoples Union (ZAPU) during and after the liberation
> war have complained that since independence in 1980, ZBC–TV has been
> screening only Zimbabwe African National Liberation Army (ZANLA)
> war documentaries. ZIPRA viewers say this implies ZANLA were the
> only ones who fought for the war. According to the paper, ZAPU view-
> ers claim that the ZBC was given the footage of ZIPRA guerrillas just
> after the cease-fire agreement with the Rhodesian military in 1979. At
> the time, ZAPU officials reportedly claimed that government had banned

ZIPRA war documentaries after Nkomo was accused of sponsoring rebels in Matabeleland.[16]

Other common complaints—in both government-owned and independent newspapers—address license fees, irrelevant previews, excessive religious programming, repeats, subtitles, and broadcasters' failure to respond to viewer feedback.

Foreign and Local Favorites

Many viewers list imported programs as their favorites: among the top twenty-four programs listed by people I consulted in 2001, only six were made in Zimbabwe. Table 4.2 summarizes these results.

Other favorite titles and genres included domestically made programs such as *Afrobeat, Gospel Hour, High School Debates, Mabhuku na Vanyori* (Books and Writers), *Madzidza neMutupo* (Customs and Totems), *Mukadota Family, Mutendi waNhasi* (Today's Believer), *National High School Quiz, News Hour, Nzira yeMutendi* (Path of the Believer), *Royco Recipes, Tambai, Teen Scene,* and *Waiters*. Imported favorites included British shows such as *BBC News*, sitcoms *'Allo 'Allo!* and *Thin Blue Line,* the hospital drama *Casualty,* and the slapstick comedy *Mr. Bean;* American imports such as 1980s prime-time soap opera *Falcon Crest,* daytime soaps *Santa Barbara* and *The Bold and the Beautiful,* sitcoms *Family Matters, Fresh Prince of Bel Air, Golden Girls, Malcolm & Eddie, Malcolm,* and *Moesha,* action films such as *Hard Target* and *Mortal Kombat,* court show *Judge Joe Brown,* and children's programs such as *GI Joe, My Little Pony,* and *Pinocchio;* and imports from other countries such as Bruce Lee's kung fu film *Game of Death,* Australian soap opera *Neighbors,* and the general category "African movies," which were typically from Ghana. Some viewers listed genres that include both local and imported programs: news, drama, comedies, movies, soccer, educational programming, romances, and sports.[17]

What does it mean to be a "favorite" program or a "popular" one? The 2000 Zimbabwe All Media and Products and Services survey of five thousand adults makes clear that viewers' favorite programs do not always coincide with what they actually watch. For example, 44 percent of ZAMPS respondents indicated that the Shona and Ndebele music video program *Mutinhimira/Ezomgido* was their favorite, making it the most popular program in the country for the third year in a row. But the most viewed program was actually ZBC's *Main News at Eight,* which aired daily and was the second-most popular. A viewer may watch the news every night, but it may not be his or her favorite program. In contrast to the results obtained in my questionnaire, the ZAMPS survey found that four of the top six favorite programs were domestically made, while the fourth-most favorite, soccer, included both local and imported broadcasts. The two that tied for fifth place among the top favorites were *Afrobeat,* a locally produced music show, and *Walker, Texas Ranger,* an action-filled drama made in the United States.[18]

TABLE 4.2. Programs enjoyed by Zimbabweans polled in 2001

Rank	Title/category	Number	%
1	*Gringo Ndiani?**	11	15.28
2	*Sunset Beach*	8	11.11
3	*Miami Sands*	7	9.72
4	news	6	8.33
5	local drama*	5	6.94
5	*Mutinhimira weMimhanzi/Ezomghido**	5	6.94
6	drama	4	5.56
7	*Coke on the Beat**	3	4.17
7	comedies	3	4.17
7	movies	3	4.17
7	soccer	3	4.17
7	wrestling	3	4.17
8	*Days of Our Lives*	2	2.78
8	*Friends*	2	2.78
8	*Generations*	2	2.78
8	*Madzinza eZimbabwe**	2	2.78
8	*Martial Law*	2	2.78
8	*Passions*	2	2.78
8	*Mudzimai wa Nhasi**	2	2.78
8	*Peter Pan*	2	2.78
8	*Psalmody*	2	2.78
8	soaps	2	2.78
8	*Suburban Bliss*	2	2.78
8	*Walker, Texas Ranger*	2	2.78
8	*The Young and the Restless*	2	2.78

* Titles marked with asterisks were domestically produced.

Conversations with viewers further illustrate the popularity of both local and imported programming. In the following excerpt, I speak with three of my Shona host-sisters (Nyaradzai, age 12, Sisasenkosi, 17, and Charity, 21) in the bedroom the four of us shared in a high-density suburb of Kadoma, a city in the Mashonaland West province, about ninety miles southwest of Harare.

KDT: How often do you watch television?

Charity: All the time.

Nyaradzai: Every day.

KDT: Which programs do you like to watch?

Charity: I like comedies.

KDT: Like what?

Sisasenkosi: The South African comedies and sometimes the movies.

Charity: The African movies are quite nice.

Nyaradzai: I like cartoons!

Charity: [Making fun of her younger sister] She just yells, "I like cartoons!"

KDT: Do you remember the names of any cartoons you like?

Charity: Or soaps.

Nyaradzai: *Miami Sands.*

Sisasenkosi: Oh ya, the soaps. And then . . .

Sisasenkosi and Charity: *Passions* . . .

Charity: Wow, that was nice.

Sisasenkosi: On ABN, the African Broadcast Network. For comedies, I like the one we watched, *Suburban Bliss.*

Charity: I used to enjoy *Friends.*

Sisasenkosi: And one on Thursdays, *The Hughleys.*

Nyaradzai: *GI Joe.*

Charity: And the other one, *Power Rangers,* a cartoon.

Nyaradzai: *Madeleine.*

The African Broadcast Network provided ZBC with a suite of imported programs for a few months in 2001. With the exception of South African comedies like *Suburban Bliss* and the movies from Ghana, most of the programs the girls mention are produced in the United States. But after listing all of these imported programs, the girls go on to praise several local programs that they count among their favorites.

KDT: Are there any programs that you make a point to watch every time?

Charity: Local drama.

> Sisasenkosi: Local drama.
> Nyaradzai: It's very funny.
> Sisasenkosi: Yes, it's funny.
> Charity: And *Coke on the Beat.*
> Sisasenkosi: Oh, yes.

It is difficult to pinpoint the popularity of local versus imported programming. These three girls are typical in including programs from both categories as both their favorites and their most frequently viewed. Both have large numbers of viewers.

"Untold Embarrassment in African Homes": Attitudes toward the Foreign

Zimbabweans' mixed reactions to imported TV programs is part and parcel of their mixed reactions to "foreign" goods, ideas, and cultures more generally. In the ZAMPS 2000 survey, respondents were asked to agree or disagree with the statement "I like to be exposed to foreign culture/ideas." Nearly half agreed, but about 40 percent disagreed. Similarly, about 40 percent of ZAMPS respondents agreed with the statement "I believe imported products are better than local ones," while almost the same percentage disagreed.[19] Virtually all Zimbabweans have some access to imported cinematic arts, and many enjoy them, but others critique the programs on their screens. For example, television critic Tazzen Mandizvidza writes, "We want them to show us programmes that promote the local and not foreign cultures."[20] Even Alexander Kanengoni, who worked for ZBC, lamented the effect of imported television on local cultures:

> Television is powerful—it is literally shaping people's attitudes and per-
> ceptions. It's dangerous, actually, because culturally it is . . . oh goodness!
> We have a lot of work to be done to try to control what we show there;
> otherwise, goodness me! It is very powerful; it is powerful. You will be
> surprised if you walk along the street you will see young boys calling
> themselves Will Smith, and so on. Very powerful! Unfortunately, we do
> not have the money to put out the kind of programs that we would
> want. So we will always be open to that kind of influence. We don't have
> the money to buy programs of our choice; we don't have the money to
> produce programs of our own, so we consider buying programs about
> the Mafia in the USA, whatever. It's a powerful means of communication.

It is telling that when asked about television generally, Zimbabweans will often first mention imported programs. Kanengoni was careful not to openly criticize the station's programming. Nevertheless, his use of "the Mafia" contributes to his construction of programming as "dangerous" and in need of "control." When he comments on how "unfortunate" it is that Zimbabweans are prey to "that kind of influence," it is clear just what kind of influence he refers to: a negative one.

What is the alternative? The "programs that we would want," "the programs of our choice," would be "programs of our own."

Imported media are criticized not only for being foreign, thereby displacing local productions, but also for introducing foreign values. A Harare viewer, Dr. Onesimus A. Ngundu, in a 1 January 2001 letter to the editor of the government-owned *Herald,* complained of the nudity in a Palmolive soap commercial aired on Joy TV during the soap opera *Sunset Beach:*

> Since TV watching, especially during the evenings, has become a family affair (parents, teenage children, and sometimes grandparents, or in-laws, etc.) in most homes, nude commercials have resulted in untold embarrassment in African homes. Culturally, there are certain things (e.g., soap operas, nude commercials, etc.) which are off limit. Please, don't label or sideline these cultural ideas as backward. Instead, these cultural values, heritage, and ethos should continue to be preserved.

Palmolive is a U.S. soap company, and the ad is in English, but the accent of the voice-over in the commercial is African, possibly Zimbabwean. The origin of the commercial is unclear, but Ngundu interprets the values it represents as foreign. The fact that it offends his values, which he represents as African cultural values, is more important to him than its origin. This commercial only aired during *Sunset Beach,* a U.S. soap opera that included not only partial nudity but also scenes of physical intimacy between both married and unmarried couples. Ngundu and his family could only have seen the commercial if they were watching *Sunset Beach,* so it is ironic that he includes soap operas among things that are culturally "off limit."

The above examples illustrate that any potential impact that imported productions might have on viewers is mediated by their own interpretations of that programming, connections they draw between it and their own cultures and personal beliefs, conversations with family or friends about what they watch, as well as criticism they may level against it.

"TV and Shona Culture Do Not Get Along Well": Critiquing Foreign Values on TV

The portrayal of a culture radically different from what viewers think of as "traditional" Shona culture is often precisely what they critique. For example, Mrs. Tichafara, a forty-something Shona woman in Chitungwiza, described to me the embarrassment she feels when watching a U.S. soap opera with the children in her extended family.

KDT: *Ndeupi ukama uri pakati peterevhizheni netsika dzechiShona?*

Tichafara: *A-ah terevhizheni chaiyo haina hukama chaihwo . . . , nokuti zvinhu zvinoitwa muT.V. tikazviisa kutsika dzeChiShona hazviwirirane, kana tichiona fanike isusu vabereki sonemakuriro atakaita isusu nemakuriro*

ari kuita vana vedu mazuva anoka zvimwe zvinoitwa muterevhizheni
nemamwe maprogrammes . . . tsika dzacho dziri kunosiyana manje. Isusu
tsika dzatakararama tiri nedzatava kuona zvimwe zvacho zvinoitwa
muterevhizheni zvimwe zvacho zvinonyadzisa zvimwe hazvinyadzisi,
zvimwe zvakanaka, zvimwe hazvitikosheri isusu vabereki, totosimuka
totosiyawo vana vacho vakagara muterevhizheni toti regai tibve zvedu
tiende nekuti tinenge tanyatsoona kuti izvi manje kuti mwana wangu
awone apa saiye Dambu uyu. Ini ndiri pano fanike especially mamwe
maprogrammes akaita saSunset Beach ava kuti tichiona nevana nguve
imwe chete isu naamai vacho takunyara navanababa. Tobva tasimuka
tosiya vana vedu vachidii, vachiona. Ehe.

KDT: What is the relationship between television and Shona culture?

Tichafara: A-ah television itself does not have a true relationship . . .
because if we put things that are done on TV in Shona culture they
do not get along well. If we look at, for example, we parents, like
with the ways we behave and the ways our children behave these
days, some of the things that are done on television and some of
the programs, . . . their culture is so different. The culture which
we live with and that which we saw. Some of what is done on television, some of it is very embarrassing, some is not embarrassing, some is good, some does not respect us parents. We parents
just stand up and leave the children sitting at the television, just
saying, "Let us go for our own sake. Let's go," because we would
see very well these things that my child sees here, like this one,
this Dambudzo [*pointing to her nephew*]. . . . For example, especially
some programs like *Sunset Beach,* which we were watching together
with the children one time, we, the mother and the father, were
ashamed. So we just got up and left the children doing what they
do, watching. Yes. (*Laughs*)

Mrs. Tichafara is critical of the differences between Shona culture and contemporary cinematic culture, presenting them not only as a cultural clash but also a
generational one. Her critique is mild, however. She does not deny her children
access to imported programming, but she chooses not to watch it with them. In
our May 2001 conversation, Mr. Ndhlovu, a Ndebele man who lives in Kadoma
and speaks both Ndebele and Shona, raised similar concerns and criticized what he
saw as the Europeanization of Africans in an imported South African soap opera:

Generations is really popular; even the children like it. Ya, it's very popular. However, some scenes, you know, it's a drama where you find a
mixture of culture. There is the European culture and the African background. And if you watch, you'll find that the African way of life is get-

ting absorbed into the European lifestyle. There are certain things that we don't do as blacks that whites just do and it's normal. That's one thing that I didn't really appreciate in *Generations*. Because you find a young black man with a young black woman kissing publicly. You know? Hugging and the like, that kind of thing. This is taboo. It's taboo. That's one thing that I don't like. There are certain programs that will come a bit late which I don't even like my children to watch. It's not everything which is good that comes on TV. So it's very important to know which program to watch, what time to close to go to bed, that kind of thing. You see? So whilst the TV will be very educative, it can be very dangerous as well.

In both examples, open displays of romance and sexuality, which Mrs. Tichafara alludes to and Mr. Ndhlovu explicitly criticizes, are measures of the disjuncture between the cultures presented in imported programs and local "traditional" (in these cases, Shona and Ndebele) cultural values. Notably, it is not only programs imported from the West that highlight this disjuncture; sometimes values Zimbabweans perceive as Western or European can also make their way into the country via another African country, usually South Africa or Ghana.

Viewers' critiques of television's "foreign" values mitigate the effect those values might have on Zimbabwean cultures. Nevertheless, these examples illustrate that imported television has the potential to negatively alter the values they perceive as "traditional" or essential to their cultures. Older viewers may hold this view more than younger ones, a phenomenon we also saw in responses to *Jit*.

Earlier we witnessed viewers using their knowledge of Shona cultural values to imagine alternative endings to *Yellow Card*, even though the dialogue was in English and the filmmaker was from the United States. Similarly with imported cinematic arts, viewers often subtly resist the values of a particular text or genre even if they do not critique imported programming on the whole. My conversation with Mrs. Tichafara turned to locally produced dramas. She told me:

Madrama anodzidzisa, zvavakwauri iwe muridzi manje kuti uchitsvaga chakanaka nechakaipa nokuti pane nguva yekuti unodzidziswa zvinhu zvamanga musingazivewoso. Wotoona kuti apa tanga tichirasika takadai. Ugozowona pamwe paunoona kuti dzidziso yacho imwe inenge isisiriyo yakanyatsoti tsvikitiwo. Iwe zvaakwauriwo uri kuona drama kusarudza.

Dramas teach. It, however, depends on you, the owner of the television, to seek out the good and the bad because at times you are taught things which you did not know. You already see that here we were going astray in such a way. Ultimately sometimes you see that its lesson might not be a healthy one. It therefore depends on you who are watching the drama to choose.

The educational value of programming is important to Mrs. Tichafara, but she is not passively absorbing all of television's "lessons." Viewers often adopt critical methods while watching an imported drama such as a soap opera, just as they do when watching local films and dramas. Furthermore, imported programming may also offer viewers a means to resist oppressive aspects of local culture.

"A Potential Reservoir of Criticism": Resisting the Local through the Foreign

In 2000 and 2001, *Sunset Beach* was one of the most popular programs on Zimbabwean television. Since Joy TV's broadcast range extended only seventy kilometers beyond Harare, it is important to look at its programs' popularity with urban viewers rather than with the population at large, among which *Sunset Beach* ranked much lower. According to the ZAMPS 2000 survey, it was the most frequently viewed Joy TV program, ranked at number five among high-density city viewers and number two among low-density city viewers.[21]

"Stories That Flow": The Popularity of Soaps

Viewers worldwide have come to associate U.S. TV with soap operas, starting with the remarkable success of *Dallas* and *Dynasty* in the early 1980s. Many countries import U.S., British, and Australian soap operas, and some non-Western countries have also begun to create their own versions. South Africa, Kenya, and the Ivory Coast, for example, have created soap operas not only to entertain but also to educate viewers about social issues such as AIDS, ethnic rivalries, and population control. Many other African countries import all of their soap operas, choosing other genres for their own productions; prior to the 2001 Broadcasting Services Act, Zimbabwe was one of them.[22]

There are several reasons why imported soap operas were a popular choice for ZTV and Joy TV. The cost to air soaps is relatively minimal, and the large number of episodes produced means that they can be aired either once or several times a week. Airing a daily show only once or twice a week creates a growing lag time between the episodes aired in Zimbabwe and the current episodes being aired elsewhere. By my reckoning, in 2001 *Days of Our Lives* was about thirteen years behind the episodes airing in the United States. Zimbabwean fans occasionally become disconcerted when they somehow learn of events that are still years to come on their soap.

> Sisasenkosi: For soaps, I also like *Days of Our Lives*.
> Charity: Not these old ones; the current one is exciting.
> Sisasenkosi: What do you mean, "old ones"?

Charity: Ah, they're showing old episodes. Like if you watch SABC,
they've got current episodes, very much ahead. I think, four years.

Here Charity, the oldest sister, flaunts her access to South African Broadcasting
Corporation programming, which she has access to via satellite dish at her work-
place in Zvishavane, while her younger sisters, who still live at home in Kadoma,
only have ZBC because they live outside of Joy TV's radius and their family cannot
afford a satellite dish.

In *Soap Operas Worldwide,* Marilyn Matelski suggests that one reason for the
global popularity of U.S. soaps is that viewers "can feed their seemingly insatiable
hunger for American culture. More important, they can enjoy watching story lines
filled with glamour, sex, adventure, and opulence, as well as actors and actresses
who also represent [these things]." Pedzisai Mashiri argues that for Zimbabweans,
imported soaps "offer a sense of freedom, cheap thrills, and pleasure to viewers" in
contrast to the "morality, discipline, and social control portrayed in local drama."
However, it would be an oversimplification to assume that access to Western culture, or the freedom it represents, is the sole reason for Zimbabweans' enjoyment
of soap operas. Many other opportunities exist for accessing Western culture.
Television offers U.S. and British films, dramas, sitcoms, talk shows, news, music
videos, and so on, many replete with "glamour, sex, adventure, and opulence" as
well as "freedom, cheap thrills, and pleasure." Zimbabwean viewers do not need
soaps to fulfill their desire for these things. My conversations with viewers suggest that what is unique about soaps is their long duration, as well as the specific
story lines, which draw viewers in and with which Zimbabwean viewers compare
and contrast their own lives. Their timing is also important: choosing to watch a
foreign soap can mean a deliberate choice not to watch the local news.[23]

Three soaps were particularly popular during my fieldwork: *Generations,*
which aired every Sunday on ZBC, *Days of Our Lives,* which aired on Saturdays
and Sundays on ZBC, and *Sunset Beach,* which aired Monday through Friday on Joy
TV. Commenting on these shows' popularity in his 14 January 2001 TV column for
Sunday Mail Magazine, Garikai Mazara says that Zimbabweans "drool over" *Days
of Our Lives* and *Sunset Beach.* Their popularity was widely recognized.

Generations is a South African soap purchased by ZBC as part of the broadcaster's attempt to supply more African content. According to the catalog of
California Newsreel, which distributes the South African prime-time program,
"*Generations* . . . made history as the first soap produced, directed, and written by
black South Africans. It portrays a society obsessed with power, money, and sex,
in other words a world not dissimilar to that of our own [U.S.] soaps. It differs in
that South Africa's black majority can now fantasize about glamorous characters
who share their skin color and speak the usual clichés in a variety of indigenous
languages."[24]

Generations has been on the air in South Africa since 1995, when it became the
first soap that the SABC broadcast daily during prime time.[25] In 2001 it aired
every Sunday evening in Zimbabwe. Although California Newsreel criticized the
program in 1995 for "mut[ing] potentially divisive, inter-racial issues by portray-
ing a largely black world focused around a flourishing advertizing agency, New
Horizons, owned by Paul Moroka and his family," this criticism no longer held
true by 2001. The episodes that were airing in Zimbabwe at that time featured
not only black characters but also whites, Indians, and people of mixed race.
Although the program is primarily in English, characters do code switch between
English, Afrikaans, and a variety of indigenous South African languages, which
are subtitled in English. One character on the show even spoke Shona, which was
a source of pleasure for some of the viewers with whom I spoke. Most of the
cinematic texts Zimbabwean viewers have access to portray characters speaking
only English, only Shona, or only Ndebele. *Generations* is a much more accurate
representation of language use in most Africans' lives, in which multilingualism
and code switching are the norm.

Days of Our Lives has been on the air in the United States since November 1965.
NBC calls the program "the powerhouse of NBC's soap opera lineup and a true
classic in television history." According to the broadcaster, "*Days of Our Lives* is set
in the fictitious midwestern town of Salem. The core families are the Hortons and
Bradys, and the multi-layered storylines involve elements of romance, adventure,
mystery, comedy, and drama." Because of the haphazardness and inaccuracy of
Zimbabwean program listings and the National Archives' records on television, it
is impossible to determine with any degree of accuracy how long a given program
has been on the air, but *Days* had been airing in Zimbabwe for several years when
I arrived in 2000.

Sunset Beach was broadcast in the United States on NBC from January 6, 1997
to December 31, 1999. Its creator, Aaron Spelling, was well known for *Dynasty*,
Beverly Hills 90210, and other popular evening dramas; it marked his first foray into
the world of daytime soaps. In fact, it was Spelling's reputation that made broadcasters eager to add *Sunset Beach* to their lineups: "Before the soap was ever aired,
Worldvision Entertainment (Spelling Productions' export subsidiary) had already
sold 260 episodes to the UK, France, Germany, Sweden, Norway, Denmark,
Belgium, Greece, the Middle East, North Africa, and Latin America."[26]

Initial interest soon petered out, though, and the series was canceled. But its
popularity in Zimbabwe stayed strong. When Joy TV marked its two-year anniver-
sary as a station in 1999, it was already counting the soap among its most popular
programs.[27] The show aired there until June 2001.

The long duration of soaps is one reason for their popularity. Some soaps
have been on the air for more than thirty years in the States, so fans may feel that
they have developed a relationship with the characters. Likewise, in Zimbabwe,

viewers enjoy returning to a beloved program daily or weekly. A 23-year-old Shona man in a high-density suburb of Kadoma told me that long running times are his main reason for preferring imported programs, since most local dramas run for thirteen weeks or less. Another Shona viewer told me, "I enjoy stories that flow," echoing what soap scholar Christine Geraghty calls "that sense of endless but organised time which characterises soap operas."[28] When a soap comes to an end, as *Santa Barbara* did in 1997 and *Sunset Beach* in 2001, Zimbabwean fans can be distraught.

Ien Ang notes that in Europe and the United States, prime-time soaps have a more heterogeneous audience than daytime soaps, with a wider range of themes, scenes, and plots and a greater number of male characters.[29] The distinction between daytime and prime-time soaps, however, is blurred when they are imported. What have been daytime soaps in the States become evening soaps when aired in Zimbabwe, where ZBC defines prime time as 6 PM to midnight. In 2001, ZBC aired *Days of Our Lives* shortly after 9 PM on Saturdays and Sundays, and Joy TV aired *Sunset Beach* at 8:15 PM Monday through Friday, opposite the local news on ZTV.

Viewers Respond

Zimbabweans love to talk about soaps. R. C. Allen writes that "regardless of the cultural context of their production and reception, regardless of their plot or themes, television serials around the world seem more than any other form of programming to provoke talk about them among their viewers."[30] In talking with Zimbabwean television viewers, I found that they had much to say about both local and imported series, especially soaps. In this excerpt I return to my conversation with my host sisters in Kadoma.

> KDT: Do you ever discuss what you watch on TV with other people?
>
> Sisasenkosi: Afterwards? With other people? Ya. Especially at school. Usually on Tuesdays we talk about the local drama. (*Laughs*) Especially the funny parts.
>
> Charity: Ya, soaps, ya.
>
> KDT: What about other programs?
>
> Charity: Ya, sometimes. Like the films? Ya. For example, with *Passions* [a U.S. soap aired on ZBC], you would know that all of your friends are watching. So later on when you meet tomorrow you'll be like, "Oh, did you see that part?" The cutest guys.
>
> Sisasenkosi: And their clothes and their hairstyles and everything.

John Fiske argues that a text "can be made popular only if it offers meanings that are relevant to the everyday lives of subordinate people, and these meanings will be pleasurable only if they are made *out of* [the text], not *by* [the text]."[31] Zimbabwean viewers have clearly made soap operas popular, so we must ask: what meanings do these programs offer that are relevant to their lives? For young women, fashion and sexuality may be the most relevant aspects of an American soap.

An older woman's pleasures may be quite different from those of younger women. In Kadoma, I spoke with Mrs. Mavenge, a Shona mother of two, and Sisasenkosi, her 17-year-old niece.

> KDT: How often do you usually watch television?
>
> Mavenge: Every day.
>
> KDT: Do you have any favorite programs?
>
> Mavenge: Usually the movies, the musical programs, the children's pro-
> grams, and some talk shows.
>
> KDT: Do you know the names of any of the movies that you liked?
>
> Mavenge: Well, my favorites were *Broken Hearts;* then there is *Maya,*
> then there is *The Sacred Tree,* then *Yellow Card.* Most of them are
> Ghanaian. Then our soap, *Days of Our Lives.* I don't miss that one.
> (*Laughs*)
>
> KDT: Do you have any preference for programs in English versus pro-
> grams in Shona?
>
> Mavenge: I prefer both. I don't mind. Especially the talk shows. We have
> liked one talk show in Shona that came just after the 6 o'clock news.
> The one by Rebecca Chisamba called *With Women in Mind.* I usually
> enjoy that. The presenter is very dynamic. Ya. She is rich in her own
> language, her questioning techniques. She is quite good. So I like it.
> As a result, her shows are quite lively, so I listen to those.
>
> KDT: Do you think the issues talked about on her shows are issues you
> can relate to?
>
> Mavenge: Yes, they are everyday things. Really things that we talk about
> at work, at home. Things that are affecting our daily lives. Like
> sometimes they talk about inheritance, sometimes they talk about
> health issues, sometimes they talk about *lobola* [bridewealth] issues,
> sometimes they talk about issues affecting children. So things that
> generally affect our day-to-day living.
>
> KDT: You mentioned that one of your favorite shows is *Days of Our Lives.*
> Can you tell me why?
>
> Mavenge: I enjoy soaps; I enjoy stories that flow. It is not very violent;
> it's sort of romantic . . .
>
> Sisasenkosi: Emotional.
>
> Mavenge: Emotional. I enjoy it so much.

KDT: Is there anything in the story of *Days of Our Lives* that is relevant to your life?

Mavenge: Yes, I think . . . you know, like the way the doctor . . . I never understood. . . . Was it really ever finalized that the pregnancy was not the husband's? So that was sort of a secret she kept. So I think, yes, that's relevant. We have got lots of secrets. In our Zimbabwean culture, there are lots of secrets that are kept among women from their husbands, husbands from their wives, or from relations. You find some of them keep something to themselves: "No, no, no! This thing should never be heard!" Things like that. So I think that's relevant. And also the issue of burying people alive. I think we have heard stories that some people were buried alive. It's left me on some uneasy level, because I'm not very sure when people die. (*Laughs*) Maybe I want to say, "Are you really dead?"

KDT: You mean in real life?

Mavenge: Yes! (*Laughs*) I think it changed my perception, because I think from the stories that we gather, some people are being buried alive. So these days when people die, I'm not very sure whether they are completely dead or half-dead! So I think that's another issue that affected me. And also the issue of jealousy, with Vivian, Nicky, and the son [*Days* characters]. She went in between them, trying to ruin their relationship. We are living with that. We have our relatives who come in between relationships and try to tear people apart. It's quite good, because we are living among some of those situations.

Mrs. Mavenge clearly finds television important. The differences between her discussion of a local talk show and an imported soap opera illustrate the comparative emotional impact of the two genres. *With Women in Mind* is relevant to her way of thinking about Shona culture and Zimbabwean society, but *Days of Our Lives* engages her emotions. She recalls elements of the story to explain the depth of her emotional engagement with the program. The soap opera, in its focus on human relationships through storytelling—"stories that flow"—draws her in more than the talk show, which focuses on issues that are important to Shona culture.

A Clash between Programs

"Some of the programs clash, like *ZBC News* and Joy TV's *Sunset Beach*," a 20-year-old woman in Chitungwiza told me. *Sunset Beach* was a common topic in my conversations with viewers, and it was frequently mentioned in television columns and letters to the editors of several newspapers. But it wasn't the content of the program that inspired such discourse. Instead, most viewers and critics drew attention to the time the show aired: opposite the local news at 8 PM. Viewers and critics variously interpreted the decision to watch the news versus a soap opera in terms of different but overlapping dichotomies: between men who are thought to watch news and women who are thought to watch soaps, between fact and fiction, and between local and foreign. These dichotomies raise issues that are important not only to the specific clash between these two programs but also to the globalization of Zimbabwean television more generally and to viewers' responses to local and imported programming.

Soaps for Women, News for Men?

In the United States and Britain, women are the primary viewers of soaps. According to Mary Ellen Brown, 70 percent of U.S. viewers are women. Therefore, most research on soaps has focused on its female characters and viewers.[32] David Morley shows that British women prefer fiction while British men prefer factual programming.[33] Many Zimbabweans *perceive* soap operas as women's television and news as men's television. But more than half of the men I consulted in Zimbabwe listed soaps as among their favorite programs.

The time at which soaps are broadcast in Zimbabwe has an effect on the number of men and women who watch them. In the States, where soaps air in the afternoons Monday through Friday, women are more likely than men to be at home. But in Zimbabwe, where soaps are broadcast during prime time and/or on the weekends, both men and women are at home and many women are busy with domestic work.

Zimbabwean men and women may watch soaps in more or less equal numbers, but the perception remains strong that soaps are for women and factual genres are for men. For example, television reviewer Sam Mawokamatanda complained in his 4 February 2001 column for the *Sunday Mail Magazine*, "Can't Joy TV move *Sunset Beach* to an earlier slot than 8 PM? Some families are finding it increasingly difficult to watch the main news bulletin on ZTV while daughters and wives are clamouring for their popular soap on the other channel. Well we all can't own two television sets! I suppose that is the competition." The notion that women are the main audience for soaps affects not only decisions within families about what to watch but also the programming decisions of broadcasters. When Dexter Mushaka was planning for his short-lived station LDM, which broadcast from 2 to 5 PM on ZTV2 in 1997, he said that his "prime audience will be women and children so that the foreign content will consist of a smattering of soaps, drama, [and] cookery."[34] This perception tells us something about gender in Zimbabwe, where women are perceived as having greater competency than men in the domestic sphere and where television may play a role in socializing them into this sphere. Conversely, Zimbabwean men, who supposedly prefer news and talk shows, are perceived to be more competent in politics, economics, and sports. Mrs. Mavenge constructs these gendered differences:

> I hate television when it comes to the soccer season because I don't like soccer. It will be soccer! My husband will be very happy because he's into soccer. So he watches soccer alone or he goes to his friend's house to watch soccer, because I would rather read or knit. I fail to understand and appreciate soccer. (*Laughs*) So when it's the soccer season, I feel I could do something. But if my husband is going to watch soccer, I will have no option. He will be very happy, but I . . . He usually complains that I am not into soccer. He also says to me, "You are into *Days of Our Lives*," and he doesn't like it, but these days he is much better. When he saw that part where Katrina was being buried alive, that's when he developed an interest. So from that time, he has been watching, and he has been asking questions if he is not home. Then he asks you tomorrow, "So what happened?" (*Laughs*) So we have our different tastes.

On the surface, Mrs. Mavenge suggests that men enjoy sports while women enjoy soaps, but her talk reveals that her husband does in fact enjoy *Days of Our Lives*. Popular perceptions of men's and women's differing competencies and tastes are interesting precisely because they do not reflect the reality of what Shona men and women are actually watching.

In analyzing viewers' readings of *Sunset Beach* in relation to gender, it is important not to interpret the program in a vacuum but to understand how its depiction of gender relates to "other sets of representations, images, stereotypes that the audience is familiar with," as David Morley writes. Juxtaposing imported soaps with other media, one can see that soap operas are one of the few genres available to Zimbabweans in which female characters play a primary role. For example, Hilde Arnsten argues that women are underrepresented in Zimbabwean media *except* in women's magazines and soaps.[35]

Zimbabwean literature and oral traditions are another source of images of women, though usually not as primary characters. Woman as mother, the primary image in the country's literary and oral traditions, finds its counterpart in soaps like *Sunset Beach*, where characters like Bette Katzenkazrahi and Joan Cummings are mothers or mother substitutes to various characters. But most soaps go beyond this image to present a wide range of characters who occupy different social positions and relationships to one another such as daughters, sisters, girlfriends, business owners, and workers. Such characters, though varied, do not necessarily represent positive or progressive images, however. To the contrary, soaps have prompted both fans and critics to complain about stereotyped portrayals. In fact, Mary Ellen Brown writes that soaps are "one cultural site" at which "hegemonic notions of femininity and womanhood develop." Nevertheless, just as I argue that Shona viewers of U.S. soaps are not victims of foreign television, Brown argues that "hegemony is leaky" and that stereotyped images of women "can be accepted, resisted, and/or negotiated in the process of consumption."[36]

Furthermore, negative or stereotypical images of women are found not only in imported dramas but also in local ones. Mashiri writes that in local dramas they are confined to two stereotypes, "the educated modern working woman and the uneducated traditional woman." The former is used to represent promiscuity, rebellion against cultural norms, and a loss of morality, while the latter represents cultural authenticity and normative femininity based in motherhood.[37] Imported and local dramas are both produced in patriarchal societies in which men largely control the media. It is important to recognize that both present stereotypical and negative images of women. Stereotypes thrive in popular culture wherever it is produced, wherever it is consumed.

We have seen that gendered viewing habits in Zimbabwe are quite different from those in the West. It is unlikely, however, that such differences can be attributed to great differences in taste between Zimbabwean men and their Western counterparts; more likely the difference boils down to the degree of choice available to viewers in Zimbabwe versus those in the United States and Britain, where a greater variety of programs is available and can be tailored to subsections of the population. If given the choice of a variety of programs on different networks, would Zimbabwean men choose to watch soap operas?

Are Soaps Really Fiction? Is News Really Fact?

One of soaps' pleasures can be found in the respite the fiction genre gives viewers from "reality." For many viewers, "soap operas [are like a] place of safety, a refuge from . . . the more serious news and documentaries."[38] To switch from the local news on ZTV1 to watch a soap on Joy TV is, for some viewers, to momentarily escape from their daily lives and to enter the fantasy world of Sunset Beach, California.

For others, however, there is not such a clear distinction to be made between news "reality" or "seriousness" and soap opera fantasy or fiction. Garikai Mazara commented on letters he received from viewers about ZTV's change from a thirty-minute to sixty-minute English-language news broadcast:

> One viewer is of the opinion that ZTV's *News Hour* is to counter *Sunset Beach*. Many viewers were watching the 30-minute news bulletin, then switching over to *Sunset Beach* (with soaps, one wouldn't have missed much), but now the one-hour completely wipes out *Sunset Beach*—one has to choose between *News Hour* and the soap. Which is which?

Mazara's rhetorical question "Which is which?" constructs the news as indistinguishable from fiction and other entertainment programming. This notion crópped up repeatedly in newspapers. As early as 1984, ZBC director Grey Tichaona defended the network from such criticisms: "Let me make it clear that ZBC does not manufacture programmes from the figment of its imagination."[39] Viewers remain skeptical of such claims.

Throughout the 1990s and up to 2001, the ZBC "local" news was actually an amalgamation of local and international news, the latter purchased from the BBC, Reuters, CNN, and other agencies. The Media Monitoring Project of Zimbabwe, a local NGO, found that imported news was sometimes spliced into local footage in ways that served the ruling party agenda. For example, whenever the news featured a state spokesperson invoking claims that the MDC party was white-funded, ZTV replayed CNN footage of MDC leader Morgan Tsvangirai receiving campaign funds from white farmers. The broadcaster even dug up footage from the archives: "Other footage of colonial era abuses or—quite extraordinarily— clips from fiction films about colonial British military exploits in Africa were also employed in the TV bulletins to bolster ZBC's propaganda campaign and the image projected by ZANU-PF, and especially President Mugabe, that the MDC was a 'stooge' of Western and colonial forces."[40]

The montage of news items gave viewers who did watch the *Main News at Eight* on ZTV1 the opportunity to compare local and foreign, often criticizing the former. Michael Bruun Andersen argued that there was "a very clear difference between ZBC reports and reports bought from, say, Reuters." The "sound of the ZBC reports, especially the voice-over, is strangely detached from the pictures . . . due to insufficient sound facilities [which] endows the reports with a surplus meaning of constructedness." This "constructedness" drew viewers' attention to the similarities between news and other programming: "On Monday someone made a mistake and put in the montage [an advertisement] for soaps during the long and boring news hour. It made the one-side-of-the-story news bulletin look like a soap opera. It's starting to look like one any[way]," commented television critic Tazzen Mandizvidza. Another TV critic, Itayi Viriri, wrote, "Sometimes, one is not sure whether one is watching the news or *Whose Line Is It Anyway?*" Comparing the news with an imported British sketch comedy show, Viriri suggested that the announcers for the *Main News at Eight* made up the news as they went along, with laughable results.[41]

Comparing entertainment programs with the news was a way to criticize ZBC through humor. Contrasting the genres is used similarly. For example, in a *Daily News* comic strip called *Nyati*, Watson Mukutirwa depicted a man and woman sitting on their sofa watching a local music program on television. When the phone rings, the man tells the caller, "We are busy watching *Mvengemvenge*," and in the next frame, "Please phone during the news hour!" Mukutirwa illus- trates the popular opinion that entertainment programs are preferable to the news and merit more attention.

What is the implication of the local news failing to compete with and distinguish itself from fiction? Despite the fact that many Zimbabweans criticize ZBC and ZTV1 for offering little more than government propaganda masked as news, the blatancy of this bias may actually bode well for viewers. John Fiske argues that it is important that news *not* try to be objective and completely accurate, because doing so will "increase its authority and decrease people's opportunity to 'argue' with it, to negotiate with it."[42] It may be that ZBC has unwittingly given Zimbabweans the means to criticize the government's message through its overt failure to be objective and accurate.

Zimbabweans cite information, education, and entertainment as their main reasons for watching television. One might expect news to offer information and education, and drama to offer entertainment, but many viewers actually perceive both program genres as providing all three components of viewing pleasure. "Television news *is* watched for pleasure, as well as for top-down information; it is watched for its relevance to everyday life," Fiske writes in *Reading the Popular.*[43]

Soap operas and other dramas, conversely, give viewers not only entertainment but also information. For example, a 19-year-old Shona woman in Kadoma told me that through imported fiction, "One gets to know more from other countries, their culture, behavior, as well as dressing and above all, different languages spoken." Viewers support Morley's claim that "there is, in television, no such thing as 'an innocent text'—no programme which is not worthy of serious attention, no programme which can claim to provide only 'entertainment' rather than messages about society."[44] What kind of messages? I asked two teenage sisters in Chitungwiza, both *Sunset Beach* fans, about what the program taught them:

> KDT: *Ndeupi hukama hwuripo pakati peterevhizheni netsika dzeChishona?*
>
> Iris: *Eh, mamwe maprogrammes avanobudidisa vanenge vachiti, ah, like, for example, if it's drama, when they're acting, zvimwe zvavanenge vachiactor vachiita zvinenge zvichitidzidzisa, there's a lesson behind it.*
>
> Melissa: *Tsika nemagariro.*
>
> KDT: *Ko,* Sunset Beach?
>
> Melissa: *Zvirimo zvaunodzidza.*
>
> Iris: You learn more about love. (*Laughs*)
>
> KDT: What is the relationship between television and Shona culture?
>
> Iris: Eh, some of the programs which they show us are didactic, ah, like, for example, if it's drama, when they're acting, some of what they may act, while they are doing it, it may be teaching us, there's a lesson behind it.
>
> Melissa: Customs and ways of living.

KDT: What about *Sunset Beach?*

Melissa: It has its lessons.

Iris: You learn more about love. *(Laughs)*

These young women couch their discussion of the program in terms of its "lesson," illustrating a common notion among Shona viewers that programs, regardless of genre or origin, "all have a lesson somehow," as a 20-year-old man in downtown Harare told me. When the "lessons" a drama offers are more relevant to viewers than the news, *Sunset Beach* wins out.

Choosing the Foreign, Critiquing the Local

Despite the overlap between news and entertainment in general, in the case of ZTV1's *Main News at Eight* and Joy TV's *Sunset Beach,* viewers were required to choose between the two genres because they aired simultaneously. The dichotomy in this case runs parallel to that between local and imported programming. In Zimbabwe "most fiction is of foreign origin and most fact is nationally produced," Andersen observed.[45] It is telling, then, that when viewers chose fiction over "fact" by choosing *Sunset Beach* over the *Main News,* they were also choosing imported over local. For some, this choice served as a critique of the government-controlled news.

The boundaries between fact and fiction are blurred on the *Main News* by ZBC. They were similarly blurred by viewers of *Sunset Beach,* who saw soaps as a realistic representation of everyday life in the United States. The boundaries between foreign and local television were also blurred. On the one hand, viewers can and do distinguish between locally produced and imported programs. The latter produce feelings of pride in seeing local settings, actors, and themes portrayed on their screens. On the other hand, imported programs are sometimes "localized" by viewers and can have greater relevance for viewers than does a domestically produced program like the *Main News.* The perception of the news as biased, unprofessional, and repressive of various segments of the population is more important to most viewers than is its status as "local." Likewise the perception of *Sunset Beach* as entertaining, educational, and relevant to viewers' everyday lives was more important to them than is its status as "foreign."

Critics Respond

Soaps and other dramatic programs attract viewers more than other genres, and this is one reason that Zimbabwean critics fear their "effects" on audiences. This fear is heightened when dramas are imported, since they are perceived as undermining local cultures. For example, the disparity between the relative wealth of U.S. soap characters and the relative poverty of Zimbabwean viewers has given a number of Zimbabwean media critics a reason to denounce imported films and series. On *Sunset Beach,* for example, characters Gregory Richards, the corrupt head of Liberty Corporation, and his wife, Olivia, owner of a radio station, live in a mansion with their two children. Similarly, Ben Evans owns a coffeehouse and a nightclub, has numerous other business ventures, and lives in a luxurious beach-front house. Even on *Generations,* where many of the main characters are black South Africans, most are wealthy. Zimbabwean viewers are well aware of this. A 21-year-old Shona viewer explained to me that *Generations* "has to do with inheritance. It focuses on one particular family, a rich family. And in that family, the kids will be working and they've got an organization they run . . . a family organization." The wealthy characters on Zimbabwe's most popular imported soaps stand in sharp contrast to the middle- or lower-class black families typically portrayed on local Zimbabwean dramas. Geraghty argues that, even for U.S. viewers, soaps "invite us to observe with amusement, amazement, or wonder the behaviour of a nouveau riche upper class." Similarly, Andrea Press writes of *Dynasty:* "The show offers to us a vision of what it would be like were our wildest fantasies of material success fulfilled." Yet even when characters are middle class by U.S. standards, their lives, homes, and commodities may seem luxurious to Zimbabweans.[46]

Zimbabwean filmmakers and critics have been extremely critical of the display of first world wealth on local screens. Filmmaker Ollie Maruma contended that imported programming "reinforces a desire for the culture and lifestyles of the colonial forces who undermined African culture through centuries of corrosive indoctrination which was part and parcel of slavery and colonisation." Similarly, media studies scholar Munashe Furusa argues that "people who have been trained, throughout their lives, to think that all European things are modern, universal, and, thus, superior to those of other races might be fooled into thinking that the films present models of life they should imitate." At the same time, Furusa fears the opposite: that images of wealth in U.S. soap operas can actually help keep Zimbabwean viewers in a subordinate position by *reducing* their desire for wealth. He writes that imported dramas "reinforce the belief that riches make people unhappy and miserable. Such an objective obviously protects the status quo by reducing our envy for the rich." Furusa seems not to notice the contradiction here: are Zimbabwean television viewers made to desire Western luxury or to see it as the source of misery? Moreover, the question remains as to whose goal it is to keep Zimbabweans subordinate: the U.S. producers who create imported programming, or the state-run Zimbabwean broadcaster who purchases their material and transmits it to the nation?[47]

Statements about the effects of foreign images of wealth on local viewers remain unsubstantiated without research into viewers' actual reactions to and readings of imported film and television. One can see, however, that, in contrast to Maruma's and Furusa's claims, some images of wealth actually present progressive images to Zimbabwean viewers. Mavis Moyo, assistant head of broadcasting for ZBC's Radio 4, wrote about TV and radio depictions of women in the 1980s: "In general little attention is paid in broadcasting to issues of specific importance to women, such as those pertaining to women's movements, or to the contributions made to society by independent and talented women. Women are depicted both on radio and television as dependent, irrational, and over-emotional." Stereotyped depictions of women are arguably common in U.S. programs as well, but there is more variety. For example, whereas women in Zimbabwe are traditionally not allowed to own property in their own names, or may not be aware of their legal right to do so, women in U.S. soaps are well-off, often own their own homes and/ or businesses, and control their own finances. The fact that Zimbabwean viewers may learn of a more financially equal role for women from watching U.S. soaps can be seen as a potentially positive effect of imported programming. In local dramas, one finds that "ideological and legal changes that challenge the status quo and facilitate the empowerment of women and gender equality are depicted as Eurocentric and destructive," as Mashiri writes, but imported programs that challenge Zimbabwe's status quo are likewise depicted by critics as destructive. As we have seen, many viewers would disagree.[48]

Conclusion

Cultural imperialism is inherent in the sheer number of imported programs that find their way to African screens, as well as in the fact that by purchasing foreign programs, African broadcasters have little money left for the production of local content. Broadcasters are more likely to produce "factual" programming such as news, talk shows, game shows, and sports matches rather than expensive dramas. Cultural imperialism has a greater impact on the means of production and distribution of programming than it does on viewers themselves. In other words, depictions of foreign cultures do not necessarily exert imperialism over Zimbabwean viewers.

For viewers, imported television's real potential is as a device for progressive change. I agree with Michael Bruun Andersen, one of the few media critics who have seen the potential of Zimbabwean viewers to move beyond victimhood, when he asserts that the cinematic arts allow Zimbabweans to see that "there are other possibilities and models stemming from foreign material, mostly fictitious. Images and models of that kind are stored, and a potential reservoir of criticism makes it possible for the viewers to see that the way we do it here is not necessarily the only way or the best way."[49] The key word in Andersen's account of television in Zimbabwe, as in my own, is *potential*. I see examples of imported content that potentially allow viewers to critique their own culture and create progressive change in their own lives, but viewers rarely brought up such examples when answering my questionnaires or talking with me. In fact, I found little evidence that the content of imported television was helping viewers critique local political culture. Instead, critiques of the government were displaced onto the state broadcaster. I did find, however, that imported soap operas allowed viewers to connect with elements of their own culture that are not often portrayed on-screen, simply because few local productions are available. Moreover, in a situation where viewers often feel like they have no choice with regard to television and other media, having the power to watch an imported soap opera rather than the local news gave viewers just that: a choice. In this case, viewers seized the opportunity to back up their complaints about the biases of ZBC and its *Main News at Eight* with action: they changed the channel.

* * * * * * * *

CHAPTER 5

Power, Citizenship, and Local Content:
A Critical Reading of the
Broadcasting Services Act

The interests which a discourse serves may be very far from those which it appears, at first sight, to represent.

—Chris Weedon, *Feminist Practice and Poststructuralist Theory*

There is a history of common stereotypes used in Zimbabwean discourse, which are, in complex ways, sometimes reinforced and sometimes subverted in Zimbabwean media. Viewers play an active role in selecting which stereotypes will and will not have power in their own identities. These discourses have tremendous power, so much so that the government transformed them into legislation, the 2001 Broadcasting Services Act.

The BBC's recommendations that Zimbabwe privatize the ZBC went unheeded. For over thirty years, broadcasting in Zimbabwe has been organized as a state monopoly governed by the 1973 Broadcasting Act inherited from Rhodesia. A challenge to this monopoly came for the first time from private radio broadcasters in 2000, leading to the BSA. The act had two main goals: to restrict the possibility of real liberalization and to mandate local content. Unfortunately, the public conversations about the act among culture workers focused almost entirely on the latter. Their conversations revealed nuanced approaches to national culture and the concept of "the local," but they ignored the immediate effects of the act for the state's control of information. The state-owned media encouraged a focus on the local content component of the act in order to deflect attention from its restrictive effects, which were to distribute local propaganda and to limit foreign news, thereby restricting Zimbabwe's public image to one produced by the state.

The discourse examined in this chapter includes the text of the 2001 Broadcasting Services Act, newspaper editorial commentary, and the opinions of culture workers. My goal is not to exhaustively describe the act but to focus on those features within it that appear to be what critical discourse analyst Thomas Huckin calls "textual manipulations serving non-democratic purposes."[1]

The act's legal technicality serves a purpose, ostensibly establishing the Broadcasting Authority of Zimbabwe as a beneficent institution with liberal democratic goals, while giving unrestricted powers to the president to control

Zimbabweans' access to information. The BSA operates on at least three levels of discourse: it specifies how discursive power—the ability to circulate information via broadcasting—is to be limited by the state; it specifies how power should be distributed among agents of the state; and it sets up particular positions for its readers. As legislation, the text has practical effects on people's lives, both framing their experience of "foreign" and "local" cultures and restricting their access to information.

No Room for "Nutties": A History of Control

Zimbabwe announced its commitment to deregulating broadcasting in 1995 in response to both external and internal pressures to liberalize. External pressures included increased liberalization of broadcasting in Europe, the 1991 Declaration of Windhoek on press freedom and media pluralism in the Southern African Development Community (SADC) region, the establishment of the Media Institute of Southern Africa (MISA), and the 1992 SADC Declaration Treaty and Protocol, which advocated governmental support for increased popular participation in democracy. Internal pressures included those of local unions and NGOs, such as the Zimbabwe Union of Journalists and the Zimbabwe branch of MISA. The unlikelihood of achieving true deregulation was revealed that same year when Information Minister Jonathan Moyo said, "You don't know what a non-state radio station might broadcast," constructing independent media as dangerous to the state and using that claim to justify state control of information.[2]

In 1998, the Ministry of Information introduced a draft communications bill, aimed at establishing a body to regulate and ostensibly license private broadcasters as well as telecommunication and postal service providers. However, many commentators saw the bill as the state's attempt not to liberalize broadcasting but to consolidate its control of it. The bill led to ongoing confrontations between government and private newspapers, cell phone providers, and Internet service providers for the next two years. Eventually it was reworked into the Postal and Telecommunication Bill, passed into a law that focused on cell phones rather than broadcasting.[3]

The government continued to send mixed messages about its commitment to liberalization. State spokesmen made, on the one hand, verbal commitments to broadcasting reform and, on the other, paranoid claims about the role of "foreign" media in undermining Zimbabwe. For example, Chen Chimutengwende, then minister of information, was interviewed during a question-and-answer slot on ZTV's *Main News at Eight* just before the 2000 parliamentary election. He claimed that the liberalization of the airwaves would be a top priority in the next Parliament, yet went on to attack a Netherlands-based radio station that had begun broadcasting in Zimbabwe earlier that month, as well as the BBC World

Service, CNN, and other international broadcasters, accusing them of trying to destabilize the country and keep Zimbabwe under Western influence. He said Zimbabwe needed to intensify its efforts to channel "the correct information" about the country and to "counter the propaganda churned out" by international broadcasters. His comments eerily echo colonial cinematographer Geoffrey Mangin's about propaganda used by the Rhodesian Front government to "keep their world viewers correctly informed about the true facts of a peaceful Southern Africa" and counteract the "distorted stories" produced by "visitors."[4]

After Chimutengwende won a parliamentary seat in the June elections, the government restructured the Ministry of Information, Posts, and Telecommunications, separating telecommunications from other media, which were moved under the Ministry of Information and Publicity, and appointing Jonathan Moyo as the new minister. Moyo had served as ZANU-PF's campaign manager in the 2000 parliamentary elections. He was charged with pursuing media law reform and regulating broadcasting.[5] Like the proposed communications bill, such reform was ostensibly aimed at liberalizing broadcasting but in fact further limited it.

The first real challenge to the state's monopoly over broadcasting came in September 2000 from a private radio station, Capital Radio, established by two white Zimbabweans, Mike Auret Jr. and Gerry Jackson. The Munhumatapa African Broadcasting Corporation—the short-lived private network that had rented airtime from ZBC on ZTV2—and Capital Radio both challenged the ZBC monopoly in the Supreme Court. In September 2000 the Court found in favor of Capital Radio, declaring that the state's monopoly on broadcasting violated section 20 of the constitution, which allows individual freedom of expression.[6]

The Supreme Court's ruling was a victory for liberalization, but the government immediately countered by invoking the Presidential Powers (Temporary Measures) Act of 1986, which allows the president to enact emergency laws that are valid for up to six months without going through Parliament. Under these laws, according to Ndlela, Mugabe ordered the seizure of Capital Radio's equipment. Dumisani Moyo writes that the resulting legislation, the 2000 Presidential Powers (Temporary Measures) (Broadcasting) Regulations, "further tightened the conditions of entry into the sector." MISA called the temporary regulations "draconian" and criticized them for "giving Moyo—and ultimately President Mugabe— unfettered powers to dictate how the whole broadcasting system should work." Eric Mazango, in a report written for the Zimbabwe chapter of MISA, argues that while the emergency regulations drew on liberalization legislation from other parts of the world, "the imperative control, limits, and prohibitions inherent in many provisions shows that they were hastily drawn up and structured to deal with the Capital Radio saga." The temporary regulations formed the core of the 2001 BSA.[7]

The temporary laws created the Broadcasting Authority of Zimbabwe to review applications for broadcasting licenses, but the Authority never granted

Capital Radio a license. In public commentary on the case, Jonathan Moyo announced that no "foreigners" would own media in Zimbabwe, insinuating that Auret's and Jackson's whiteness made them foreign. Moyo also indicated his opposition to liberalization: "Liberalisation is a political and not a legal concept. Taken to its extreme, it might mean nutties should be given as much room as Christians, and certainly any democratic society cannot tolerate that."[8] The temporary broadcasting laws, alongside the mobilization of a racialized discourse disguised in terms of "foreign" and "local" and other attempts to define which Zimbabweans should be "given room" in the country's media culture, paved the way for the 2001 BSA. The battle for broadcasting deregulation had begun, and the state had made clear that it would make that battle very difficult for its opponents.

"A Good Idea about the Local Content": Hopes for Change

Before the bill was enacted, many culture workers were excited about the legislation, seeing it as opening up real possibilities for a pluralistic broadcasting environment. For example, in my 2001 conversation with film producer Simon Bright, he told me that he saw possibilities for more collaboration between TV and film: "I hope that the Broadcasting Act will create an outlet for a lot more guys to emerge with a ready market waiting for their material, and that's essentially what's going to stimulate production." Arthur Chikuhwa, director of the Capricorn Video Unit, told me he hoped that the potential growth in the market would lead not only to increased production but also to employment opportunities for filmmakers:

> I think it is a good idea about the local content, because we have writers here; we have actors here. The skill—it is here. It's so painful to make a good film here, a documentary—it is seen in South Africa or Australia, but your own people don't see it. It is very painful. But with this kind of an approach, if we can have more of that, if money is available, I know that material will be made. That means more work for the artists—actors, technical crew. More work and more business for us.

Even state-affiliated culture workers expected changes. Alexander Kanengoni, head of research at ZBC, saw the potential for more broadcasters to inject much-needed competition into the mediascape. After explaining Joy TV's limited broadcasting range and times in relation to ZTV's dominance, he shared with me his prediction that change would occur because of the BSA:

> It will change. There's no doubt about that. Because of the little competition we are getting from Joy, it is quite significant. If we introduce someone completely new who is able to reach the whole country, it will be serious competition. Given that ZBC does not have any money at all,

the new players will take care of that at the beginning—to make sure that they have got the money. Once they come with the money, that is a big problem for ZBC.

Kanengoni presents change as imminent and inevitable. Zimbabweans' hopes for the Broadcasting Services Act were high.

Initial reactions to the BSA may have been largely positive, but when the legislation was enacted and its text was released to the public, people began to assess it. Surprisingly, their critiques were largely restricted to the local content portions of the BSA, a reading I call "uncritical" because it ignores the ways the state used the act to consolidate its power.

An Uncritical Reading

The 2001 BSA is divided into nine parts, which are then subdivided into forty-eight sections, followed by six appendixes called "schedules." On its title page, the act is summarized in terms of the actions it aims to accomplish.

AN ACT to provide for the functions, powers, and duties of the Broadcasting Authority of Zimbabwe; to provide for the constitution of the Authority; to provide for the planning, management, allocation, regulation, and protection of the broadcasting frequency spectrum and the regulation and licensing of broadcasting services and systems; to provide for programme standards; to regulate and license signal carriers; to encourage and develop the creative arts through broadcasting content standards; to create a sense of national identity through broadcasting services; to create a Broadcasting Fund to help finance local broadcasting and for related purposes; and to provide for matters incidental to or connected with the foregoing.

Focusing on the verbs, at face value one might conclude that the president and the Parliament are motivated by magnanimous goals of *providing, encouraging,* and *creating* a broadcasting culture that will benefit Zimbabwe. The only verb without connotations of generosity is *regulate,* but because of its occurrence in the phrase "regulate and license signal carriers," it suggests a move toward liberalization of broadcasting. An uncritical reading of the act assumes that the state has the best interests of Zimbabweans at heart. Nothing could be further from the truth.

A Critical Reading

Raising questions about the goals, functions, and interpretations of the text reveals that it actually prevents broadcast liberalization by strengthening the powers of the president, the minister of information and publicity, and the police, creating citizenship and residency requirements for broadcasters, and limiting the freedom of expression of broadcasters. The act's use of legal discourse is an impediment to public understanding of the legislation, and it establishes power relationships among people and institutions.

The eight goals listed in the above summary of the BSA fit into two broad themes:

1. establishing legislation to control licensing of new broadcasters, and
2. encouraging national identity through local production and broadcasting.

The first theme is textually dominant, addressed in sections 3–27, sections 36–48, and schedules 1–5—approximately twenty pages of the thirty-page document. The second theme is confined to sections 28–35 and schedule 6—approximately four pages. The other six pages are devoted to the summary, table of contents, and definitions of the terms used. The BSA emphasizes state control of licenses over its commitment to national identity and "local" media.

Legislating Licensure: Technicality, Power, and Citizenship

In establishing legislation to control licensing of new broadcasters, the BSA achieves three effects. First, it uses technicality to encourage an uncritical reading. Second, it establishes important power relationships among people and institutions that allow the state to retain authority over broadcasting and limit democratic access to information. Third, it establishes citizenship and residency requirements for broadcasters.

Technicality

The BSA is relatively conventional in its use of legal discourse notoriously difficult for lay readers to understand. "The main lexical characteristic of the law is large-scale technicality," John Gibbons argues.[9] Typical of the genre, the BSA is marked by difficult vocabulary, long noun phrases, and intratextuality. Legal jargon, specialized use of common words, and technological terms make the portions that deal with licensing technically difficult.

The preliminary part of the act includes two sections that define forty-three terms used. Among these are the types of broadcasting, including cable, commercial, community, free-to-air, national, public, subscription, subscription cable, and subscription satellite broadcasting services, as well as datacasting, diffusion, open narrowcasting, subscription narrowcasting, and webcasting.[10] By including all of these types, many of which have never existed in Zimbabwe, the BSA suggests that broadcasting will indeed be liberalized. At the same time, by providing explicit definitions for all foreseeable broadcasting services, it reduces the possibility that a potential broadcaster might find a loophole to broadcast without a license. Moreover, while the use of such technical terms is necessary given the content of the BSA, the layperson's lack of familiarity with these technologies contributes to its impenetrability.

Power Relations

The BSA establishes power relations between individuals and institutions with interest in broadcasting. These include powerful agents of the state, including the Broadcasting Authority of Zimbabwe and its board members, the minister of information, the police, and the president, as well as those subject to state power, including broadcasting stations, their owners and employees, content providers, and audiences.

Part II, section 4.2 of the BSA establishes the Broadcasting Authority of Zimbabwe to oversee the distribution of broadcasting licenses to new broadcasters, and it outlines the procedures to be followed both by the Authority and would-be broadcasters. It gives legal status to the Authority, a board of advisors to the minister of information and publicity, whose members are appointed by the minister in consultation with the president "and in accordance with any directions that the president may give him."

By the time the BSA was passed, the Authority had already been widely criticized by media analysts starting from the time the board had been established through temporary regulations in October 2000. Eric Mazango suggests that the initial members of the Authority had no professional qualifications and were chosen with no clear criteria; essentially, they were Mugabe's cronies.

An examination of the actions to be performed by the Authority, however, reveals that its agency is minimal. Among the seventeen "powers and functions" of the Authority listed in part II, section 3, five of them speak to the Authority's role as an agent of the minister.

> Subject to this Act, the powers and functions of the Authority shall be— . . .
>
> (b) to advise the Minister on the adoption and establishment of standards and codes relating to equipment attached to broadcasting systems;
>
> (c) to receive, evaluate, and consider applications for the issue of any broadcasting licence or signal carrier licence for the purpose of advising the Minister on whether or not he should grant the licence; . . .

(e) to advise the Minister on ways of improving and promoting a
regulatory environment that will facilitate the development of a
broadcasting industry in Zimbabwe that is efficient, competitive,
and responsive to audience needs and the national interest; . . .

(p) generally, to advise the Minister on all matters relating to broadcasting systems and services;

(q) subject to this Act, to carry out any function or act as may be
prescribed by the Minister.

In contrast to the Authority, the minister is constructed as a powerful agent.
He causes the Authority to act: he may *direct* the Authority to notify an applicant
or licensee in writing of his decisions; he may *request* the Authority to institute a
public inquiry into a licensee suspected of criminal activity; and he may *require* the
Authority to determine program standards. Moreover, the minister has the power
to appoint and dismiss members of the Authority's board. In addition to making
explicit various reasons why a board member might be dismissed, the act gives the
minister discretion to dismiss any board member who has "conducted himself in
a manner that renders him unsuitable as a member."[11]

The minister may be the most textually prominent agent in the act, but his
authority is ultimately subject to the approval of the president, as the act's definition of "minister" makes clear:

"Minister" means the minister of state for information and publicity in
the president's office or any other minister to whom the president may,
from time to time, assign the administration of this Act.

Not only is the minister located physically and organizationally "in the president's
office," but also the position is one appointed by the president rather than an
elected office. If at any time the president is displeased with the minister's administration of the act, he may call on any other minister to take over these duties.
Moreover, though not mentioned in the act, the president may also opt to remove
him from office completely and appoint a new minister of state for information
and publicity, as President Mugabe eventually did when he fired Jonathan Moyo
in February 2005. Finally, although the act itself was written by Moyo, it was
"ENACTED by the President and the Parliament of Zimbabwe"—with capital-
ization in the original text. Although the act theoretically provides mechanisms
for liberalizing Zimbabwean broadcasting, it actually gives the president ultimate
power over the airwaves.

The president's authority extends not only over the minister, through whom
licenses may be granted or revoked, but also over the police, through whom vio-
lators of the act may be physically controlled. In section 42, "Inspections," the
act grants the police a number of powers: to "require a person whom [sic] he has

reasonable cause to suspect is a person required in terms of this Act to possess a licence to produce his licence"; to enter the premises of a licensee or anyone suspected of broadcasting without a license; to seize broadcasting equipment or any other material used in contravention of the act; to retain such material "for so long as may be necessary for the purpose of any examination, investigation, trial, or inquiry"; and to order anyone, whether licensed or not, to cease broadcasting. Those who fail to comply with police requests and orders may be arrested or fined.

In contrast to agents of the state whose powers are described and effected by the act, broadcasting stations, their owners and employees, and audiences are depicted as powerless. We have already seen how an applicant for a broadcasting license is powerless in relation to the Broadcasting Authority, the minister of information and publicity, and ultimately the president. Even if licensed, a broadcaster remains under threat of government surveillance, equipment seizure, and arrest.

If the act marks potential broadcasters as relatively powerless in relation to the state, it marks the public—viewers and listeners—as entirely without agency. For example, one function of the Authority is "to advise the Minister on ways of improving and promoting a regulatory environment that will facilitate the development of a broadcasting industry in Zimbabwe that is efficient, competitive, and *responsive to audience needs* and the national interest." In some cases the term *community* is used to stand in for *audience*, with repeated claims that broadcasting must respect "community standards and values."[12] All applicants for broadcasting licenses must develop a code of conduct in which "community attitudes to the following matters are to be taken into account":

(a) the portrayal in programmes of physical and psychological violence;

(b) the portrayal in programmes of sexual conduct and nudity;

(c) the use in programmes of offensive language, including hate speech;

(d) the portrayal in programmes of the use of drugs, including alcohol;

(e) the portrayal in programmes of matter that is likely to incite or perpetuate hatred against, or vilifies, any person or group on the basis of ethnicity, nationality, race, gender, natural difference or condition, age, religion, or physical or mental disability;

(f) the reasonable protection of an individual's name and reputation;

(g) such other matters relating to programme content as are of concern to the community.[13]

Despite this level of detail, the act neither defines *community* nor explains how "community values" will be assessed or concerns collected. Nowhere in the act are the audience or the community treated as agents. Zimbabwean viewers have long aired their concerns about the differences between their "traditional values" and those in TV programs and films, especially imported ones, and yet they continue to watch them. The act's treatment of the public as powerless and devoid of agency, subject to paternalistic claims about their needs and concerns with no authorized means of voicing them, stands in stark contrast to Zimbabwe's active viewers.

Citizenship and Residency

The act restricts involvement in broadcasting, in any capacity, to Zimbabwean citizens living in Zimbabwe. Section 8.1 states that a broadcasting license can only be granted to "individuals who are citizens of Zimbabwe and ordinarily resident in Zimbabwe" or to a "body corporate" in which a controlling interest is held by one or more citizens who are normally resident in the country. "Controlling interest" typically implies 51 percent of voting stock shares, but section 8.2 defines the term restrictively to mean 100 percent of the body corporate's securities, shares, or votes. Moreover, a licensed broadcaster cannot even employ someone who is not a citizen ordinarily residing in Zimbabwe, although the minister has the authority to make exceptions to this rule. Additionally, according to section 11.8, all members of the Broadcasting Authority board must be Zimbabwean citizens.

Through citizenship and residency requirements, the act effectively makes almost any viable broadcaster ineligible, since most citizens ordinarily residing in Zimbabwe do not have access to the capital, equipment, and training required to operate a radio or television station. With more than three hundred Zimbabweans per month emigrating legally and countless more illegally, the act's stipulation that only those "ordinarily resident in Zimbabwe" can own broadcasting licenses ensures that critics of ZANU-PF now living in exile will have minimal influence in the country's cinematic and broadcasting culture.[14] In conjunction, sections 8, 11, and 12 prevent anyone who is not a citizen of Zimbabwe, as well as Zimbabweans who have left the country, from playing any role in the country's broadcasting system, either as financial backers or as employees.

(Not) Defining National Identity

Sections 3.2(e) through (h) make use of a number of terms that are not defined in section 2: "audience needs," "national interest," "diversity," "Zimbabweans," and "Zimbabwean identity, character and cultural diversity." By neglecting to define these terms, the act suggests that their meanings are what critical discourse analyst Norman Fairclough calls "taken-for-granted background knowledge." Background knowledge "subsumes 'naturalized' ideological representations, i.e., ideological representations which come to be seen as nonideological 'common sense.'"[15] These terms have contested meanings that must be historicized. Little is known about what audiences in Zimbabwe "need," a term reminiscent of the paternalism of colonial broadcasting and cinema. "National interest" presumes that everyone within the boundaries of the nation has interests that are shared among them as well as aligned with the government's interests. Diversity is often defined in terms of racial, linguistic, ethnic, geographic, and socioeconomic binaries that are in fact fluid and hybrid. The label *Zimbabweans* is often used not to mean all citizens of Zimbabwe but rather black citizens of Zimbabwe. Identity and character are constructed by individuals engaged with cultural texts, not merely developed and reflected by broadcasters, and may take forms other than national ones, including identities constructed through ethnicity and language, gender, educational level, or socioeconomic class. The framing of broadcasting legislation in terms of national interests and Zimbabwean identity encourages Zimbabweans to think about themselves in certain ways, and places them in particular relations to state power.

With regard to broadcasting, with the transmission of TV or radio programs from a distance, the term *national* has an important spatial meaning. The act defines "national broadcasting service" using *national* in the geographic sense: "a free-to-air community or commercial broadcasting service whose licence area is the whole of Zimbabwe." In this context *national* is distinct from the *state* and *national broadcasting service* is distinct from *public broadcaster,* defined in part I of the act as "the Zimbabwe Broadcasting Corporation referred to in section 3 of the Zimbabwe Broadcasting Corporation Act [chapter 12:01] or any other broadcasting entity established by law which is wholly owned or controlled by the state." Section 9 of the act dictates that only one television license can be issued to a national free-to-air broadcaster other than ZBC, effectively limiting national broadcasting service providers to two: ZBC and one other. In other words, if liberalization were to take place, it would do so regionally rather than nationally. The ability to reach only a regional audience means not only that potential broadcasters would not be able to compete for advertising dollars but also that alternative viewpoints would not be made accessible at the national level.

Although the act does not make this explicit, its local content provisions are presumably an important mechanism by which it supports the creation of a "national identity." Various sections of the act address "local content." Section 11.3 says that "every licence for the provision of a radio, television, or subscription cable broadcasting service shall be issued subject to the local content conditions specified in the Sixth Schedule." Section 2.1 of the Sixth Schedule states that a free-to-air television broadcasting licensee must ensure that at least 75 percent of its total programming, as well as 75 percent of its prime-time (6 PM to 10 PM) programming, is "local television content and material from Africa," including repeats (the local term for what Americans call "reruns"). Furthermore, section 2.3 breaks down the requirement along the lines of program genres, summarized in table 5.1.

Even subscription television services, such as satellite broadcasters, must air at least 30 percent "local television content."[16] Furthermore, section 4 stipulates that 40 percent of local programming must be "independent television productions,"

TABLE 5.1. Local content requirements by genre

Drama	70%
Current affairs	80%
Social documentary	70%
Informal knowledge-building	70%
Educational	80%
Children's	80%

meaning 30 percent of total programming for free-to-air TV broadcasters and 9 percent for subscription TV broadcasters. While the act fails to define "independent television productions," I believe it refers to productions made outside of a broadcaster's own studios, such as domestically produced films. Section 7(a) of the schedule gives the minister the discretion to prescribe other local content conditions to any licensee, or to extend the period in which a broadcaster must meet local content percentages, effectively granting ZBC permission to continue broadcasting much lower percentages of local content than the act requires for other potential broadcasters.

In addition to prescribing local content quotas, the act also establishes a language policy for broadcasting for the first time in Zimbabwe's history. Section 4(a) requires all licensees to broadcast at least 10 percent of their programming in "any of the national aboriginal languages of Zimbabwe other than Shona and Ndebele," while section 4(b) requires that at least 10 percent of programming must cater to the hearing-impaired. Since neither "national languages" nor "national aboriginal languages" are defined in the Zimbabwean constitution, one can only assume that this section refers to the various languages used in Zimbabwe by its minority ethnic groups. This policy would be a welcome change from the English-dominated broadcasting environment in place before the act, but it is noteworthy that the act still neglects to dictate minimums for Shona and Ndebele. Neither was broadcast for more than 8 percent at the time this legislation was enacted.

Conflicting Channels of Dialogue and Debate

In the six months between the establishment of the temporary Broadcasting Regulations on 4 October 2000 and the passage of the BSA on 4 April 2001, advocates of broadcasting law reform repeatedly urged the government to "foster all-inclusive dialogue and debate that takes into account the views and interests of the diversity of groups in Zimbabwe" by subjecting the proposed regulations to "public debate and scrutiny" by the public, professional bodies, advertisers, cinematic arts producers, academics, and other media experts before they were presented to Parliament.[17] The Zimbabwe chapter of MISA recommended the establishment of a National Media Advisory Panel tasked with advising the government on national broadcasting priorities. In December 2000, the government did create a panel bearing this name, but many journalists saw it not as fulfilling MISA's recommendation but rather as a "media watchdog" that would do more harm than good to press freedom.[18] Speaking at a panel discussion about the act a few months after it was passed, novelist and poet Chenjerai Hove commented, "It needed a dialog between filmmakers, broadcasters, and all the stakeholders to discuss it before they came out with this requirement. Because nobody was consulted, I don't think, about this matter. I don't remember any consultation about this matter. So it has problems, as far as I can see, real problems. It is local, but it has problems which were not looked into before it was put on paper to become law." With the aside "It is local," Hove differentiates the act from other policies that have been criticized for being imposed on Zimbabwe from elsewhere—such as the Economic Structural Adjustment Program in the early 1990s. "It is local, but it has problems." Hove's remarks are a pithy reminder that being produced locally does not guarantee that a text serves the interests of Zimbabweans.

The government may have followed the letter rather than the spirit of MISA's suggestion, but outside of official channels the BSA *was* subjected to extensive public debate and scrutiny, particularly among cultural workers like Hove. However, state discourse framed interpretation of the act in terms of its less prominent theme, national identity, constraining public discourse about the legislation to conversations about foreign and local content and preventing discussion of the act's repressive effect on independent broadcasting.

Throughout 2001, debates over "the local content act," as the BSA was popularly known, filled local newspapers and TV talk shows and were frequent among film, TV, and other cultural workers. Despite its primary concern with TV and radio broadcasting, the act affected filmmakers as well because most of them either produce films or videos that are eventually broadcast on television or they work in both film and television.

There are important similarities between state-affiliated interpretations of the act and the independent interpretations of culture workers and the public. By restricting their conversations about the act to its local content sections, they unwittingly took up a state-sponsored uncritical reading of it that supports the status quo. Although they come to different conclusions, both interpretations focus on the costs, benefits, and feasibility of increasing local content. Where they differ more markedly is in the nuanced approach that culture workers bring to questions of localness, citizenship, globalization, colonialism, and national culture—terms that state-affiliated interpretations encourage Zimbabweans to take for granted.

"A Sharp Change on Our Local Television Screens":
State-Affiliated Readings of the Act

Coverage of the BSA in state-owned media reveals an emphasis on the effect of its local content provisions on audiences, with limited discussion of its restrictive license terms for new broadcasters. Moreover, discussion of the legislation in the state press was largely positive, lauding its support for Zimbabwean values and identity. Editorials published in state-owned Zimbabwean newspapers provide numerous examples of uncritical readings of the act. Two days after the act was passed by Parliament and signed by President Mugabe, the state-owned *Herald* published three articles about the legislation. First, TV reviewer Elton Dzikiti wrote, "Will the New Broadcasting Act Bring Change to ZBC?" In it, he writes:

> Without doubt, the biggest story in broadcast media circles this week is the newly introduced Broadcasting Services Act. Passed, signed, and gazetted on Wednesday, the new law also affects ZBC, particularly on the clause regarding local programme content. According to the act, a television broadcasting licensee must ensure that at least 75 [*sic*] percent of its drama, 80 percent of its current affairs, 75 [*sic*] percent of social documentaries, 75 [*sic*] percent of informal knowledge building programmes, 80 percent of educational programmes, and 80 percent of children's programmes are Zimbabwean. We should be seeing a sharp change on our local television screens soon.

Dzikiti's remarks are typical of state-affiliated interpretations of the act in several ways. He focuses on "the clause regarding local programme content" at the expense of the sections of the act that deal with licensure. He says that this clause "in particular" will affect ZBC, but he doesn't address any other clause. His statement that the "new law also affects ZBC" presents the act as fair: it will affect ZBC as well as others. It also implies that the act will lead to the establishment of other broadcasters or even—although pointedly untrue—that there already are other broadcasters. His comments on local programming requirements merely summarize the text of the act without offering any critique or questioning. Finally, his forecast for imminent change suggests either naïve assumptions about the state's enforcement of the act vis-à-vis ZTV or a deliberate attempt to circulate this interpretation among readers.

Second, the *Herald* ran an anonymous editorial, "Act Opens New Era in Broadcasting." The author calls the act "a piece of legislation which gives Zimbabweans the ammunition to restore their values" and its enactment "yet another important milestone in our quest to forge national and cultural identity, dignity, and sovereignty." It also claims that the act "ensur[es] that licenses will be awarded to locals," suggesting that licenses will in fact be awarded. On the one hand, the editorial rejects "foreigners" and "foreign programmes, most of which are trash," and on the other hand, it uses legislation from other parts of the world to give credence to the BSA. Using citizenship and residency as license requirements "is critical and in line with worldwide trends where foreigners are not allowed to own and run radio and television stations." The use of foreign legislation to justify the exclusion of foreign broadcasters is highly ironic.

The editorial also addresses public concerns about Zimbabwean broadcasters' capacity to meet the local content requirements: "Granted, the capacity to produce quality local productions is limited, but that should not mean that we accept as normal being overwhelmed by foreign programmes, most of which are trash." The author frames the act as a cultural tool that will be used to promote Zimbabwean values and identity, constraining how the Zimbabwean public, most of whom will not have read the act, can interpret it. "Restoring" Zimbabwean values suggests a return to past values that have been lost. The editorial continues: "Our values cannot continue to be eroded and rubbished in the name of democracy." The values and identity reflected in the legislation remain nebulous, but its antidemocratic agenda is clear.

A third anonymous piece on page 9 of the *Herald* offered an ostensibly more balanced approach to the act, but one that nevertheless favored the state's paternalistic claims to protect Zimbabweans from foreign elements. Titled "New Broadcasting Services Act Generates Mixed Feelings," the article surveys "most players in the broadcasting sector" and concludes that the act "has generated mixed feelings, with most people interviewed welcoming it while others say it has clauses that are unconstitutional." After this introductory paragraph, twenty-two paragraphs present positive interpretations of the act, with four individuals quoted in favor of the legislation, plus additional indirect speech from Minister Jonathan Moyo, the author of the act. In contrast, only five paragraphs present negative views of the legislation, with only one individual quoted plus indirect speech from two others. The only negative view quoted is from Mike Auret Jr., whose attempt to start Capital Radio had spurred the state to establish the act.

Diluting Quality: Public Interpretations of the Act

In contrast to the state-owned papers and television, the independent press provided a more negative view of the BSA. For example, on 8 April 2001, Itayi Viriri, a TV columnist for the *Standard,* quoted a letter from a viewer: "I seldom watch *Insight* but decided to hear what Gideon Gono had to say about the station's restructuring and the Broadcasting Act last Sunday night." Viriri doesn't include the viewer's comments on what he or she learned from ZBC chairman Gideon Gono, but he adds his own commentary: "Well, we don't know anything new, least of all how ZTV is going to produce 75 percent local content in an 18-hour viewing day." Not having read the act themselves, viewers rely on other media to interpret it, including the state-run TV news. In the absence of useful information on the act, they restrict their commentary to the 75 percent local content rule.

Even while criticizing the legislation, the independent press focused almost entirely on the local content portions. For example, according to an anonymous editorial in the *Daily News* published on 7 April 2001, "New Broadcasting Act Reflects Rabid Paranoia," Eddison Zvobgo chaired a parliamentary legal committee that reviewed the act and found that eight sections were inconsistent with section 20 of the constitution, which protects freedom of expression:

> This was obviously a reference to the Act's numerous restrictive clauses, in particular those dealing with the programming content as they stipulate that every television licensee must ensure that at least 75 percent of what they air is Zimbabwean. That stipulation does not only impinge on the broadcasters' rights to freedom of expression but also violates audiences' freedom of choice of what to watch by so limiting variety of what stations can offer that they will more or less be homogenous. Exasperatingly enough, in that homogeneity, all broadcasting services will be made to look like clones of the ZBC, nauseating as it is.

Newspaper coverage of the BSA petered out in the months following its enactment, but culture workers continued to debate it. A prime example of such a debate took place at the Book Café, a restaurant frequented by Harare's intellectuals and artists, where readings, panel discussions, film screenings, and other cultural events often took place. On 8 August 2001, a panel that included novelist Chenjerai Hove and journalists Chido Makunike and Ish Mafundikwa came together. The chair of the panel announced:

> The topic we are going to discuss is a focus on the newly enacted broadcasting law in Zimbabwe. And that law basically says all materials to be broadcast on national television and national radio, and I believe even private stations as well, should have a 75 percent Zimbabwean content. So, we have our panel here which will look at whether that local content for broadcasting media is feasible, and whether it will boost local arts or dilute quality, and what place that leaves for other cultures from Africa— African cultures—and whether that allows diversity.

The chair's summary offers a reading of the act that mirrors the state's framing of the legislation as primarily concerned with local content.

Hove, Makunike, and Mafundikwa are culture workers and intellectuals, but they are also part of broadcasting's public. As viewers of local and foreign television and film, they take up positions similar to other Zimbabweans. Their comments are typical of audience reactions to the act, taking up concerns about pleasure, quality, and quantity similar to those raised but dismissed by the editorials in the *Herald* I discussed above.

Audience fears about boring television and radio filled with reruns were couched in discussions of the economic feasibility of developing enough local content to fill the 75 percent quota stipulated by the act, however that local content might be defined. Mafundikwa, for example, opined, "Excuse me if I am wrong, but I suspect that we do not have the capacity to produce the 75 percent."

The BSA defined the powers of the Broadcasting Authority to include promoting "the provision of high quality and innovative programming by providers of broadcasting services," but many people questioned not only the quantity of available resources but also the quality. Hove, for example, commented, "I don't think we have resources enough to be able to match certain technical qualities which we can source from other places." And Mafundikwa asked, "Will [the act] boost local arts or dilute quality? I have worked on local radio, and one of the reasons cited by local DJs for not playing local music is the poor quality of locally produced music. This sometimes is a legitimate excuse." Later he added, "If we are going to record merely to fill a quota, this 75 percent, then just about anybody who can afford to go into a studio will go in and record, in spite of the quality. We might end up having very monotonous, uninspired recordings to deal with." One reason that the money needed to produce local programs is scarce is that the same pool of money is used to purchase the imported TV shows that dominate ZTV. Spending its limited resources on imported shows undermines ZBC's ability to produce its own. The 75 percent local content requirement seems to address this problem, but it fails to specify how the state will provide the financial resources.[19]

Many viewers and culture workers lamented the anticipated low quality of local broadcasting, but most failed to see the connection between restrictions on foreign content and the licensing of new broadcasters. Mike Auret Jr. and Gerry Jackson were an exception:

> Anyone in the industry can tell you that the cost of local production is much higher than that of buying international productions and these provisions would immediately make broadcasting nonviable and unsustainable and the Ministry will have achieved its objective of constraining freedom of expression since no one will be able to afford to broadcast under these provisions.[20]

Mafundikwa elaborated on the reasons musicians—and one can add filmmakers—cannot afford to produce more high-quality work: the cost of equipment is high, most of it must be imported, and then a heavy import tax is levied against it, difficulties that are compounded by the decreasing value of the Zimbabwean dollar. So Auret and Jackson's prediction of a nonviable and unsustainable local industry seems well founded.

As film and television viewers, Hove and Mafundikwa take up widespread concerns about the effects of the BSA on viewers' everyday experience of film and television, what kinds of programs they will have access to, and what level of quality those programs will offer. They seem to take the state's framing of the act as primarily concerned with local content at face value. Yet the panel opened up a space for public discourse that went beyond this frame, offering nuanced views of contested terms such as *authentic, local,* and even *Zimbabwean.*

Hove began by likening Zimbabwe's attempts to expunge imported programming from television to other African governments' attempts to create an artificially "authentic" African national culture after independence:

> Now what it reminds me of is what happened in Zaire during the time of Mobutu Sese Seko. He decreed under his philosophy of authenticity —Do you remember those days?—that there is no other music on Zairian television except Zairian music. That's why he changed his name to Mobutu Sese Seko; he was called something else. People began to take local names. Because it worked somehow. It worked because that's why there is Zairian music all over the place. But also that's why the Zairian musicians, most of them, are based in Paris.... So I don't really think that art works through dictatorship. It might work that if you order poets to write good poems about socialism, they will stop writing those poems at all. You see? So that's one of my worries.

Here Hove uses an example from Zaire (now the Democratic Republic of the Congo), a shift of context that allows him to criticize Mugabe without naming him; Mobutu's dictatorship stands in for another dictatorship closer to home. We can find similar examples of Mobutu's "philosophy of authenticity" in Zimbabwe itself. Like Mobutu's self-naming, the renaming of Rhodesia as Zimbabwe imposed an "authentic" African identity on the country. Tropes of tradition and authenticity in the cinematic arts, like the African drummer who introduces ZTV news, are abstract but without a superior role in Zimbabwean identity. Hove presents these tropes as dangerous for the arts because they limit freedom of artistic expression.

Hove continued:

> What do we mean by "local content"? I have problems with that. Because I can do a film myself with all foreign actors, set here in Zimbabwe with foreign actors. And the crew and the cameraman and the producers are all Zimbabweans. Is that going to be local content or not local content? What do you mean? So I have problems with that, and I always think that it has got an element of racism in it.

Hove uses a hypothetical film made with foreign actors and a local crew to illustrate a point, but the example is all too familiar, almost exactly the state of cinematic arts in the 1980s when Hollywood filmmakers were using Zimbabwe as a location. Chido Makunike raised similar concerns, asking a series of rhetorical questions:

What is local? Are Shona lyrics backing with Western instruments local, or is that not local? Must local necessarily mean Shona or Ndebele lyrics with *mbira* [a thumb piano] or other local instruments? Is it okay, then, to amplify them, or is it not okay to amplify them? Just by asking these questions I hope I have shown how absurd it is to say, "This is local, this is foreign, this is Zimbabwean, this is Western, this is black, this is white." We don't live in a situation where those kinds of demarcations are possible any more. I think we waste a lot of time when we try to force them on ourselves. And we make ourselves look absurd and silly.

The cultural ramifications of designating some texts and practices as local and others as foreign represent the concerns of cultural workers and public intellectuals in the midst of a national crisis of representation and identity.

Calls for Democratic Change

Media watchdogs continue to criticize the 2001 Broadcasting Services Act for preventing liberalization. Calls to revise the act continue. In 2007, Mugabe appointed a new minister of information and publicity, Sikhanyiso Ndlovu, whose response to such calls illustrates how little has changed since 2001. Consider the following excerpts from an anonymous article from the state-owned *Herald*, "Be Patient, Minister Urges Prospective Broadcasters," published on 7 September 2007, which quotes Ndlovu extensively:

> The Minister of Information and Publicity, Cde Sikhanyiso Ndlovu, has urged those who want to establish radio and television stations to be patient while he studies the Broadcasting Services Act.
>
> "I am still studying the Act so that we can formulate policies and regulations that are user friendly to all our people. We don't serve the nation to be confrontational.
>
> "These regulations will ensure the development of the media and protect the nation's values and traditions from undue disturbance by other countries," he said.
>
> "I have been attacked that I am maintaining the monopoly and I don't want other players to be licensed.
>
> "There are certain implications or bottlenecks which need refinement for applicants to meet the requirements. Meeting the requirements is not on paper," he said.

Like most stories in state newspapers and on television, the article relies heavily on quotes from a government spokesperson rather than investigative reporting. Throughout the article, Ndlovu is referred to repeatedly using the abbreviated Marxist appellation *Cde*, a return to the widespread use of the title *Comrade* during the liberation struggle and the early years of majority rule. "The word 'Comrade,' as used in Zimbabwe's mass media," according to Winston Mano, "especially refers to the country's cabinet ministers and top ruling party officials," while other politicians are only selectively referred to as Comrades, depending on their relationship to ZANU-PF.[21] Referring to Ndlovu as Comrade marks him as particularly close to Mugabe. In the above excerpt, Ndlovu initially frames himself as patient and willing to compromise, in contrast to those calling for change who are "confrontational" and attacking. By claiming that the act "protect[s] the nation's values and traditions from undue disturbance by other countries," he suggests that the nation has a set of shared values and traditions, that broadcasting is an important means by which other countries "disturb" these values, and that Zimbabweans need protection by a paternalistic state. By implication, those who do not share the values he alludes to are excluded from Ndlovu's definition of the nation and thereby are not truly Zimbabwean. Although he claims willingness to revise the act, he suggests that the revision needed is minor, mere "refinement," making it more "user friendly." But his final sentence, "meeting the requirements is not on paper," confirms what many critics have suggested, that the act allows the Broadcasting Authority to deny licenses even to applicants who have met all the legal requirements.

The same article reveals that unwritten requirements include questions of identity, patriotism, and nationalism:

> [Ndlovu] said there were fundamental principles that applicants of broadcasting licences should be aware of.
>
> "Applicants should know that they are Zimbabweans. If you bring in foreigners, they have their own agenda to pursue," he said.
>
> The minister said people who chose to work with other players should be Zimbabweans and patriotic for the good of the country.
>
> "For example, in the U.S., you cannot go there and set up a radio station or a newspaper if you are a foreigner," said Cde Ndlovu.
>
> He said Press freedom should be practiced with responsibility.
>
> Cde Ndlovu said his concern was to build the nation and not to destroy.
>
> "And to any applicants, the principle is to be patriotic, be constructive, and not to destroy. Some say Zimbabwe is undemocratic since "it has State media." We have licensed newspapers. But how can we have newspapers called opposition media or those called independent media? Independent media or opposition media to what?
>
> "These questions must be asked. We must have media that should be primarily for the nation, which is concerned with Zimbabwe's problems and development," he said.

Since the BSA already specifies that licensees and their employees must be Zimbabwean citizens residing in Zimbabwe, Ndlovu's statement that "Applicants should know that they are Zimbabweans" suggests that being Zimbabwean requires more than just citizenship and residency; it also demands allegiance to the image of the nation constructed by the current government. He depicts those who lack allegiance to this narrowly defined construction of the nation as destructive and lacking concern for Zimbabwe. Finally, he uses terms like *nation* and *Zimbabwean* as if they are "common sense," but he questions the meanings of the terms *independent* and *opposition*. Although *opposition* is widely understood as opposing the ruling party, Ndlovu's question suggests that non-state media are opposed to Zimbabwean values and even to Zimbabwe itself.

Disrupting Hegemonic Discourse

Although the BSA ensures that state discourse like Ndlovu's dominates the media, other voices continue to disrupt its hegemony and offer alternative discourse. An examination of film and television in Zimbabwe that relies on the ruling party's statements about those media, or on the opinions of culture workers, would suggest a polarized culture. The state attempts to rid the nation of foreign elements, including foreign media and popular culture. On the other hand, film and TV workers perceived as foreign by the state defend their work as local. These polarities do exist, but they do not give a full picture of the everyday use of film and television by ordinary people.

In watching film and television, viewers make choices about the incorporation of foreign and local cultures into their homes. They make clear that "foreign versus local" is not a meaningful distinction for them. Some question the very categories. Foreign and local elements—actors, films, TV programs, cultural practices, and languages—exist side by side and intermingle. When a foreign practice is seen negatively, it is criticized in relation to local ones, such as one viewer's horror at kissing in public. But many foreign elements are indigenized by viewers who relate them to elements in their cultures, like the woman who compared keeping secrets in Shona culture to the dramatic irony employed by U.S. soap operas. Moreover, there is recognition that what constitutes local cultures may be changing—a television scene embarrassing to adult Shona viewers may be watched with pleasure by younger viewers, often with their parents' permission. The public complicates the foreign/local binary despite the BSA's attempt to polarize the message and dominate the airwaves with it.

Conclusion

The 2001 Broadcasting Services Act was the Zimbabwean government's response to two challenges: pressure to liberalize the airwaves and a rejection of Western influence. Comments from President Mugabe and the men he appointed to serve as minister of information and publicity, Chen Chimutengwende and Jonathan Moyo, reveal that liberalization was never their goal. A critical reading of the act itself demonstrates that not only does it actually create legal mechanisms for the state to consolidate its monopoly over broadcasting, but it also obfuscates this consolidation through local content requirements. For many viewers, local content quotas sparked fears of low-quality programming. By focusing on the impracticality of achieving 75 percent local content rather than on the political ramifications of the act, viewers and culture workers failed to recognize the act's impending negative effects on media freedoms. Yet concerns raised by culture workers about the nature of authenticity, government interference in the culture industries, and the difficulty of pinpointing the national origins of collaboratively authored texts or those created with "Western" technologies point to the larger issues that the legislation glosses over. By failing to address these issues, the BSA puts the lie to its claims to create "radio and television stations that are truly Zimbabwean in every respect." Instead, the legislation advances an antidemocratic agenda that oversimplifies who Zimbabweans are. By narrowly defining national identity, the state justifies limiting the public's access to information. If an "authentic" Zimbabwean is one who supports the status quo, then Zimbabweans have no need for independent information from new broadcasters.

One way the act oversimplifies Zimbabwean identities is in its language policy. The use of African languages other than English would create greater access for Zimbabweans, particularly in the rural areas, and when they are used, they play an important role in how people construct their identities. Monolingual programming also does not accurately represent language use in urban areas. The act addresses the languages of Zimbabwe's minority groups but fails to address Shona and Ndebele, languages spoken by 95 percent of the country and yet grossly underrepresented in the cinematic arts. A more democratic approach to language offers potential solutions to Zimbabwe's media situation.

CHAPTER 6

• • • • • • • •

Language as a Form of Social Change: Public Debate in Local Languages

In many countries, media in a common language play a primary role in the creation of a "national" identity. Unfortunately, in multilingual countries they also promote one language at the expense of others and thus favor the speakers of the national language at the expense of those who do not speak it fluently. In Zimbabwe, the English language has served this purpose since English speakers arrived in Southern Rhodesia. Its use in the cinematic arts and other media continues to support the interests of highly educated elites and those in power and to disadvantage those who don't know it well. At least fifteen other Zimbabwean languages as well as hybrid codes are used in everyday talk, but these seldom find their way onto film and TV screens. What if all the country's languages were used in the cinematic arts, if rural and urban viewers had equal access to film and television, if the power of language to unite as well as to divide were acknowledged? If such a scenario seems far-fetched, consider South Africa, which has attempted such a democratic approach with eleven official languages.[1] Any discussion of how ordinary people construct Zimbabwean identities must take the languages they use into consideration.

Many of Zimbabwe's filmmakers and cultural critics are concerned about the perceived erosion of "indigenous" cultures by the dominance of imported cinematic texts. Surprisingly, the related dominance of English-language media has gone largely ignored. In contrast to Shona, Ndebele, and other Zimbabwean languages, English can be described using the very adjectives that frequently stand in for *foreign* in Zimbabwean discourse: multicultural, colonial, European, white, imported, international, and urban. In all these ways it is associated with the "foreign" elements that the ruling party criticizes, and yet it continues to be used as the language of education, political discourse, and the media.

English allows communication across ethnic groups and avoids ethnic favoritism, but its use also misrepresents linguistic realities and restricts access to information. While depicted as enabling the inclusion of every group in the nation, its use in fact creates exclusion of the majority. In other words, language is part of the problem in Zimbabwe. Viewers' attitudes toward local language programming vary, but many favor increased use of their mother tongues in cinematic texts. Among the genres of television that do use Shona and Ndebele, "factual" programming is dominant. But "factual" programs like the news do not fulfill the informational needs of the majority because they tend to be monolingual, monologic, and edited to avoid controversy. In the first major exception to such patterns, a live talk show called *Talk to the Nation* that aired in May 2001, the threat of a local language public sphere to the authoritarian state becomes clear. The program represented a form of what Norman Fairclough calls "intervention involving language"—both language choice and a transformation of discourse patterns. Because "language change [is] a form of social change," such changes present a challenge to the status quo.[2]

Ignoring the Realities of a Hybrid Nation: A History of English Dominance

Relatively few Zimbabweans had high proficiency levels in English at the time of independence. Its use as the sole official language and one of three national languages has been legitimated as both providing national unity among diverse ethnic groups and giving the nation access to modernity and development. This national language ideology dovetails with a cultural ideology that dichotomizes the "modern" and the "traditional," so that English is seen as modern while Shona and Ndebele are traditional, and the minority languages are rarely even registered. African languages other than English are used extensively on the radio, an older and less expensive medium that reaches large audiences in rural areas, but very little on television or in films, newer and more expensive media that are more accessible in urban areas. These patterns of media use both reflect and contribute to binary discourse about urban/rural and modern/traditional identities.

One might assume that the large percentage of English programming is due to the correspondingly large percentage of foreign programming, but this is not entirely the case. Even if one only examines locally made programming, one still finds a much larger percentage of English than the other national languages, as table 6.1 illustrates.

Not only do languages other than English deserve greater representation, but also language use could be represented more accurately. In Pedzisai Mashiri's study of Zimbabwe's "local dramas," the only fictional TV programming that uses languages other than English, he demonstrates that although such programs use Shona and Ndebele, they do so in ways that do not accurately depict Zimbabwe's linguistic and ethnic realities. Shona dramas depict code switching from standard Shona to English, and Ndebele dramas show code switching from standard Ndebele to English, but neither shows code switching between Shona, Ndebele, and other languages nor even between different dialects of one language. The absence of code switching in cinematic texts is not only linguistically inaccurate but "also shows no interaction between Ndebele and Shona speakers as if to suggest the existence of two separate and distinct tribal communities."[3] The depiction of ethnic isolation contributes to a narrow definition of the national in

TABLE 6.1. Languages used on ZTV1 local programs, Monday, 25 May 2001

	English	Shona	Ndebele	Mixing Shona & Ndebele	Total
Number of Minutes	286	62	44	52	444
Percentage	64.41	13.96	9.91	11.71	100

which ethnicity is either ignored or used to divide. A more accurate depiction of multilingualism would show that Zimbabweans of various ethnicities are finding ways to talk to one another through many languages.

The multilingual South African soap opera *Generations* was one of the most popular programs among Zimbabwean viewers with whom I spoke. *Generations* includes code switching among English, Afrikaans, Setswana, Shangaan, Sotho, Venda, Xhosa, and even Shona, making clear that monolingualism is not a necessary feature of cinematic texts. By providing English subtitles throughout, the program is able to reach over seven million South Africans every day and it has been the most popular program in South Africa almost since its inception.[4] Through export to Zimbabwe and elsewhere, it reaches even more viewers. The program takes up multilingualism explicitly. Citing *Generations* and several other programs as examples, Ian Barnard argues:

> Current South African television programming enact[s] a multilingualism designed to mirror the realities of a hybrid nation and move its peoples towards national reconciliation, but it also thematises language, as the issue of what language a character is speaking or how characters can deceive one another by speaking a particular language become central plot twists in locally produced soap operas and sitcoms.[5]

In contrast to South Africa, which favors multilingualism both in official language policies and in cinematic texts, Zimbabwe has largely brushed language under the rug in favor of a policy that favors English in all realms of public discourse, including the cinematic arts.

"We Just Enjoy the Pictures, But We Don't Understand What Is Said": Viewer Critiques of English Dominance

In a 2001 survey conducted on behalf of Media for Development Trust, young viewers in Chitungwiza were asked how they interpreted *Yellow Card*, one of the seven feature films produced in Zimbabwe before 2001, all of which use

English. Although they were mostly able to comprehend *Yellow Card* in English, a number of them criticized the film for not using Shona. Tiyane's father tells him in the film, "My aunt in Rusape is colored. But she speaks our language. She wears a *dhuku* [a headwrap]. She's fine." Like many Shona speakers, Tiyane's father sees their language as both a carrier of, and an indicator of inclusion in, their culture. Contrasting Shona and colored Zimbabweans only to dismiss their differences as unimportant, he constructs language as more important than race for Zimbabwean identity.

The survey of young Chitungwiza viewers was conducted in English, but viewers' comments make clear that in some cases they misunderstood the questions they were asked and even key elements of the film. If urban youth, mostly secondary-school students, don't fully understand an English-language film, what about rural viewers? They are considerably less likely to understand English than are their urban counterparts. When viewers don't understand the language of a cinematic text, they lose their power as critics and cannot participate in discussions of how their identities are constructed.

English is the most widely used language on television, even on local programs, but it is not the most practical language through which to reach viewers. In a conversation in a small village in Chiweshe Communal Lands in May 2001, Mrs. Jaunda explains how her fluency in English and Shona affect her enjoyment of television.

> KDT: *Munofarira zvirongwa zvakaitwa muno kana kunze?*
>
> Jaunda: *Tinofarira zvemuno.*
>
> KDT: *Nemhaka yei?*
>
> Jaunda: *Tinonzwa zvinotaurwaka. Tinenge tichinzwa zvinotaurwaka ndozvatinoda, nekuti kana zviri zvekunze uko zvinenge zvaakuda vaye vakadzidza chaizvo ndokuti vazvinzwe. Zvino isu tisina kudzidza chaizvo chaizvo hatizvinzwe. Tinongonakidzwa nemapikicha chete, zvinotaurwa zviya hatizvinzwe.*
>
> KDT: *Nokuti munotaura . . . ?*
>
> Jaunda: *Ehe mutauro.*
>
> KDT: *Saka munofarira zvirongwa zveChiShona pane zveChirungu?*
>
> Jaunda: *Ehe ndinofarira zvechiShona.*
>
> KDT: *Muchiona navamwe vanofarira zvirongwa zveChiShona kana zveChirungu?*
>
> Jaunda: *Ehe vamwe variko asi vamwe kana kuri kuradio uku vanofarira Radio Three. Vanonzwa zvinotaurwa zvese. Kuradio tinongodawo Shona sezvatinongoitawo kuterevhizhoni. Tinodawo Shona kuitira kunzwa mutauro.*

KDT: Do you enjoy local or foreign made programs?

Jaunda: We enjoy local ones.

KDT: For what reason?

Jaunda: We understand what is said. When we understand what is said we like it, because if it is foreign, one who understands it will like it and learn more. Now we who are not very educated can't understand the foreign programs. We just enjoy the pictures, but we don't understand what is said.

KDT: Is it because you speak Shona?

Jaunda: Yes, [because of] the language.

KDT: So you enjoy Shona programs more than English?

Jaunda: Yes.

KDT: When you watch with others, do they enjoy Shona or English programs?

Jaunda: Yes, there are some who like Shona, but there are also others who even enjoy Radio Three. They understand everything that is said. On the radio, we also like Shona just like on television. We want Shona in order to understand the language.

Here Mrs. Jaunda uses the first-person plural "we" to mark her identity as part of the group "we who are not very educated," and the third-person plural "they" to describe others, those who "enjoy Radio Three," a station that broadcast in English and played mostly imported music. On the one hand, she presents Shona TV programs as beneficial to and enjoyed by people like her. On the other hand, she associates English-language TV and radio with the "foreign" and as privileging the educated.

I also consulted viewers like those Mrs. Jaunde associates with Radio Three. Comments from viewers who speak English well and may prefer cinematic texts in English suggest that they are nevertheless aware of the way English excludes others. For example, a 19-year-old male secondary-school student in a high-density suburb of Kadoma told me that there should be more broadcasting in Shona "so that our grandmothers and elders can understand." Similarly, Tsitsi, a 17-year-old girl in Chiweshe Communal Lands, said, "Here in Zimbabwe there are grandmothers and grandfathers who are not able to understand English. So it annoys them to see television because there is nothing which they can understand." Despite their own understanding and enjoyment of English language cinematic texts, these viewers recognize that the use of English prevents a majority of Zimbabweans, including many rural and older people who lack formal education, from understanding their country's media.

Many viewers told me that they would like to see more television programs made in Shona. Their reasons fall into four general categories: to promote Shona language and culture for its own sake; to allow those with less education than themselves access to the cinematic arts; to allow the majority of Zimbabweans access to the cinematic arts; and to assert the value of Shona vis-à-vis other languages, especially English.

Viewers maintain that more cinematic texts in Shona would encourage the development of the language as well as Shona values. Tawanda Gunda, then a young filmmaker studying at the UNESCO Film and Video Training Project in Harare, told me in 2001, "It's always nice to hear your own language. And I think it's also good for foreign audiences as well." Musiiwa, a 17-year-old in Chiweshe Communal Lands, argued that Shona cinematic arts are needed "so that we of our Shona ethnic group may live knowing good behavior and customs."

Some participants would like to see more Shona films and television programs not for their own sake but for their elders, who are less likely to understand English. A young man in Harare believes that Shona cinematic arts are good "for the elderly and young to learn and appreciate together and share an afterthought," serving as a talking point for discussions after the film or television program has ended. Enock, a 19-year-old in Chiweshe Communal Lands, explained that "most people are being educated, so Shona is an advantage to those who are not educated, especially older people." Young viewers may not perceive Shona as necessary to their own lives, but they still value it for the connection it allows them with their elders. They associate Shona with the past, like Rebecca Chisamba's construction of "deep Shona" as "speaking like an *ambuya*." But Shona can also be used to bring the past into the present: the same viewer who wanted more Shona TV for the sake of "our grandmothers and our elders" added: *Uye vana vadiki vakwanisawao kunzwa zvekare,* "And small children can also understand the past." His construction of Shona as a language that can help young people "understand the past" is again similar to Chisamba's use of "deep Shona" on TV, presenting tradition in a modern way and apparently inspiring young people to value the language.

Other viewers point to the fact that Shona is the majority language in Zimbabwe and is understood by more people than is English. Tenderai in Seke, Harare, argued that Shona cinematic arts are needed "to reach as much people as possible." Tendai, a 25-year-old in a high-density suburb of Kadoma, said that with Shona cinematic arts, "more people will understand the theme of the movie. . . . Our main language in Zimbabwe is Shona, so we need to promote it, and a lot of people will understand the programs." A 46-year-old in Chiweshe Communal Lands argued for more Shona cinematic texts *ndiko kuti vanhu vazhinji vaanzwisisi,* "so that the majority can understand them."

Some viewers argue that, because Shona is more widely understood than other Zimbabwean languages, audiences are more likely to receive the educational benefits of cinematic texts in Shona. They learn from local dramas, Rebecca Chisamba's talk shows, and the news "because they give lessons to the whole Zimbabwean family, adults and children," as a Chitungwiza viewer explained. Two viewers in a high-density suburb of Kadoma told me they want more Shona films "because we are Shonas, therefore they should be numerous" and "becoz we are Shona's here we musn't follow at the back of white[s]." Such strongly worded responses construct Shona superiority over other Zimbabwean ethnic groups and reject white superiority.

"Winning the Minds of Our People": The Language of Entertainment and Information

Media studies worldwide have demonstrated the ability of audiences to enjoy entertainment programming in languages they do not fully understand. Recall Mrs. Jaunda's comment, "We just enjoy the pictures, but we don't understand what is said." Zimbabweans are big fans of martial arts films and chase scenes, where they can "just enjoy the pictures." These genres are particularly popular in high-density suburbs without full-fledged cinemas and where residents have few financial resources. One likely reason for their popularity is that they have limited dialogue and thus can be easily understood even when the viewer does not understand Chinese or English. As filmmaker Tawanda Gunda told me in our 2001 interview, "Sometimes you can concentrate on the action to understand the story."

Unlike entertainment programming, which can offer visual pleasures, most informational programming requires verbal comprehension. In a case study of media use in a rural Zimbabwean growth point, Knut Lundby found that the "language of the mediascape, as it opens to people in Tsanzaguru, is mainly English" and that English was a barrier to his participants' understanding of cinematic texts, even programs they enjoyed. For example, even though all of Lundby's interviewees were "literate and able to read English," one woman reported, "I do not always understand English." Similarly, many Shona speakers can read and write English better than they can speak and comprehend it. Kedmon Hungwe, in a study of media use in Zimbabwean schools, considers imbalanced proficiency in English a barrier to cultural and educational development. Of the potential barriers to children being able to understand imported films, he considers language "the most important, because without the tool of language it is extremely difficult to even begin to learn from imported film." Even when schoolchildren have mastered Zimbabwean English to a reasonable degree, British and American accents are "unusual," and this hinders understanding.[6]

My own research supports these findings about viewers' varied fluency and literacy. Zimbabwe's high literacy rates, if they can be trusted at all, are not indicative of speaking and listening proficiency, nor do they indicate which languages

Zimbabweans can read. Among viewers I consulted, a significant number reportedly spoke English, but almost all reportedly read English. In addition to "knowing" English and Shona to varying degrees, participants also indicated that each language was used in a different domain and for different functions. In this diglossic context, Shona dominates in informal settings such as at home, on public transportation, and with friends, performing "low" functions, while English dominates in the formal settings of work and school, performing a "high" function. The only formal setting in which Shona is regularly used is in church, and the Bible has been translated into Shona. Television and film are usually viewed in informal settings such as at home, in a cinema, at a friend's or family member's home, or in a public hall, all locales where Shona is more likely to be used than English.[7] The dominance of English on screens stands in stark contrast to the conversations taking place about the films and TV programs people are watching.

The state, despite using English as the language of official discourse, recognizes that Zimbabweans understand local languages more so than spoken English. For example, Mugabe consistently uses Shona when addressing rural audiences. The government has also expressed fears about the use of languages other than English in the independent media. For example, Radio Netherlands began broadcasting short wave radio signals into Zimbabwe in June 2000, using not only English but also Shona and Ndebele. Minister of Information Chen Chimutengwende responded:

> The Netherlands has decided to broadcast directly to Southern African and Zimbabwe *in our own languages* and we think this is still part of the same international co-ordinated western plan to destabilize developing countries. . . . It is because they want to control this region. That is why they are putting in so many resources in trying to win the minds of our people.[8]

Supposed Western conspiracies to overthrow ZANU-PF are seen as effective, and thus dangerous, when they are broadcast using languages that the majority of Zimbabweans can understand.

Zimbabwean society at large supports the dominance of English by actively participating in a system that favors English over other languages, in particular, by pursuing increased access to English-medium schooling. Yet outside of formal education, Zimbabweans exhibit varied stances toward the use of English vis-à-vis their mother tongues.

A majority of Zimbabwe's filmmakers have been resistant to using languages other than English because they want to reach international audiences. However, many later dub their films into Shona, Ndebele, and other Zimbabwean languages. The Capricorn Video Unit dubs English-language films from throughout the Southern African Development Community region into Shona and Ndebele for use by mobile cinema units in Zimbabwe. *Yellow Card* was subsequently dubbed into Shona, despite the director's misgivings about doing so. John Riber told me in March 2001, "I don't think audiences really like the Shona dubs that much. They're sort of like, 'Why are you dubbing this? We know this is in English.'" Riber constructs Zimbabwean viewers as preferring films in their original language over films in languages they can understand well. Similarly, filmmaker Tawanda Gunda makes short films in Shona but says, "I find it very disturbing to watch dubbed movies," expressing a common complaint among viewers that dubbed texts are "unnatural" because of imperfect lip-synchronicity. For example, the Matabeleland Aids Council suggests that when Ndebele speakers watch a film dubbed from English to Ndebele and "see that the way the mouth of the speaker on the screen does not correspond to the sound, they are likely to dismiss the film/video as 'just acting,'" thus limiting the ability of a social message film to impart information.[9]

Because of such complaints, NGOs working with rural populations have argued that the opposite strategy would be more effective: films should be made first in a local language for Zimbabwean viewers and later dubbed or subtitled in English for international viewers. ZBC has tried this strategy with local dramas, making them first in Shona or Ndebele and later subtitling them into English for potential sale to other African countries. I sat in on a subtitling session at ZBC during my fieldwork and observed that the producer's English writing proficiency and translation skills were quite low, resulting in a number of mistranslations. Skilled translators with high proficiency in both languages are needed if this strategy is to be profitable and thereby viable.

English continues to be the most commonly used language on both film and television screens, as it was before independence. Its use is problematic in news broadcasts and other informational programming. In fiction or entertainment programming, English can also serve the interests of those in power. Television and "movies are not just a commercial product—they constitute a powerful instrument that records and affirms its own language and culture and its dissemination across borders."[10] The borders that English, as a global language, crosses can include not only national ones but also linguistic or ethnic borders. We witness the former when English-language films and TV programs are imported into Zimbabwe, and the latter when English is used as the official language and the major language of the media, allowing communication among a diverse population. In both types of border crossing, films and TV programs affirm the English language and its culture, even when they are produced locally. In this way, the use of English further blurs the line between foreign and local. But "English culture" may differ depending on where those films and TV programs are made. For example, the "American message" in English-language productions imported from the United States may be that of capitalism, while the Zimbabwean message in locally produced English-language productions is that of nationalism and upward mobility via education.

Implanting a "Superior" Language: Controlling the Nation through English

The elevation of English to the status of official language has strengthened the socioeconomic and educational divide between rural and urban, poor and wealthy. In this excerpt from my 2001 email exchange with white filmmaker Rory Kilalea, he describes his experience with Zimbabwean languages:

> Zimbabwe is a country which has not been unified by language—and regrettably, the *lingua franca* has perforce become ENGLISH. . . . Colonialism destroyed the essential dignity of the people—by implanting a "superior" language, a culture, a life style—and thus the traditions—be it with the Amandebele or with the Manyika or the Shona or Karanga—have been denigrated. This has resulted in the narrative traditions being eroded— and I personally believe that this lack of self-worth—of self-confidence— has actually reduced the effort, the means, for the Zimbabwe people to wish to step into medium of narrative television or film making. . . . Whereas in Kenya even whites speak Swahili, Zimbabwe[,] . . . which has largely become separated by the middle class and the rural, has also been segmented by this language barrier. Young girls—friends of my daughter—have laughed when they hear the accented English spoken by the rural folk . . . and they do not speak Shona unless they have to. English has become the preferred means of class distinction.

Kilalea's comments clarify the social purpose that English serves in Zimbabwe. As the dominant language of the media and educational systems, English elevates those who can understand it to an elite status. Broadcasting in English parallels the distribution of high art or what Garcia Canclini calls "select art" in contrast to folk art or popular cultural forms: "At the same time that mass distribution of 'select' art is a socializing action, it also is a procedure for securing the distinction of those who are familiar with it. . . . The mechanisms of reinforcement of distinction tend to be resources for reproducing hegemony."[11] In the same way, broadcasting in English secures the distinction of those who can speak and understand spoken English, those who can understand English in a foreign accent, those who are familiar with American or British programming genres, and those who know how to make meaning from an English-language comedy, talk show, drama, or news broadcast. English, in this way, reproduces the state's hegemony over the majority of Zimbabweans, whose degree of fluency in English is low but who nevertheless aspire to speak it (or have their children speak it).

Because English is the language of official nationalism, chosen by the government as the language that will unite Zimbabweans despite their ethnic differences, I read viewers' desire for Shona programming as a rejection of the discourse of official nationalism and linguistic hegemony. To quote Kembo-Sure and Vic Webb, "In recent years, the use of one's cultural language has become a human rights issue, so that a national legal system that encourages the suppression of a minority language and imposes the use of a majority language is considered to be promoting linguistic hegemony."[12] In Zimbabwe's case, however, in addition to the national legal system, the national broadcasting system and the national education system also encourage the suppression of languages other than English—both majority languages like Shona and Ndebele and the numerous minority languages. Viewers don't address the country's language policy directly, but their comments on language use in cinematic texts suggest support for linguistic pluralism that could extend from the cinematic arts to national policy.

The government's control over which foreign news may be broadcast parallels the choice of which languages it uses for which purposes. Important news about the local economy or international events is broadcast in English, thus reaching a smaller local audience, while news of lesser importance, such as the funeral ceremony of a local politician, is broadcast at great length in Shona. *The Main News at Eight* is broadcast every evening for an hour in English, but Shona and Ndebele language news are each given only fifteen minutes of airtime in the late afternoon, a time when fewer people are at home. I discussed this issue with Alexander Kanengoni, novelist and head of research at ZBC, in March 2001:

> KDT: I've noticed that the news is an hour long in English but only a half hour in Shona and Ndebele.
>
> Kanengoni: We raised that point to the Minister actually at a seminar some time. We said, "You are talking about 75 percent local content. You should begin with the news. Make them one hour, in local languages." In fact there were some complaints about how all resources in the news department seem to be channeled toward the English bulletin rather than the local news. There are no reporters, for instance, for the local news. And if cameras are made available at all for local stories, it's as if you have to fight first to get the camera.

Because of the disproportionate resources given the English-language news, those who watch the Shona and Ndebele news find English interviews with government officials, which comprise the majority of news stories, either subtitled or summarized by the news anchor, leaving room for deliberate or accidental mistranslation. The relative emphasis given to news in each language also influences viewers' choices about which version of the news to watch. Whereas one might expect viewers to prefer news in their own language, in fact some prefer the English news simply because it is, as one viewer told me, "more detailed than the brief broadcast in Ndebele and Shona."

"You Can't Build a Nation by Talking to Yourself": Viewers Talk to the Nation

Analysis of a May 2001 episode of *Talk to the Nation* illustrates problems of language conflict, popular support for linguistic pluralism, and, unfortunately, government resistance to public debate. The program was sponsored by the National Development Assembly (NDA), "a civic grouping largely made up of black business persons, championing what has come to be called the indigenisation of the economy."[13] The episode in question, which aired on 31 May 2001, is particularly relevant to the issue of language conflict because it dramatized the ability of ordinary Zimbabweans to challenge the imposition of English in the realm of popular culture and in discussions of politics.

Talk to the Nation was the first live talk show ever aired on Zimbabwean television, a fact about which viewers were quite excited. Zimbabweans have seen live television since 1983, but it has been largely limited to sporting events. *Talk to the Nation* was broadcast immediately after the *Main News at Eight,* one of the country's most watched programs, so it drew a large audience. Talk shows are not new to Zimbabweans, but most talk shows are either imported (such as *Jenny Jones* or *Oprah*) or deal primarily with cultural topics such as the one described in March 2001 by local talk show host Rebecca Chisamba:

> I spoke to my producer, and we agreed that it was unfair for the elders— parents—to be always talking about the teenagers and so forth. "Why don't we invite them and hear from them?" And so we talked about them, and one of the topics was, "What kind of a spouse would you want for a life partner?" The type of dressing, the tights—some of them are un-African. They are coming in; they are new, and some families will not accept. We wanted to hear what our young people think about such things. Some were saying, "No, it's fine. You have to dress what you think is fine with you and what will make you comfortable." Some were saying, "Because my parents do 1, 2, 3, I am frustrated, and then I end up doing 1, 2, 3."

Such topics may be of interest to viewers on a cultural level, but they do not allow them to actively engage with national politics. Moreover, even if such programs were to take up political issues directly, because the programs are not live, the participation they would offer viewers would be limited and its content likely edited to support the ruling party's perspective. *Talk to the Nation* attracted viewers because of its difference from their typical TV options, which are imported or engage with "local" realities culturally rather than politically.

Research in other countries has shown that talk shows offer a forum for participatory democracy, public discourse, and critiques of the status quo. In fact, Livingstone and Lunt argue that "the mass media are the *only* institution which can provide a space for public debate in modern society." Moreover, we know that media do not merely reflect, transmit, or express political culture, but that they also play an active role in *creating* a political culture by encouraging viewers to form opinions about issues of public concern. Engagement with news media has been shown to encourage political conversations. *Talk to the Nation,* as one of the first Zimbabwean talk shows to deal with national politics, provides a window into the country's political culture. It was also a mechanism used by the NDA to create a more open political culture, by viewers to negotiate it, and by the government to suppress it.[14]

Opinion formation, group discussion, and public debate "are potentially colonized and undermined by media institutions and by experts and politicians who represent established power," according to Livingstone and Lunt. In Zimbabwe one finds these processes, discussions, and debates colonized by the state, via legislation, harassment, physical violence, and censorship. One mechanism used to discourage audience interpretation, negotiation, and resistance is through the structuring of local news. Prior to the Broadcasting Services Act, CNN news was spliced into ZTV's *Main News at Eight.* In CNN news, on-site reporters address the audience directly, but in those portions of the news produced by ZBC, the reporter rarely questions his interviewees on-screen. Instead, we see reaction shots of the reporter. Andersen observed, "The reporter is turned into a mute, humble listener, he or she becomes the listener, a very special (representative of the) audience built into the visuals of the sutured whole of textual fragments which makes out the body of the single news story." Through such mechanisms, the state-run ZBC places viewers in the position of passive mass audience / consumers. In contrast, *Talk to the Nation* engaged with them as viewers and citizens, a position that is increasingly threatened by the actions of the state toward the media.[15]

The format of *Talk to the Nation* was a question-and-answer panel, with a conservative moderator, Mutumwa Mawere, a businessman who chaired the NDA. On the 31 May episode, the panel included two members of Parliament: a representative from ZANU-PF, the ruling party, and one from the Movement for Democratic Change (MDC), the main opposition party. Both were members of the Parliamentary Budget and Finance Committee. ZANU-PF was represented by that committee's chairman, David Chapfika, and the MDC by another committee member, the shadow minister of finance, Tapiwa Mashakada. Mawere introduced the program by describing its purpose: to educate viewers about how Parliament and its various committees operate, so that they might better understand, and therefore participate in, their government.

"Nation-building" has been a prominent theme in discussions of the cinematic arts. This theme was taken up in early post-independence discourse about Zimbabwe's cinematic culture and in the 2001 Broadcasting Services Act. Various elements of *Talk to the Nation* served to highlight its attempts to participate in this discourse, not the least of which was the moderator's and panelists' frequent use of the term *nation-building*. First, the program's name significantly unites the concept of "nation" with that of the "talk" show, in particular a show in which viewers would be given meaningful opportunities to talk *about* the nation, and to have their talk broadcast *to* the nation. Mawere described the program in these terms: "We see nation-building as an enterprise whose keystone is the regeneration, processing, and implementation of ideas. You can't build a nation alone or by talking to yourself, hence our theme 'Talk to the Nation.'"[16]

Second, *Talk to the Nation* was produced by the National Development Assembly, an organization whose name clearly indicates its interests in "national" concerns. In order to emphasize the "nationalness" of the NDA and of *Talk to the Nation*, the program begins with images that evoke Zimbabwe as a nation: farmland, rural areas, two urban scenes, the Kariba dam, and finally the famous conical tower of Great Zimbabwe, "the central trope in the Shona symbolism that inspires and informs Zimbabwean national culture."[17] The same images, along with the NDA logo, are repeated at the end of the program.

In addition to focusing on the nation, the program centered on the concept of democracy. Mawere opened the program with this statement:

> A healthy democratic society is not only measured by the regular conduct of general elections, but also by other windows open for civic participation in governance. A democratic system of governance ensures that citizens participate in the political process between elections and are represented in Parliament. It also provides the mechanisms and resources necessary to achieve these goals.

Although Mawere went on to emphasize what Livingstone and Lunt call "elite democracy"—the workings of Parliament and its various committees—I read his opening statement as a call for viewer/citizen participation in Zimbabwean society. Implicit in his comments is the claim that *Talk to the Nation* is actually a discursive forum for such participation, not just educating viewers about how Parliament works, but also giving them the opportunity to air their opinions and openly engage in debate with their elected representatives. Mawere's commitment to viewer/citizen participation becomes clear through his privileging of viewers' comments over those of the representatives, whom he gave very little time to answer questions. He repeatedly interrupted Chapfika and Mashakada in order to take phone calls from viewers, and he allowed twenty-six viewers to speak during the hour-long program.

Seizing the opportunity to participate in a public debate, the viewers who called in to *Talk to the Nation* transformed the program in two significant ways. First, the viewers changed the format from an informative question-and-answer session to an unprecedented public debate between political parties. Caller after caller challenged the two representatives to speak on behalf of ZANU-PF or the MDC rather than on behalf of the committee they jointly represented. One caller asked Chapfika to account for the money ZANU-PF spends on election campaigns: does it come from the state or from party members? Another asked Mashakada to explain the MDC's alleged promotion of violence as a way to overthrow the current government. Again and again, Mawere tried to steer the conversation back to its stated purpose, reminding viewers that this was not a political debate but an hour to discuss the finance committee. But viewers ignored him. In the absence of other opportunities to engage in such a debate, viewers were unwilling to give up the opportunity when it presented itself. Furthermore, Mawere allowed callers to engage at greater length with Mashakada, who was allowed to answer nine questions, than with Chapfika, who was allowed to answer eight questions.

The MDC's representation on the program was noteworthy for its rarity. In a report on the 2000 constitutional election, the Media Monitoring Project Zimbabwe demonstrated that in the state press, "there was a virtual boycott of stories quoting MDC leader Morgan Tsvangirai, except where his statements or activities were vulnerable to attack." Two years later it reported that "out of a total of 14 hours and 25 minutes that ZBC television news bulletins devoted to the presidential election campaign, ZANU-PF's candidate was granted a total of 13 hours and 34 minutes, or a little more than 94%. This compares to the national broadcaster's TV coverage of the MDC and its candidate, of just 31 minutes and 30 seconds, a paltry 4%." Because of such limited media coverage of the MDC, *Talk to the Nation* viewers took advantage of this opportunity to learn more about, and debate with, the opposition party.[18]

The second way that viewers transformed *Talk to the Nation* was through their choice of language. Like most programming, *Talk to the Nation* was to be aired in English. The conversation began in English, with Mawere asking questions of the two representatives, and each giving answers of one to two minutes in length. This went on for five minutes, after which Mawere began to allow viewers to phone in with questions. The first caller, rather than using solely English, switched between Shona and English in the course of his question. Mashakada responded in English. The second caller switched entirely into Shona; his question was a repeat of the first question and so was not answered. The third caller used English, and Mashakada responded in English. The fourth caller greeted Mawere in English but asked his question in Shona. Again, Mashakada answered in English. The fifth caller used only Shona, addressing his question to Chapfika. Chapfika responded briefly in English, but then announced, "Since you asked your question in the vernacular language, I think I'm obliged to answer or to respond in Shona as well." His response not only differentiated him from Mashakada, who used only English, but also aligned him more with "the people," those who speak "the vernacular." From the sixth caller on, the convention was established: the caller determined the language of the conversation, and both Mawere and Chapfika followed the caller's lead. The viewers, represented by those who phoned in, staged a linguistic coup, virtually taking over the program, forcing the participants to use a language that the majority of Zimbabweans can understand. Of the twenty-six callers, fifteen spoke primarily Shona, nine spoke primarily English, and two practiced significant code switching between the two languages. Viewers demanded political pluralism by engaging in a public debate over their economy and political system. By using a language other than English, they also demanded linguistic pluralism, a policy that would afford "all languages space to develop, to be recognized, and to be used for crucial private and public purposes."[19]

Nevertheless, there was one resister to the linguistic convention viewers established; Mashakada, who responded only in English. He is ethnically Shona and understood the questions, responding appropriately whether they were asked in Shona or English. Why then would he never use Shona? It seems likely that Mashakada wanted to remain comprehensible to his constituency. The MDC has won a lot of votes in Matabeleland, where Ndebele is the major language, and is backed by a large number of whites, most of whom do not speak Zimbabwean languages other than English. I saw great hope in the Shona speakers' taking linguistic control of this program, but Mashakada's position serves as a reminder that any language, even a majority one like Shona, cannot be understood by the entire nation and may also be used to serve the interests of those in power. Just as the use of English restricts the information available to Shona speakers, the use of Shona may restrict the information available to those who speak other languages.

The use of English and Shona on *Talk to the Nation* and the absence of Ndebele mirror the dominance of Shona over Ndebele in other media and in the culture at large. For example, although ZBC's reported aim is to alternate between Shona and Ndebele local dramas, most are in Shona because the broadcaster has more producers in Harare than in Bulawayo. Andersen argues that in Matabeleland, "the ZBC is experienced as not only the national channel, but also as an agent of Shona cultural dominance."[20] Because of their proximity to the border of South Africa, many Ndebele viewers watch SABC programming, an act of resistance to ZBC and to Shona dominance.

Zimbabweans in both rural and urban areas are aware that other languages are even more poorly served than Shona. Smith Mbedzi, a Venda speaker, describes the areas outside of Mashonaland and Matabeleland as marginalized areas: "The Zimbabwean government-controlled radio and TV stations operate as if there were only three languages in the country—English, Shona, and Ndebele. Consequently, some of the national announcements made on radio and TV were incomprehensible to people living in the marginalized areas."[21] A viewer in Harare told me that there is a need for the cinematic arts "to accommodate other languages." Another in Chiweshe Communal Lands commented that television needs "to allow other Ndebele, Tonga programs and other languages." Juniel, a 23-year-old in Rimuka, Kadoma, offered two important reminders: "We are not all able to speak Shona," and Shona cinematic texts are not "helpful" to everyone "because those who do not know Shona would not be helped by that film."

At the end of *Talk to the Nation*, Mawere summed up the program in English, providing viewers with a reminder of its message: "As long as you are a citizen of Zimbabwe, you are entitled to talk to this nation; you are entitled to contribute. So I think it is incumbent upon all of us to contribute." In his final statement, Mawere emphasized the key themes of the program: citizenship, nationhood, participation, and talk.

In response to the first televised forum for live public debate, the government reacted swiftly and forcefully: less than a week after the program aired, on 5 June 2001, ZBC canceled *Talk to the Nation*. The station had already agreed to broadcast twenty-six episodes, stood to gain a much-needed $4 million from the program's producers and advertising revenues, and would have increased its local content in line with the 75 percent quota established by the Broadcasting Services Act. Nevertheless, ZBC refused to honor its contract with the NDA and banned the remaining episodes from future broadcast. According to Kindness Paradza, the program's executive producer for the NDA, the decision to cancel the program came not from ZBC but from Jonathan Moyo, minister of information and publicity. Many people believed that Mashakada, the MDC representative, had debated more effectively than the ZANU-PF representative, Chapfika. Moyo claimed that the NDA had given too much exposure to the MDC.[22]

In a public statement, Moyo made clear that the decision to cancel *Talk to the Nation* stemmed directly from government fear of public debate. According to Moyo, "Live productions can be tricky and dangerous. The setting on the NDA production was professionally done, but maybe the programme should not have been broadcast live. You do not know what someone will come and say, and there is no way of controlling it." He also told Mutumwa Mawere, chairman of the NDA and moderator of the program, that "his Ministry could not allow a situation where the ZBC surrenders ownership of a live programme to a civic organization or such other outside person."[23] Here Moyo constructs the state as responsible for controlling what Zimbabweans are allowed to say about their own society.

The government's response to *Talk to the Nation* revealed MDC representatives, civic organizations, and the general public—viewers/citizens—as threats to the status quo.

The cancellation's implications for democracy did not go unnoticed by Zimbabwean media workers. MISA reported:

> The banning of the programme underscores a skewed understanding of the role of public broadcasting in a democratic country. The intolerance of opposing views that has been shown by ZBC and those who run it is not in the interests of Zimbabwe. There is a need for everyone, no matter their background, race, gender, or political affiliation, to be heard through the only public broadcasting station that Zimbabwe has. The banning strengthens the call for the disentanglement of ZBC from the shackles of politicians who feel that the corporation is their personal fiefdom for the peddling of partisan views. MISA-Zimbabwe has repeatedly called for the opening up of the airwaves and the revising of the new broadcasting law, which is inherently flawed and undemocratic. It must be noted that as long as the ZBC continues to operate under the authoritarian arm of the government, as the current Act provides, its role as a public broadcaster will forever be compromised. The banning of the NDA programme does not augur well for the development of a free broadcasting industry. MISA-Zimbabwe, therefore calls for the unconditional lifting of the ban and the implementation of the NDA-ZBC contract as previously agreed. The ZBC is a public broadcaster, supported by the taxpayers, and as such it must be representative of all the people of Zimbabwe.[24]

The banning of *Talk to the Nation* illustrates the government's commitment to curtailing free speech and public debate, especially when that debate takes place in a language that the majority of the country can understand. Chapfika reinforced this commitment at the end of the program when he summed up the ZANU-PF position:

> We need to speak with one voice. We need to be united. If we are not united . . . , our enemies will strike. It becomes easier for them to strike. What's important now is for us to speak with one voice in the national interest.

Clearly the "one voice" ZANU-PF has in mind is the government's voice. In contrast to this "one voice," which represents an elite democracy rather than a participatory one, the viewers who engaged with *Talk to the Nation* illustrate the potential of such a program as a discursive forum in which ordinary people can speak in their own voices. It is precisely because of this potential—which briefly became a reality—that the government canceled *Talk to the Nation.* For one evening, the public spoke not with the government but with multiple voices, debating the issues that matter most to them and using the language that they know best.

Conclusion

Zimbabwe's diverse languages present a challenge to forming a democratic media and a national identity. Despite a national and international language ideology that favors English, there are internal pressures toward a more democratic use of Zimbabwean languages. A small group of education policy researchers advocate not only equitable use of Zimbabwe's languages in schools and the media but also a concern for the local contexts in which each language is used.[25]

In a multilingual nation, what would a democratic use of languages look and sound like? The example of South Africa's soap opera *Generations* shows that there are models for cinematic multilingualism in neighboring countries on which Zimbabwean filmmakers and broadcasters could draw. Shona written literature and oral traditions also offer examples of different dialects and code switching. The hybrid language use of urban and diaspora Zimbabweans in popular music and Internet chat rooms is another model, one that not only disrupts the notion of "pure" languages but also connects Zimbabweans to global communities, breaking down distinctions between "local" and "foreign" and subverting concepts of "tradition" and "authenticity." But there is also a need to make sure that "urban vernaculars" are not reified at the expense of rural access to the media. Migration between rural and urban areas "links them [and] means that their linguistic fates are inextricably intertwined."[26] The cinematic arts can also link them. The subversive potential of multilingualism is what makes it dangerous to the state, which has a stake in imagining Zimbabwe as monolithic and unchanging. At the same time, its subversiveness is what makes democratic multilingualism a valuable resource for ordinary Zimbabweans as they construct complex identities, not in terms dictated by those in power but in their own words.

CONCLUSION

• • • • • • • • • • •

Possibilities for Democratic Change

As popular cultural phenomena, film and television are by definition shifting, as are the ways Zimbabweans talk about them, making them an amorphous, moving target. So far we have examined the period 1980–2001, when Zimbabwe's film and television culture was recovering from its colonization by foreign elements, developing local talents and themes, and was finally legislated to serve the interests of the state. More than a decade has passed since my fieldwork in Zimbabwe, *Yellow Card*'s screening on ZTV, and the Broadcasting Services Act's passage into law. In an excerpt from our June 2011 exchange on Facebook, actor and comedian Edgar Langeveldt recalls the events of 2001 and their effect on Zimbabwe's cinematic arts in the decade that followed:

> 2001 is a critical watershed year in terms of Zimbabwean socio-politics: it was the dawn of a new millennium . . . , we had just had hotly contested, "harmonized" elections the year before and the Opposition had announced its arrival with serious intent. Our economy was in free fall following the 1997 War Vet Payout Scheme / Dollar Crash, the 1998 Costly Congo Caper with Kabila Senior, the 1999 invasion and "reformative re-conquest" of land, commercial farms, private residences and businesses, etc., and generally we were under pressure as citizens. Because film/TV require resources, teamwork, and skills to aggregate at the right time, we were obviously blown off course by this set of background facts and events.

But time has not stood still. If the international news is anything to go by, Zimbabwe is falling apart. The year after the act was passed, the European Union and the United States implemented targeted sanctions on President Mugabe and senior members of his government, buttressing British "smart sanctions" that had begun in 2000. All three avoided full economic sanctions out of fear of harming ordinary Zimbabweans, but the loss of International Monetary Fund and other loans for Zimbabwe nevertheless meant that the decade was a devastating one for all but the wealthiest Zimbabweans. Only since 2008, when the Zimbabwe dollar was officially abandoned in favor of the U.S. dollar and the South African rand, has hyperinflation been brought under control and the economy begun to stabilize.[1]

The Government of National Unity (GNU) was formed in September 2008 through a power-sharing agreement between ZANU-PF and the MDC. The GNU was intended to end the crisis of the contested 2008 presidential elections, which had involved several rounds, delayed release of results, and ultimately led to Mugabe's reelection—despite observers' claims that the elections were neither free nor fair. Although MDC leader Morgan Tsvangirai won 48 percent of the votes in the first round of the elections, he consented to the power-sharing agreement primarily to end the violence that was inflicted on MDC supporters during the run-offs, including systematic rape and torture of women supporters by men affiliated with "Mugabe's ZANU-PF youth militia, agents of Zimbabwe's Central Intelligence Organization, and people who identify themselves as veterans of the liberation war (known as war veterans) affiliated with ZANU-PF."[2]

In the new government, Mugabe remains president of Zimbabwe and head of the cabinet, while Tsvangirai is prime minister and chair of a council of ministers that ostensibly supervises the cabinet. Although the 2009 documentary *Shungu* depicts what director Saki Mafundikwa calls the "eventual reconciliation between President Robert Mugabe and opposition leader Morgan Tsvangirai," many question the real value of this reconciliation.[3] Political scientists argue that the GNU has actually created barriers to reform, leaving Mugabe with most of the executive powers he wielded previously, as well as control over the state's security apparatus. Political tensions and distrust between Mugabe and Tsvangirai, notably over failure to implement fully the arrangements underpinning the power-sharing agreement, remain high. State-sponsored violence toward the MDC and other opposition parties, Morgan Tsvangirai, and ordinary citizens continues. Mugabe continues to push for elections which he hopes will dissolve the GNU, while Tsvangirai hopes to see both a new constitution and promised reforms in place before holding elections.[4]

As has proven typical during Zimbabwe's election cycles during the last decade, 2011 saw an increase in reports of politically motivated intimidation and violence, which were linked to issues of access to the media. When Egyptian uprisings began on 25 January 2011, eventually driving Hosni Mubarak out of power, many who hope for democratic change in Zimbabwe debated whether similar mass protests might be adapted to Zimbabwean conditions. For example, Leonard Makombe wrote an editorial titled "Mubarak, Mugabe Regimes— So Many Parallels to Draw" for the 25 February 2011 edition of the *Zimbabwe Independent*, drawing explicit comparisons between Mubarak and Mugabe, including their three decades in power, use of emergency law, and reliance on the military and police.

Because of ZBC's monopoly on the airwaves, most Zimbabweans had limited access to news coverage of the Egyptian uprisings and had to seek out alternative sources of information. When a small group of lawyers, trade unionists, and students gathered to watch and discuss DVD recordings of Al Jazeera and BBC coverage of the Egyptian protests on 19 February, police seized their projector, DVDs, and laptop, jailed the viewers at a maximum security prison, and charged them with treason—an indictment that carries the death penalty. Later reports indicated that a number of them were tortured while awaiting charges. Most were released sixteen days later, with charges dropped, while the remaining six were released on bail after almost a month in jail. The same week, the German press reported that two women and a man were arrested for singing a parody of a ZBC television jingle that mocked Mugabe. Both incidents illustrate that Zimbabweans continue not only to watch both local and imported television but also to make unintended uses of them. Freedom of expression, freedom of assembly, and freedom to access information nevertheless remain limited.

Such an outline, however, tells us little about how the people I spoke with in 2001 are faring today. One can keep up with political events in Zimbabwe through the international news, but my experience in talking with filmmakers and viewers in 2001 left me hungry for more substantial news about how Zimbabwean culture has developed over the last decade and how ordinary people are engaging with local and international events. In an effort to find out, between June and August 2011 I conducted several new interviews with filmmakers via email, Facebook, and telephone, including Simon Bright, Tsitsi Dangarembga, Edgar Langeveldt, and Ben Mahaka. I draw on these interviews to assess Zimbabwe's current cinematic culture in light of the foreign and local elements that pervade discourse about both Zimbabwean identity and the cinematic arts, using my analysis to show how filmmakers and viewers are creating and envisioning change in the midst of challenges to their freedom.

Television remains problematic, with attempts to develop a strong local industry hindered by state control of the airwaves, mismanagement of financial resources, and Zimbabweans' continued search for more viewing choices than the national broadcaster is willing and able to offer. The film industry, however, has not only continued to develop, but it has done so in a more local way than ever before, with greater involvement of black filmmakers, less funding from NGOs with development agendas, and greater use of local languages. The most striking theme in the new interviews I conducted is *hope*. Whether working in film, television, or new media, filmmakers still see the development of a vibrant cinematic culture that represents their nation and connects them with others beyond Zimbabwe's borders as a real possibility, and their comments gesture toward its realization.

Television since 2001

It is difficult to get accurate information about Zimbabwean television from outside of the country, because the available information—mostly in Zimbabwean newspapers—is extremely polarized, either reflecting the view of the ruling party, which controls ZBC, or condemning everything on ZTV. Filmmakers, who are also TV viewers, can offer some perspective on television since 2001, but their comments often blur the line between facts and opinions. For example, Edgar Langeveldt believes that ZTV has surpassed the BSA's goal of airing 75 percent local content, while filmmaker Ben Mahaka believes ZTV has come nowhere near that goal. Both use these opinions, however, to criticize the national broadcaster, Langeveldt for its airing of low-quality programs and government propaganda, and Mahaka for its failure to work with advertisers to produce enough high-quality programming.

The main development on Zimbabwean television since 2001 has been the production of local soap operas in an attempt to build on the popularity of the soap genre, while also indigenizing it with local themes and actors. The first of these locally produced soaps was *Studio 263*, which began in 2002 and on which both Langeveldt and Mahaka acted. The soap, shown in thirty-minute episodes three times a week, was funded by Population Services International (PSI) as "an HIV and AIDS awareness soap," a social message program with a development agenda. Foreign funding meant that the cast and crew were initially well paid compared with those of ZBC-produced local dramas such as *Gringo*, whose writer Enock Chihombori quit in 2003 citing the broadcaster's unprofessionalism and failure to pay adequate salaries. However, Mahaka explains that as the value of the Zimbabwe dollar continued to plummet, PSI failed to keep up with inflation and eventually pulled out altogether. On his production company's website, Mahaka writes about the popularity of the soap in its early days, when he played the lead character, Tom, a womanizer:

> *Studio 263* gets addictive. People start scheduling their evenings around the show. Men who usually stop by the pub for a pint or two rush home to catch the show. Prostitutes go out later because they don't want to miss it. The whole nation is rooting for Vimbai (who seems oblivious to Tom's intentions) and her wholesome boyfriend, James. ZTV has a hit.[5]

However, after PSI stopped funding the soap, "ZTV did nothing to support their biggest cash earner and eventually all the professional crew and cast left," leading to the program's demise in 2009, Mahaka told me.

Building on the initial success and relatively long run of *Studio 263*, in 2003 ZBC invited independent producers to submit concepts for feature films, soap operas, documentaries, local dramas, and children's cartoons, despite the uncertainty of funding for production. Since then a number of prime time soap operas have launched and then waned, including *Fragments* (2003), *Amakorokoza* (2004), *Estate Blues* (2005), *Smallhouse Saga* (2006), and *Fading Pictures* (2009).

In news reports about the launch of such programs, ZBC continues to explicitly contrast local productions with the imported ones they replaced, with *Fragments*, for example, advertised as a replacement for the imported *Kids Say the Darndest Things.* Locally produced soaps have continued to function as social message programming, covering topics such as child abuse, domestic violence, HIV/AIDS, and nepotism. Viewers continue to critique new programs using measures of localness. Writing about *Smallhouse Saga* in his 15 October 2006 *Zimbabwe Standard* television column, John Mokwetsi complained that "the story itself is hardly indigenous," and he criticized the "international soundtrack," while a viewer told him, "It is too English; really, there is no Zimbabwean story in that script." Localness continues to lie in the eye of the beholder, regardless of the national broadcaster's intentions.

The limited availability of high-quality locally produced television content creates a cycle that perpetuates ZTV's failure. "Because very few people are watching ZTV," Mahaka wrote to me, "advertisers are spending their money in the print media and outdoor advertising," leaving ZTV without money to create the high-quality program that would attract viewers and advertisers. The state broadcaster's biases lead to similar problems: "The fact that ZTV is used—quite blatantly—as a platform for ZANU-PF alienates a lot of possible advertisers which means that there's even less money to fund programming."

A second major development since 2001 has been the increased availability of satellite broadcasts. CNN's and BBC's images of Zimbabwe on the news are now absent from television thanks to the Broadcasting Services Act, so regional and international satellite TV have become Zimbabweans' main source of independent news. Although few Zimbabweans can afford to legally subscribe to satellite TV, decoders that unscramble satellite signals are inexpensive and widely used. Mahaka wrote to me that "even the poorest in society use these decoders" to access high-quality international programming, both entertainment and news. Statistics support this assertion, with the most recent consumer surveys showing that 46 percent of Zimbabweans now access television via satellite—a startling increase from the 2 percent of Zimbabweans who had a satellite dish in 1999.[6] The earlier number reflected ownership, while today's figures reflect illegal access via decoders.

Further research is needed on the effects of the BSA over the last decade, but it is clear that it has been used to restrict, rather than liberalize, broadcasting. In 2003 Zimbabwe's Supreme Court struck down sections 6 and 9 of the act, thereby removing licensing authority from the minister and giving it to the Broadcasting Authority of Zimbabwe and making legal provisions for more than one broadcaster with national range. Still, no private broadcasters have been licensed. The act's legislation against broadcasting without a license has been strictly enforced, with the police raiding unlicensed stations, confiscating equipment, and arresting station trustees and journalists. Given the much higher cost of television broadcasting compared with radio, so far these unlicensed broadcasters have all been radio stations. Several would-be broadcasters have sued the ZBC and the Broadcasting Authority, contesting the ZBC's monopoly, yet the state continues to control the airwaves. In May 2011, Mugabe and Tsvangirai agreed that the Broadcasting Authority should be reconstituted, but it remains unlikely that it will move toward liberalization of the airwaves.

It is clear that the state is using the act not only to limit Zimbabweans' access to independent information but also to prevent information about local problems from reaching beyond Zimbabwe's borders. During the 2008 election cycle, for example, the act was used to justify the arrest and fining of a Reuters photographer who was covering the elections. His crime was possession of a satellite phone, included in the act's broad definition of the term *signal transmitting station*. Technical terminology continues to reinforce state power.

Because ZBC remains the sole broadcaster, even independently produced programs are subject to state censorship. Episode 61 of *Studio 263* was censored, for example, because it dealt with striking workers demanding a salary increase and would have aired at the same time that ZBC employees were striking with similar demands. When *Amakorokoza* producer Cont Mhlanga protested that ZBC was taking advantage of the soap's popularity to air campaign commercials for President Mugabe during the 2008 elections, the show was taken off the air. The *Mai Chisamba Show*, which Rebecca Chisamba began producing independently but still aired on ZBC, was canceled in 2009 after she moved from social issues to political topics.[7]

Langeveldt described censorship in more abstract terms, writing to me about the demoralization of Zimbabwean culture workers by contrasting himself with those able to work outside the country: "Those of 'us who stayed' . . . were criminalized, demonized, emasculated, abused just to get a show together." He suggests a new take on the foreign/local dichotomy, replaced by a dichotomy between those who leave, acquiring creative and political freedom, and those who stay behind, working and living in repressive conditions. His comments also reflect the importance of diaspora as a theme in current cultural discourse within and beyond Zimbabwe.

ZBC has made some effort to air more local content on television, albeit with mixed results. As I discuss below, it frequently screens short Zimbabwean films through an arrangement with the Zimbabwe International Film Festival's Short Film Project. However, ZTV's printed schedules are notoriously unreliable, and this has led to viewers' undervaluing these local productions. Although he references his own survey of "audiences in the country" without explaining the methods or location of his survey, Mhiripiri found that, "due to ZTV's tendency not to properly schedule the short films, they appear so haphazardly and unexpectedly that audiences regard them as 'fillers.'" Thus for viewers, "short films unfortunately became associated with ZTV's failure to buy foreign programmes."[8] Ironically, growth of the local industry is interpreted as a failure of the state, impacted by viewers' desires for longer programs and possibly for foreign ones.

Since 2003 there has been a "surfeit of so-called local dramas and African movies on ZTV," according to one television reviewer. Local is being defined broadly to include, for example, Zambian films that ZBC screens, enabling it to come closer to the 75 percent local content goal. Viewers continue to complain of "excruciating boredom" and "mediocrity" associated with the national broadcaster—now nicknamed "Dead BC," rhyming with the Zimbabwean English pronunciation of ZBC as "Zed BC." Speaking as a viewer, Langeveldt told me: "I enjoy ZBC for Drama, Arts, Music, Fashion, and some amazing Documentaries . . . but News & Current Affairs" offer nothing more than "another seriously irritating Jingle, Announcement or outright sick lie." Such complaints reflect both the low quality of local programming predicted in 2001 by critics of the act and the one-sided perspective provided through ZBC's monopoly of the airwaves.[9]

Film since 2001

In the last ten years, the filmmakers who were most prominent in the 1990s have left the country. John and Louise Riber moved on to Dar es Salaam, Tanzania, where they now work in radio. Simon Bright and Ingrid Sinclair moved to England in 2003, where they now run an African film festival. Michael Auret Jr., whose attempt to launch Capital Radio prompted the government to create the BSA, now works in South Africa. After running South Africa's Sithengi Film and TV Market and the Cape Town World Cinema Festival for a number of years, he now has his own production company. As Tsitsi Dangarembga put it in our 2011 phone conversation, "Most of the trained Zimbabweans have left the country. They are in South Africa, they are in Namibia. They are in England, they are in the United States. They are all over the place." Other culture workers who were involved in the cinematic arts, like Olley Maruma, Ben Zulu, Walter Maparutsa, and Ngugi wa Mirii, have since passed away.

In addition to the loss of filmmakers who were previously based in the country, as Ben Mahaka told me, "Zimbabwe has fallen off the international filmmakers' locations list," replaced by South Africa, which "offers a similar look and much better infrastructure." The loss of skilled filmmakers has shifted the playing field in Zimbabwe's cinematic culture, creating opportunities for new filmmakers to emerge and for black filmmakers to take on more prominent roles as producers and directors.

Tsitsi Dangarembga, for example, returned to Zimbabwe from Germany in 2000, with her husband, Olaf Koschke, also a filmmaker. Referring to the closure of production companies like Media for Development Trust and Zimmedia, Dangarembga told reporters in 2005, "They have since left and my time has now come."[10] In our 2011 phone interview, she argued that the loss of the most active producers of the 1990s "has really made the industry become more deeply rooted in the people. It's only those people who really feel that they have to as Zimbabweans who've stuck with it." She and her husband now run a production company called Nyerai Films, which has put out at least nine short films since 2001. In addition to her own work as a director and producer, Dangarembga also works with the Women Filmmakers of Zimbabwe—"a development organization for young women aspiring to become filmmakers"—and runs the International Images Film Festival for Women (IIFF), which screens films with female protagonists from all over the world. Her most significant work, by her own estimation, is *Kare Kare Zvako* (2005), a short musical feature based on a Shona folktale.

Ben Mahaka is another example of a film professional who was involved in the cinematic arts in the 1990s and has since opened his own production company, Mahaka Media. In the mid-1990s, Mahaka worked as a scriptwriter, coordinator for Ben Zulu's African Script Development Fund, and eventually a director for several NGO-commissioned documentaries. In the late 1990s he began writing, directing, and producing short documentaries for Simon Bright's production company, Zimmedia. He launched his acting career through a small role in *Yellow Card* in 2000, which later led to the starring role as the villain Tom Mbambo on ZTV's first soap opera, *Studio 263*, of which he also directed over 300 episodes. Since 2001, he has been involved—as writer, director, cameraman, and/or producer—in over 30 films, mostly documentaries. He also directed a short feature, *Cousin Brother* (2005), and a feature film, *Bitter Pill* (2007).

A combination of less money for filmmaking and fewer skilled filmmakers on the ground has meant that filmmakers have turned away from feature film production. As Dangarembga put it during our phone interview, a skill deficit created by the emigration of many skilled film workers has meant that "we simply do not have the capacity to make those long films." The last decade has seen huge growth in the production of short films, what Zimbabwean media studies scholar Nhamo Mhiripiri calls "a genre of convenience."[11] Production has been encouraged and financed by venues like the Zimbabwe International Film Festival's Short Film Project (SFP), prompted by the shortage of funding for feature film production. Close to twenty short films have been produced by SFP since 2001.

Compared to productions prior to 2001, the current crop of short films are less development-oriented than the social message films produced by Media for Development Trust and others. Mhiripiri argues that the new short films are "concerned (inter alia) with exploring a complex sense of Zimbabwean identity that somehow works Zimbabwean material into a cosmopolitan sensibility, and vice versa."[12] Domestic settings, the use of familiar languages, and well-known local sounds, such as *mbira*, in the soundtracks give these films a local feel. While rarely taking a critical perspective on national events, they are nevertheless contributing to national discourse that constructs Zimbabweanness.

Local Languages, Voices, and Stories

In the short films that have appeared since 2001, there is no longer a reliance on English. Many films have Shona titles and are either entirely in Shona or include code-switched conversations in English and Shona. This results in better performances as well as a greater chance that Zimbabwean viewers outside of the urban areas will understand locally made films. Dangarembga spoke with me about the advantages of directing in Shona:

> What I found about having actors who act in their mother tongue, or something very close they have an affinity for, is that it's much easier to get good performances out of them. Because they are not concentrating on forming the words; they are not thinking, "Oh my goodness, what does this word mean? Is that really what comes next?" You know? They're not concentrating on getting the intonation right. All that is natural for them so they can concentrate on actually being in the scene and not have to worry.

In contrast to the reasons earlier filmmakers gave for not using indigenous languages, using Shona or another indigenous Zimbabwean language has not prevented short films from crossing Zimbabwe's borders, as Dangarembga's *Kare Kare Zvako* exemplifies. The film was subtitled in both English and French, given an English title (*Mother's Day*), and picked up by National Geographic's All Roads Film Project, which celebrates "indigenous and underrepresented minority-culture storytellers around the world," Dangarembga told me. After being screened at the All Roads Film Festival, the film was released in the festival's "best of" DVD sold by National Geographic, through which it is now available to global audiences.

Dangarembga and I also spoke about the effect of using African languages on viewers.

> It's also very good from the point of view of African identity because you go all the way up to Kenya. It's the same language group. And there are words that are common, even as far as Cameroon, words like for the heart. And so you screen in Uganda and somebody comes up and says, "I could understand this, I could understand that." And it's really wonderful for opening the stage for more interaction on the continent.

Here Dangarembga constructs Zimbabwean cinematic texts as having an important role to play in constructing and affirming an African identity based in shared cultural and linguistic features across national borders and ethnic groups. Although not sharing an African identity, as a viewer of African cinematic texts I have experienced the pleasure she describes, of watching a film in Zulu or Ndebele and recognizing some words I know from Shona or Swahili. It does make me feel more at home in the world of the film. Excited just to hear a few cognates from a language in the same Bantu language family as their own, viewers are eager for more African-language productions. For Zimbabwean viewers, Dangarembga continues, when a film uses an indigenous language, "the resonance in the population is so much greater because everybody feels that this is something that belongs to me, and it relates to my everyday life."

Even those films that are primarily in English are making greater use of code switching and code mixing than earlier productions. As Mahaka told me, "English is still the primary language of film here, but there is a move toward more natural mixed dialogue" that reflects how urban Zimbabweans talk. "Zimbabweans generally mix Shona and English or Ndebele and English in normal conversation, and this is now reflected in productions in the last ten years—especially those done through the Zimbabwe Film Festival's Short Film Project." It remains to be seen, however, whether any films show the mixing of Ndebele and Shona or nonstandard dialects of these languages, a common practice in normal conversation that was absent from most films and TV productions before 2001. In the short films that use Shona or Ndebele at all, even for brief code switching, subtitles are provided in English. Unfortunately, those that use English do not include subtitles in any other languages, suggesting that the Short Film Project as a whole is more concerned with English-speaking viewers than with others.

Why is it at this moment that Zimbabwean filmmakers are starting to use indigenous languages in their productions? The main reason is that film production is no longer in the hands of those for whom English is a first language. And, as Dangarembga explained, using English had become part of the cinematic culture; in order for filmmakers to use indigenous languages,

> Someone has to do it. And once it's done people realize that it's permissible. It's like, oh I don't know, like having *sadza* in the hotels, you never used to until one hotel started to do it and then people realize you can actually have *sadza* in a hotel and people will buy it and eat it and enjoy it. So once one breaks through whatever psychological problem one has about that, people realize that this is the most natural thing to do.

Dangarembga compares using indigenous Zimbabwean languages in films to eating Zimbabwe's staple food, a stiff porridge made from white cornmeal, in a hotel, a setting associated with colonial culture and elite identities. Her comments connect intertextually with her novel *Nervous Conditions,* where the consumption of food is linked both to language and cultural identity. Although her novel is more ambiguous, here she suggests that such imported settings can be indigenized, and there need be no conflict with traditional elements of local life (speaking Shona, eating *sadza*) and "modern" life (making films, dining in hotels). These mixtures of foreign and local, modern and traditional elements are the stuff of Zimbabwean life, and films, she suggests, should reflect this. The growing use of indigenous languages in films indicates they are beginning to do so.

The politics of language, however, is not only about which languages are used but also about who is allowed to speak and be heard—in any language. Criticizing the Broadcasting Services Act, Langeveldt told me, "We didn't need language quotas and nasty rhetoric . . . we needed equipment and opportunities to communicate with OTHERS . . . our STORIES . . . and receive back their perspectives and digest that into our own reality." His comments not only mark the failure of the BSA to serve the national interests as it claimed to do but also construct film and television as potent mechanisms for allowing communication both among Zimbabweans and across national borders.

Langeveldt's comments also reflect a deep-seated frustration with the current opportunities for Zimbabweans to communicate. His words are echoed by those of film producer Nakai Matema, who told Mhiripiri that she sees the Short Film Project as "getting Zimbabweans to tell their own stories how they see fit." In a 2011 interview, filmmaker Rumbi Katedza spoke of the need for "telling stories so that people [within Africa] know more about what's happening in our continent." In describing her most recent project, the documentary *The Axe and the Tree*, she said that the Zimbabweans she interviewed in the film "need to speak, to be seen, to be validated." In March 2011, Wilf Mbanga, editor of the *Zimbabwean*, an independent newspaper which "since 2005 has battled to keep open a modicum of democratic space in the media," issued a call for continuing to fight for these rights. "Now, more than ever," Mbanga wrote, "we must continue to fight for freedom of speech and to tell the stories coming out of Zimbabwe. Incredibly brave, ordinary people's personal stories illustrate their battle against oppression and injustice and the huge price they have paid as a result. Their voices deserve to be heard."[13]

Critical Voices at Home and in Diaspora

Most of the films produced since 2001 are relatively apolitical, avoiding topics that might be perceived as openly criticizing the state, although some (like *The Legend of the Sky Kingdom* and *Kare Kare Zvako*) could be read as allegorical critiques of Mugabe. Dangarembga, for example, told me that she aims to be nonpartisan:

> As a professional documentary filmmaker one doesn't go in with preconceived ideas. I usually want to let people tell their stories, to make sure that I have a whole spectrum of perspectives. So, at the end of the day, the kind of the work I like to do is not really damning to any one party, unless there are glaring problems.

A handful of documentary filmmakers, however, have explicitly addressed the current crisis. For example, in 2009 Saki Mafundikwa, founder of the Zimbabwe Institute for Vigital Arts, directed *Shungu,* a documentary about ordinary people impacted during the 2008 election-year havoc. Director Simon Bright and producer Michael Auret recently released another example of a political film, *Robert Mugabe . . . What Happened?* On the film's Facebook page, Bright says that the documentary is "an exploration of what happened to a promising African leader who was well respected and it recognises his fight for freedom and against Apartheid. But it also explores the forces that caused him to effectively destroy a lot of what he built."[14] Such films are important means of letting audiences outside of Zimbabwe—including Zimbabweans now living in the diaspora—learn about what is going on there from local perspectives.

When films are critical, their political content often makes them unsafe to screen at home. *Shungu,* for example, has been screened at numerous international film festivals to high acclaim and has received several prestigious awards, but it is considered contraband in Zimbabwe, where Mafundikwa fears arrest should he dare to screen it. Such fears are not unfounded: Simon Bright was arrested when he returned to Zimbabwe in March 2004, on mere suspicion that he had helped the BBC shoot *Secrets of the Camps,* a documentary aired in Britain a month earlier that exposed widespread rape in state-run youth militia camps. In 2007, Edward Chikombo, a part-time ZBC cameraman, allegedly smuggled out of the country television footage that showed MDC leader Morgan Tsvangirai's injuries after he was beaten by police; Chikombo was found murdered soon afterward. In our 2011 email exchange, Bright used such events as evidence that "there is a militant sometimes underground culture of producing the image in spite of terrifying legislation and police brutality. . . . The underground filmmakers . . . or news camera people who smuggle footage out to BBC et al. are doing a terrific job of using the image to counter Mugabe's propaganda." Bright's comments frame filmmakers as contemporary guerillas battling against Mugabe, his security apparatus, and legislation such as the Broadcasting Services Act. Yet it is clear that while the risks are undertaken within Zimbabwe, the images they produce are mostly viewed in the diaspora.

Like *Robert Mugabe . . . What Happened?* and *Shungu,* Katedza's *The Axe and the Tree,* which features interviews with Zimbabweans tortured during the 2008 elections, has also been screened outside of the country but not yet at home. A Zimbabwean viewer recently wrote on the *Robert Mugabe . . . What Happened?* Facebook page, "We need also to see it those who are in Zimbabwe." Bright responded that the film will first air on Mnet in South Africa—which means some Zimbabweans will be able to access it via satellite—and later be released on DVD in Zimbabwe. When the film opened at the Encounters Documentary

Film Festival in Cape Town, South Africa, in June 2011, Zimbabweans living in exile were among the viewers. Bright told me in our interview via email that they "were deeply moved by the film. For some who had left Zimbabwe over a decade ago it brought back vivid and painful memories of past decades."

New disparity in access has emerged because cinematic texts that take a critical perspective on Zimbabwe are more available to viewers outside of the country than within. Since the economy started to fall apart at the turn of the century and the political situation put supporters of the opposition in danger, many Zimbabweans and expatriates have fled the country in search of better opportunities to make a living or to live without threats to their lives. The growth of a Zimbabwean diaspora has thus become an important theme in recent cinematic texts, as well as in discourse about the culture industries. Zimbabweans in the diaspora are freer to produce critical cinematic texts and to access them.

The Role of Festivals

Film screenings remain an important means by which Zimbabweans both at home and in diaspora may access alternative discourse. For example, in 2003 the Zimbabwe International Film Festival (ZIFF) showed seventy-five films from thirty-one countries across nine venues in Harare, Chitungwiza, and Bulawayo to an estimated 14,000 viewers. Another important festival is the yearly International Images Film Festival for Women, run by Tsitsi Dangarembga and the Women Filmmakers of Zimbabwe. Launched in 2002 and now held yearly in November, the IIFF includes local and international productions that feature female protagonists, and it screens films in Harare, Bulawayo, and Chimanimani.

Not only do film festivals provide urban, peri-urban, and diaspora audiences with access to media not produced by the state, but talk and texts about such festivals also offer opportunities to challenge hegemonic discourse about the role of the cinematic arts. For example, in 2004 director Rumbi Katedza described ZIFF's aim as "regenerating indigenous film production through facilitating important dialogues between aspiring/established local filmmakers and international filmmakers." While Katedza draws on the discourse of indigeneity, her use of the term is strikingly different from its use in state discourse. She constructs indigenous film production as something that is not fixed but rather subject to regeneration and renewal. Local filmmakers are contrasted not with foreign ones but rather with international filmmakers, a more inclusive category in which some Zimbabwean filmmakers may in fact find themselves. Finally, in contrast to those who would criticize foreign filmmakers for cultural imperialism, a monologue to which Zimbabweans are subjected but to which they cannot respond, she frames these two groups as in dialogue, producing an agentive identity for Zimbabwean filmmakers. In similar terms, Katedza writes, "The [Film] Forum serves to stimulate the local industry to reach larger global markets."[15] She positions Zimbabwe's film industry as contributing to global markets, rather than falling victim to them. She creates an identity for Zimbabweans as producers of their own cinematic texts rather than solely as consumers of foreign productions.

Katedza went on to describe an "open discussion" between filmmakers and the CEO of ZBC about how filmmakers might contribute local television content. Such discussions led to a deal brokered between ZIFF and ZBC in which ZTV gave the festival publicity in exchange for ZIFF's supplying films made locally for the Short Film Project to be screened on television. Since 2005, these shorts have been screened on ZBC. Dangarembga told me that ZTV recently screened her short film *Growing Stronger,* a portrait of an HIV+ model, and that she had received positive feedback from viewers. Arrangements such as this mark an important step toward making non-state discourse available outside of film festivals and therefore to audiences nationwide.

Viewers since 2001

In bringing this study of Zimbabwe's cinematic culture up to date, the absence of viewers' voices after 2001 leaves a loud silence. I hope that one contribution of this book is that we can no longer talk about Zimbabwean film and television without questioning what they mean to viewers. Likewise, we cannot talk about Zimbabwean identities without questioning what they mean to ordinary Zimbabweans. When their voices are absent, we should take notice.

Viewers' discourse about film and television is the most important source in understanding how Zimbabweans make meaning from what they watch. Yet, in the absence of such information, statistics offer a rough guide. The most recent version of the yearly Zimbabwe All Media Products and Services Survey showed that viewership of ZBC TV1 was down from 38 percent in 2008 to 24 percent in 2010. Viewership of the news hour in English (now called *Newsnight*) has also decreased, now at 26 percent but still considered viewers' favorite program. Some, however, switch from DSTV to ZTV for local news, and then back to DSTV. ZBC2 began operating again in 2010, and after an initial viewership of 14 percent in its first quarter, dropped to 10 percent in the final quarter of the year. Satellite has replaced ZTV for many viewers.[16]

While survey results don't give us viewers' voices, they do suggest that Zimbabwean viewers continue to remain active in their search for independent sources of information and entertainment. Ironically, the rising availability of regional and international satellite TV has been blamed for the lukewarm reception of locally produced films. While the feature films made in Zimbabwe before 2001 were screened and avidly watched on ZTV, today's viewers have more options via satellite and thus are watching even more foreign content than ever before.

Hopes for the Future

Given the current state of film and television in 2011, what are the possibilities for democratic change in Zimbabwe's cinematic culture, and how might such change both reflect and contribute to broader changes in society? Many culture workers recognize that new national leadership is needed, although they remain uncertain about when to expect a major political change. Media watchdog groups like MISA-Zimbabwe and some independent filmmakers have been vocal in their critique of state media and in outlining a way forward. For example, in our email exchange Simon Bright argued that ZBC must commission the work of filmmakers who are not politically appointed staff members: "The National Broadcaster should reflect the views of the diversity of Zimbabwe and Zimbabwean independent filmmakers." While such calls recognize the need for what critical applied linguist Alistair Pennycook calls "ethically argued preferred futures," they rely on change from within the state, and that change still seems uncertain at best.[17]

Many culture workers are unwilling to wait for the state to make such changes. However, there are smaller changes to which they feel they can contribute. In spite of the difficulties of working in a devastated economy and under a repressive government, filmmakers continue to create cinematic texts that satisfy their own need to create and, they hope, satisfy viewers with stories that are relevant to their experience of being Zimbabwean. Filmmakers have identified some steps to creating a flourishing cinematic culture in Zimbabwe. For example, Edgar Langeveldt writes of turning to CGI (computer-generated imagery) technology to create animation, a less expensive means of making films. Mahaka calls for the establishment of a "viable training infrastructure" for newcomers to the industry, an idea echoed by Rumbi Katedza's desire to create educational opportunities for young filmmakers and Zimbabweans returning from the diaspora,[18] and by Dangarembga's fear that young filmmakers who leave the country for training will simply not return.

Dangarembga calls for increased production of films that take up "the cultural concerns of Zimbabweans at this point in time." For example, she told me about her plans to make a film about Zimbabweans' experience of the fuel shortage that began in 2000 and still makes daily life difficult. I remember in 2001 making an appointment to meet with a colleague at the University of Zimbabwe and being told by his secretary, "He can't make it because he's been in a queue at the petrol station all afternoon." Dangarembga describes her proposed documentary as "a really simple story" about "how communities need to pull together to make things happen in times of trouble." She went on:

> A very simple message, but, hey, how many Zimbabweans come together
> in times of trouble or any other time for that matter? You know, it's these

simple things that are the basis of community, and one can see, envisage the nation as a large community. So, the same thing that holds the community together will be the things that hold a nation together. A community in a village, for example, used to gather around the storyteller, so now we have films doing the storytelling. It's in that vein that I think that one can disseminate—suggest—certain values that will be of use for a given nation.

Both Dangarembga and Bright emphasize the need for filmmakers to resist the pressure to create polarized cinematic texts that are either for or against Mugabe. Instead, Zimbabweans must "be allowed to value the diversity of their cultures," Bright argued. "Thoughtful and nuanced documentaries and films made by people driven by a passion for the art of filmmaking rather than the partisan passion of propaganda will help a process of national healing." As Dangarembga told me, "People who are partisan on one side or the other tend to have it a bit easier, but I don't really think that they leave behind a legacy."

Ironically, the illegal use of satellite television may be opening up new opportunities for filmmakers and viewers alike. While the feature films made in Zimbabwe before 2001 were screened and avidly watched on ZTV, today's viewers have more options via satellite and thus are watching even more imported content than ever before. However, coming full circle, today's imported content may include Zimbabwean productions. If picked up by South African broadcasters such as Mnet, Zimbabwean films and TV programs will be screened throughout Africa and also viewed at home. Old episodes of *Studio 263*, for example, are now available on AfricaMagic Plus, one of two digital satellite television (DSTV) stations that air solely African content. MultiChoice, Zimbabwe's DSTV provider, describes the content aired on those stations as "made by Africans, for Africans, reflecting Africa back on itself with programmes such as *Big Brother Africa, Deal or No Deal, Idols,* and *Studio 263*"[19]—ironically, all shows modeled after foreign programs. Local cinematic texts are exported only to be reimported, and foreign shows are remade with local casts. Television content has become even less clearly local or foreign, now part of a mix of African cinematic texts that are no longer constrained by national borders and where the existence of a diaspora is becoming an important part of Zimbabwe itself.

In our 2011 interview, Dangarembga spoke poignantly about the possibilities that cinematic texts can play in creating a more open Zimbabwe. I asked her, "What kinds of changes would you like to see in Zimbabwe, and what role can filmmaking play in these changes?"

I want to see a society in which people can talk openly about things and not be accused of treason or of ulterior motives against the state. I think that film can play a role there, by making those narratives, those engagements, palatable, suggestible, for populations. Once it's presented as a film, you are not saying this actually happened to me and that person did it. You are talking at the level of abstraction. But just engaging with the issue at that level is going to have some effect on behavior. And I've actually seen this happening already, with some of the films that we've screened at the [IIFF] festival. Even, for example, one of the films that the Women Filmmakers [of Zimbabwe] did about a girl child abused by her headmaster at school. And when I asked one of the main characters, who was a schoolteacher, why she wanted the role, she said to me, "It's because films like this show that you can actually talk about anything." There's so many things we don't talk about in Zimbabwe that need to be talked about, but we don't know how to start. Now in Shona when people enter into negotiations without any problematic issue, culturally we have something that is called *zarura muromo,* which is a small gift that literally means 'to open the mouth' or to begin the discussion. And so I think that film can act as such a thing. It can provide the way for people to start opening their mouths and speaking about certain things that we have not had the language for, or we have not been able to overcome certain taboos about, or certain other psychological barriers, be it fear or whatever. I think film has a big role to play in that process.

The emphasis on voices and stories in the comments of culture workers reflects a common theme emerging in Zimbabwe as culture workers and ordinary Zimbabweans try to remain hopeful during difficult times. This book echoes this theme, while also emphasizing that "stories always do something. They are never just there, as passive comments or meta-accounts of something more 'real,' but rather they actively (re)configure this reality."[20] The stories that Zimbabweans tell about themselves and others, whether through film, television, or talk about these media, actively and continually (re)constructs not only Zimbabwe's cinematic culture but also its cultural identity.

Conclusion

An examination of discourse and power in the realm of Zimbabwe's cinematic culture has shown that we should not take values and power relations for granted any more than we can take the established meanings of *local, foreign, traditional,* and *Zimbabwean* as common sense. By questioning these essentialist categories, we can create a space to hear from those Zimbabweans whose discourse is marginalized: rural people thought to exist outside of cinematic cultures and modernity; speakers of local languages whose access to televised information is limited by the use of English; people who enjoy watching foreign fiction; filmmakers trying to create "Zimbabwean films" even while their own identities may not easily fit the Zimbabwean label. By exploring how such categories are constructed, whose interests they support, and how they maintain hegemony, we can also see how they might be challenged. Challenges are coming not only from academics but also from civil society—watchdog groups such as the Media Institute of Southern Africa and the Media Monitoring Project Zimbabwe. Most important, challenges are coming from participants in film and television cultures, filmmakers, and the public. Despite the government's anti-foreign rhetoric, culture workers and the Zimbabwean public continue to value both foreign and local cultural elements, finding new ways to make do with what is available to them and to reconceive of the local.

For better or for worse, Zimbabwe has been successful in ridding itself of the more visible foreign elements in its boundaries: white citizens, expatriates, and Western television news. But with such a long history of foreign influences and current global trends, it is no longer possible for Zimbabwe to return to an unblemished past. Indeed, its involvement in media cultures precludes that return. The cinematic arts offer viewers the opportunity to move forward, to imagine new ways of being Zimbabwean and new vocabularies for constructing an inclusive national identity.

The possibilities inherent in the public's democratic vision of identities that are simultaneously foreign and local should not be mistaken for a Utopian view of Zimbabwe's future political culture; an enormous change in government and legislation needs to take place before the state will liberalize broadcasting, support cinematic production and other arts, recognize the foreign as an irrevocable element *within* the local, and support people's rights to free speech and access to information.

The people who can effect democratic change may be writers, politicians, filmmakers, and visionaries within Zimbabwe or even in another postcolonial society. But as Connell writes about the possibilities for change in cultural politics, "its field of action is the possibilities that open up in particular milieux and institutions" rather than in formal Utopias.[21] Change in Zimbabwe might come from the themes possible in particular films, the questions culture workers raise at a particular café, the critiques viewers bring to particular television news segments, the insights and pleasures they gain from particular imported soap operas, the dialogue possible at particular film festivals, or the languages used in a particular television talk show. As we listen in on these spaces, to these voices and stories, we must not let Mugabe drown out the talk of ordinary Zimbabweans.

NOTES

Introduction

1. Hall, "Cultural Identity and Diaspora," 234.

2. Ibid., 236.

3. Pennycook, *Critical Applied Linguistics*, 4.

4. Potter, *Representing Reality.*

5. Bush and Szeftel, "Editorial," 7.

6. Blommaert, *Discourse*, 35–36.

7. Makoni, Brutt-Griffler, and Mashiri, "The Use of 'Indigenous' and Urban Vernaculars in Zimbabwe," 33.

8. Diawara, *African Cinema;* Ukadike, *Black African Cinema;* Ukadike, *Questioning African Cinema Conversations with Filmmakers;* Harrow, *African Cinema: Postcolonial and Feminist Readings;* Harrow, *Postcolonial African Cinema: From Political Engagement to Postmodernism;* Barlet, *African Cinemas: Decolonizing the Gaze;* Mhando, "Approaches to African Cinema Study"; Kerr, "The Best of Both Worlds?"; Smyth, "The British Colonial Film Unit"; Burns, *Flickering Shadows.*

9. Pennycook, *Critical Applied Linguistics*, 2.

1. A Crisis of Representation

1. Appadurai, "Disjuncture and Difference in the Global Cultural Economy," 40.

2. Miller, "*The Young and the Restless* in Trinidad"; Velasco, "Imitation and Indigenization"; Liebes and Katz, *The Export of Meaning.*

3. Lundby, "Going to Tsanzaguru."

4. Fairclough, *Discourse and Social Change,* 186, 193.

5. Turino, "Are We Global Yet?" 54.

6. Jeater, *Law, Language, and Science,* 173–75.

7. Kerr, "The Best of Both Worlds?" 20, 35.

8. On African migrants, see Epprecht, "The 'Unsaying' of Indigenous Homosexualities in Zimbabwe," 7. For a related critique of the term *alien,* see Comaroff and Comaroff, "Naturing the Nation," 627.

9. Makoni, Dube, and Mashiri, "Zimbabwe Colonial and Post-Colonial Language Policy," 400–401.

10. Gwyn, "'Really Unreal,'" 324.

11. Nell, *Images of Yesteryear,* 180.

12. Mangin, *Filming Emerging Africa,* 18.

13. Ibid., 65.

14. Windrich, *The Mass Media in the Struggle for Zimbabwe,* 16. See also Stapleton and May, *African Rock.*

15. Hammar, "The Making and Unma(s)king of Local Government," 130.

16. Makoni, Dube, and Mashiri, "Zimbabwe Colonial and Post-Colonial Language Policy," 400–401.

17. Media Monitoring Project Zimbabwe, *Election 2000,* 10.

18. Mashiri, "Representations of Blacks and the City," 109.

19. Smyth, "The Development of British Colonial Film Policy," 447.

20. Government of Zimbabwe, *The Democratization of the Media,* i.

21. Campbell, *Reclaiming Zimbabwe,* 125.

22. Hammar, "The Making and Unma(s)king of Local Government," 125.

23. Hove, "Comments."

24. Muchemwa, "Galas, Biras, State Funerals, and the Necropolitan Imagination," 507–508; cf. Hammar, "The Making and Unma(s)king of Local Government," 125.

25. Zook, *Color by Fox.*

26. Hungwe, "Media in the Primary Schools of Zimbabwe," 8–9.

27. Derges, "Bringing Our Cinema Home," 48.

28. Worby, "The End of Modernity in Zimbabwe?"

29. Moyo, "From Rhodesia to Zimbabwe," 23.

30. Turino, *Nationalists, Cosmopolitans, and Popular Music in Zimbabwe.*

31. Chiumbu, "Redefining the National Agenda," 34–35.

32. Morley, *Television, Audiences, and Cultural Studies,* 6, 76.

33. Fairclough, *Critical Discourse Analysis,* 17.

34. White, *The Assassination of Herbert Chitepo,* 5–6.

35. Loomba, *Colonialism–Postcolonialism,* 2.

36. Gikandi, *Maps of Englishness,* 14.

37. One important exception is Hadland, *Re-visioning Television.*

38. Moyo, "From Rhodesia to Zimbabwe," 13.

39. Kangai, "Radio and Television Expansion in Zimbabwe."

40. Thompson, "Viewing the Foreign and the Local."

41. Barber, "Audiences in Africa."

42. Ukadike, *Black African Cinema,* 7.

2. Cinematic Arts before the 2001 Broadcasting Services Act

1. Furusa, "Television, Culture, and Development in Zimbabwe"; Zaffiro, *Media & Democracy in Zimbabwe.*

2. Kangai, "Radio and Television Expansion in Zimbabwe"; Kangai, "Radio as a Medium of Mass Communication"; Frederikse, *None but Ourselves.*

3. British Broadcasting Corporation, *Report by the Study Group,* 1.

4. Davis and Hammond, qtd. in Smyth, "The Development of British Colonial Film Policy," 447, 450; Mangin, *Filming Emerging Africa,* 38.

5. BBC, *Report by the Study Group,* 1.

6. Kangai, "Radio and Television Expansion in Zimbabwe," 11.

7. Media Institute of Southern Africa (MISA), "Minister Orders the Resignation of Entire State-Broadcasting Board."

8. Tichatonga, "Contributions of Organisations and Ministries to Radio Programmes," 8.

9. Lamb, *House of Stone,* 117; Zaffiro, *Media & Democracy in Zimbabwe,* 79; Andersen, "The Janus Face of Television in Small Countries," 56.

10. Hoad, "Between the White Man's Burden and the White Man's Disease," 563; Epprecht, "The 'Unsaying' of Indigenous Homosexualities in Zimbabwe," 10.

11. Mashiri, "Representations of Blacks and the City," 112–13.

12. O'Grady, "Shows of Independence"; Gondo interview; MISA, "Minister Goes Back on Promise to Liberalise Broadcasting."

13. MISA, "Draconian Media Bill Passed in Zimbabwe."

14. MISA, "Private Broadcasting Company"; Media Monitoring Project Zimbabwe, *Election 2000,* 102.

15. Bright, "Video for Extension Workers in Zimbabwe."

16. Burns, *Flickering Shadows,* 102.

17. Honeyman, 1986 *Audio Visual Zimbabwe;* Ukadike, *Black African Cinema,* 124.

18. Hungwe, "Narrative and Ideology."

19. Diawara, *African Cinema,* viii, 5.

20. Philander, "Hard Won Progress in Local Film Industry."

21. Hove, "Comments."

22. Gwarinda, "Development Theory and the Role of Film," 5.

23. BBC, *Report by the Study Group,* 1; Chimhundu, "The Status of African Languages in Zimbabwe"; Andersson, "Reinterpreting the Rural-Urban Connection"; Turino, *Nationalists, Cosmopolitans, and Popular Music in Zimbabwe.*

24. Kark, "Broadcasting in Zimbabwe," 14; O'Grady, "Shows of Independence"; Memper interview; Tichatonga, "Developing a Contemporary Television System in Zimbabwe," 21; Kangai, "Radio and Television Expansion in Zimbabwe."

25. Bassoppo-Moyo, qtd. in O'Grady, "Shows of Independence."

26. Mangin, *Filming Emerging Africa;* Nell, *Images of Yesteryear;* Kerr, "The Best of Both Worlds?"

27. Philander, "Hard Won Progress in Local Film Industry," n.p.

28. Lloyd, "First Local Feature Film"; Mvusi, qtd. in Munjoma, "A New Look: African Film Makers on Their Mettle," 38.

29. Furusa, "Television, Culture, and Development in Zimbabwe"; Kark, "Broadcasting in Zimbabwe."

30. Neill, "Re: [AlanB] Help—Need a Song or Two or Three"; Pickard, "Rhodesian Nostalgia"; "Telly Five Club"; Lamb, *House of Stone;* Mangin, *Filming Emerging Africa.*

31. Roberts, "RBC"; Higham, "Face from the Past a Real Jolt"; Partridge, "About Derek."

32. "Union of National Radio & Television Orgs. of Africa (URTNA)"; URTNA, "The Renaissance of a Continental Union"; Government of Zimbabwe, *The Democratization of the Media.*

33. BBC, *Report by the Study Group,* 5; Kangai, "Radio as a Medium of Mass Communication," 11.

34. O'Grady, "Shows of Independence," 119.

35. Government of Zimbabwe, *The Democratization of the Media,* 3; Ndumbu, "Africa"; Andersen, "Television, Political Culture, and the Identity of Citizenship"; Furusa, "Television, Culture, and Development in Zimbabwe," 78.

36. Summer Institute of Linguistics, "Ethnologue: Top 100 Languages by Population"; Ndlela, "Broadcasting Reforms in Southern Africa," 70.

37. Engelke, "Text and Performance in an African Church," 82. See also Lafon, "Shona Class 5 Revisited."

38. Mashiri, "Representations of Blacks and the City," 111; Lunga, "An Examination of an African Postcolonial Experience," 66.

39. Government of Zimbabwe, *The Democratization of the Media,* 1.

40. Gwarinda, "Development Theory and the Role of Film," 39.

41. Andersen, "The Janus Face of Television in Small Countries."

42. Kark, "Broadcasting in Zimbabwe," 13.

43. British Broadcasting Corporation, *Report by the Study Group,* 5.

44. Kangai, "Radio and Television Expansion in Zimbabwe," 11.

45. Lundby, "Going to Tsanzaguru."

46. Capricorn Video Unit, *Directory of Film.*

47. Zaffiro, *Media & Democracy in Zimbabwe,* 19–20.

48. Hausmann, *Bending Tradition to the Changing Times;* Riber interview.

49. Munjoma, "A New Look: African Film Makers on Their Mettle," and interviews with Arsenault, Bhagat, Bright, Chikuhwa, Riber, Sinclair, and Zulu.

50. Burns, *Flickering Shadows;* Smyth, "The Development of British Colonial Film Policy"; Kerr, "The Best of Both Worlds?"

51. Mangin, *Filming Emerging Africa,* 17.

52. Nell, *Images of Yesteryear,* 179.

53. Ibid., 126; Burns, *Flickering Shadows;* Auret interview.

54. Gecau, "Audience Responses to a Film in Rural Zimbabwe"; Nell, *Images of Yesteryear,* 203; Government of Zimbabwe, *The Democratization of the Media;* Capricorn Video Unit, *Directory of Film.*

55. Maruta interview.

56. Munjoma, "A New Look: African Film Makers on Their Mettle"; Derges, "Bringing Our Cinema Home"; Mabaso, "Southern Africa's Film Makers Fight to Control Distribution."

57. British Broadcasting Corporation, *Report by the Study Group,* 2.

58. Government of Zimbabwe, *The Democratization of the Media,* 9.

59. Chiwome, "The Interface of Orality and Literacy in the Zimbabwean Novel"; Garlake, "Prehistory and Ideology in Zimbabwe"; Makoni, Makoni, and Mashiri, "Naming Practices and Language Planning in Zimbabwe."

60. Edmondson, "National Erotica," 155; Desai, "Theater as Praxis," 68; Lamb, *House of Stone,* 177.

61. Lund, "Harmonizing the Nation," 223.

62. Andersen, "The Janus Face of Television in Small Countries," 57.

63. Makoni, Makoni, and Mashiri, "Naming Practices and Language Planning in Zimbabwe," 445; Lunga, "An Examination of an African Postcolonial Experience."

64. Dangarembga, "Film in Zimbabwe."

65. Zulu, "African Movies and the Global Mainstream."

66. Ibid.

67. Ukadike, *Black African Cinema,* 7.

3. Authorship and Identities

I am grateful to the African Literature Association for permission to include this chapter, an earlier version of which was published in *African Diasporas: Ancestors, Migrations and Boundaries,* ed. Robert Cancel and Winifred Woodhull, 184–201 (Trenton, NJ: Africa World Press, 2008).

1. Weedon, *Feminist Practice and Poststructuralist Theory,* 157.

2. Hungwe, "Narrative and Ideology," 85, 93; Brown and Singhal, "Ethical Considerations," 92.

3. Ukadike, *Black African Cinema*, 126.

4. Lee, "Desperately Seeking Tsitsi"; Kapasula, "The African Public Space," 10.

5. Boni-Claverie, "When Gazelles Fly," 58.

6. Raeburn, http://www.michaelraeburn.com; Raeburn interview by Hungwe.

7. Boni-Claverie, "When Gazelles Fly"; Bruner, "Self-Making and World-Making"; Bruner, "A Narrative Model of Self-Construction"; Bruner and Weisser, "The Invention of Self"; Raeburn interview.

8. Boni-Claverie, "When Gazelles Fly," 61.

9. Raeburn qtd. in Lloyd, "First Local Feature Film," 38; Burns, *Flickering Shadows*, 82.

10. Burns, *Flickering Shadows*, 227n67.

11. Raeburn qtd. in Lloyd, "First Local Feature Film," 38.

12. Ibid.; Raeburn interview; Reuters, "Zimbabwe's Mugabe Urges Blacks to 'Strike Fear in Heart of the White Man.'"

13. Makuvachuma qtd. in Lloyd, "First Local Feature Film," 38.

14. Qtd. in Burns, *Flickering Shadows*, 125.

15. Gwarinda, "Development Theory and the Role of Film," 84.

16. Heidegger, *Being and Time.*

17. Raeburn qtd. in Boni-Claverie, "When Gazelles Fly."

18. Gwarinda, "Development Theory and the Role of Film," 4.

19. Questionnaires #496, 579, 601; Johnson, *Yellow Card: Preview Assessment.*

20. Questionnaires #450, 340.

21. Questionnaires #348, 273, 396; Poblete, "New National Cinemas," 297; Thompson, "Imported Alternatives."

22. Johnson, *Yellow Card: Preview Assessment*, 9–10.

23. Burns, *Flickering Shadows.*

24. Questionnaires #496, 414, 333, 401.

25. Questionnaires #579, 402, 157.

26. Questionnaires #391, 385.

27. Questionnaires #143, 350, 79, 396.

28. Questionnaire #340.

29. Qtd. in Burns, *Flickering Shadows*, 143.

30. Questionnaires #333, 579, 323.

31. Johnson, *Yellow Card: Preview Assessment*, 18.

32. Kahari, *The Rise of the Shona Novel*, 84.

33. Questionnaires #360, 357, 234.

34. Johnson, *Yellow Card: Preview Assessment*, 26.

35. Collins, "Mammies, Matriarchs, and Other Controlling Images," 71.

36. Questionnaires #360, 386, 307.

37. Questionnaires #213, 231, 204.

38. Hungwe, "Putting Them in Their Place," 33.

39. Questionnaires #211, 165, 224.

40. Questionnaire #239.

41. Questionnaire #307.

42. Kahari, *The Rise of the Shona Novel*, 135.

43. Questionnaires #360, 386, 165, 333.

44. Kahari, *The Rise of the Shona Novel*, 216.

45. Gentile, *Film Feminisms*, 77; Hausmann, *Bending Tradition to the Changing Times.*

4. Changing the Channel

1. Morris, "Banality in Cultural Studies."

2. Wagnleitner and May, *Here, There, and Everywhere;* Larsen, *Import/Export;* Abercrombie, *Television and Society;* McAnany and Wilkinson, *Mass Media and Free Trade.*

3. Furusa, "Television, Culture, and Development in Zimbabwe"; Ngugi wa Mirii, "The State of Theatre in Zimbabwe"; Siwela, *"Dallas, Dynasty,* and Michael Jackson Prevail."

4. McAnany and Wilkinson, *Mass Media and Free Trade,* 18.

5. Hoskins, Finn, and McFadyen, "Television and Film in a Freer International Trade Environment," 66.

6. Mandizvidza, "ZBC/Joy Junkyards."

7. Andersen, "Television, Political Culture, and the Identity of Citizenship"; Andersen, "The Janus Face of Television in Small Countries"; Furusa, "Television, Culture, and Development in Zimbabwe"; Zindi, "Should the Media Be Concerned about the Legacy of Cultural Imperialism?"

8. Burns, "Watching Africans Watch Films"; Burns, "John Wayne on the Zambezi"; Burns, "A Source of Innocent Merriment"; Burns, *Flickering Shadows.*

9. Zulu, "African Movies and the Global Mainstream."

10. Mandizvidza, "ZBC/Joy Junkyards"; Furusa, "Television, Culture, and Development in Zimbabwe," 73, 79; Burns, "A Source of Innocent Merriment," 133.

11. Gecau, "Audience Responses to a Film in Rural Zimbabwe"; Capricorn Video Unit, *Directory of Film,* 14, 154.

12. Nell, *Images of Yesteryear;* Manhando qtd. in Rønning, "Democratisation Processes in Southern Africa," 12.

13. Auret and Jackson, "Policies and Legalities Surrounding Capital Radio."

14. Nell, *Images of Yesteryear;* Burns, "John Wayne on the Zambezi"; Burns, "A Source of Innocent Merriment"; Horne, *From the Barrel of a Gun,* 125.

15. Mashiri, "Representations of Blacks and the City," 110; Andersen, "The Janus Face of Television in Small Countries," 65.

16. Media Institute of Southern Africa, "No Trace to Documentaries."

17. Thompson, "Viewing the Foreign and the Local."

18. Probe Market Research, *Combined Summary,* 7; Probe Market Research, *2000 Zimbabwe All Media, Products and Services Survey,* fig. 3.

19. Probe Market Research, *2000 ZAMPS Survey,* fig. LIFE1A.

20. Mandizvidza, "ZBC/Joy Junkyards."

21. Probe Market Research, *2000 ZAMPS Survey,* fig. TVTJB, FAVB.

22. Allen, "As the World Turns," 117; Matelski, *Soap Operas Worldwide,* 153–54.

23. Matelski, *Soap Operas Worldwide,* 46; Mashiri, "Representations of Blacks and the City," 113.

24. California Newsreel, "Prime Time South Africa," http://newsreel.org/nav/title .asp?tc=CN0071.

25. Shepperson and Tager, "Reviews: Generations."

26. Matelski, *Soap Operas Worldwide,* 42.

27. Joy TV, "Joy TV—Family Entertainment: About Us."

28. Geraghty, *Women and Soap Opera,* 111.

29. Ang, "Melodramatic Identifications," 79.

30. Allen, "As the World Turns," 113.

31. Fiske, *Reading the Popular,* 3.

32. Brown, *Soap Opera and Women's Talk,* 54; Ang, *Watching Dallas;* Ang, "Melodramatic Identifications"; Geraghty, *Women and Soap Opera.*

33. Morley, *Television, Audiences, and Cultural Studies,* 155.

34. Morkel, "You'll Love This Station."

35. Morley, *Television, Audiences, and Cultural Studies,* 77; Arnsten, "You've Come a Long Way, Baby?"

36. Brown, *Soap Opera and Women's Talk,* xii–xiii.

37. Mashiri, "Representations of Blacks and the City," 110.

38. Geraghty, *Women and Soap Opera,* 131.

39. Tichatonga, "Contributions of Organisations and Ministries to Radio Programmes," 9.

40. Media Monitoring Project Zimbabwe, http://www.zimbabwesituation.com/jul15.html.

41. Andersen, "Television, Political Culture, and the Identity of Citizenship," 33; Mandizvidza, "ZBC/Joy Junkyards," W8; Viriri, "Bonnie and Clyde," 14.

42. Fiske, *Reading the Popular,* 176.

43. Ibid., 149.

44. Morley, *Television, Audiences, and Cultural Studies,* 82.

45. Andersen, "Television, Political Culture, and the Identity of Citizenship," 32.

46. Geraghty, *Women and Soap Opera,* 154; Press, "Class, Gender, and the Female Viewer: Women's Responses to *Dynasty,*" 163.

47. Maruma, "Indigenising the African Film," 30; Furusa, "Television, Culture, and Development in Zimbabwe," 79.

48. Moyo, "Development of Women in Broadcasting in Zimbabwe," 16; Mashiri, "Representations of Blacks and the City," 109.

49. Andersen, "Television, Political Culture, and the Identity of Citizenship," 35.

5. Power, Citizenship, and Local Content

1. Huckin, "Critical Discourse Analysis," 80.

2. Mazango, *Broadcasting;* Moyo qtd. in Ndlela, "Broadcasting Reforms in Southern Africa," 69.

3. Mazango, *Broadcasting;* Media Institute of Southern Africa (MISA), "Minister Goes Back on Promise."

4. Chimutengwende qtd. in MISA, "Minister Makes Commitment on Liberalising the Airwaves"; Mangin, *Filming Emerging Africa,* 65.

5. Mazango, *Broadcasting.*

6. MISA, "Supreme Court Rules against Monopoly of State Broadcaster."

7. Ndlela, "Broadcasting Reforms in Southern Africa"; Moyo, "From Rhodesia to Zimbabwe," 22; MISA, "Draconian New Broadcasting Regulations in Zimbabwe"; Mazango, *Broadcasting,* 39.

8. Moyo qtd. in "Rebel Radio"; Moyo qtd. in MISA, "Government Moves."

9. Gibbons, "Language and the Law," 158.

10. BSA, sec. 2.

11. BSA, schedule 3, para. 4.

12. BSA, pt. II, sec. 3.1.e, emphasis added; pt. II, sec. 3.1k; pt. IV, sec. 24.2a.

13. BSA, sec. 24.5.

14. Veit-Wild, "'Zimbolicious'—The Creative Potential of Linguistic Innovation," 688.

15. Fairclough, "Critical and Descriptive Goals in Discourse Analysis," 739.

16. BSA, schedule 6, sec. 3.1.

17. Mazango, *Broadcasting*, 43.

18. Panafrican News Agency, "Government Sets Up Media Watch Dog."

19. BSA, sec. 3.2.

20. Auret and Jackson, "Policies and Legalities Surrounding Capital Radio."

21. Mano, "The Media and Politics in Zimbabwe," 508.

6. Language as a Form of Social Change

1. Anderson, *Imagined Communities;* Chimhundu, "Language Standardization"; Mashiri, "Shona-English Code-Mixing"; Webb, *Language in South Africa.*

2. Fairclough, "A Reply to Henry Widdowson," 52.

3. Mashiri, "Representations of Blacks and the City," 111.

4. Cowling, "South Africa"; Barnes, *"Days* and *Bold."*

5. Barnard, "The Language of Multiculturalism," 49.

6. Lundby, "Going to Tsanzaguru," 30; Hungwe, "Media in the Primary Schools of Zimbabwe," 218–19, 222.

7. Thompson, "Viewing the Foreign and the Local."

8. Chen Chimutengwende, qtd. in Media Monitoring Project Zimbabwe, *Election 2000,* 98; emphasis added.

9. Capricorn Video Unit, *Directory of Film,* 106.

10. Canclini, "North Americans or Latin Americans?" 150.

11. Canclini, *Hybrid Cultures,* 104.

12. Kembo-Sure and Webb, "Languages in Competition," 114.

13. MISA, "Public Broadcaster and Information Minister Taken to Court over Ban of Television Program."

14. Livingstone and Lunt, *Talk on Television,* 2; Kim, Wyatt, and Katz, "News, Talk, Opinion, Participation."

15. Livingstone and Lunt, *Talk on Television,* 8; Andersen, "The Janus Face of Television in Small Countries," 52.

16. Mawere, "My Problem with Jonathan Moyo."

17. Court, "Dollar Falls, Transnational Dynamics, and Mediums of National Art," 10.

18. Media Monitoring Project Zimbabwe, *Election 2000;* Media Monitoring Project Zimbabwe, "Election 2002."

19. Kembo-Sure and Webb, "Languages in Competition," 119.

20. Andersen, "Television, Political Culture, and the Identity of Citizenship," 44.

21. Smith Mbedzi, qtd. in Mumpande, *Silent Voices,* 35.

22. Media Institute of Southern Africa, "Television Programme Banned"; Mawere, "My Problem with Jonathan Moyo."

23. MISA, "Public Broadcaster Ordered."

24. MISA, "MISA Zimbabwe Statement."

25. Meyer, "Voices from the Inside," 14.

26. Makoni, Brutt-Griffler, and Mashiri, "The Use of 'Indigenous' and Urban Vernaculars."

Conclusion

1. Taylor and Williams, "The Limits of Engagement"; Moyo and Yeros, "Intervention: The Zimbabwe Question and the Two Lefts."

2. AIDS-Free World, *Electing to Rape: Sexual Terror in Mugabe's Zimbabwe*, 10.

3. Mafundikwa, "About the Film."

4. Cheeseman and Tendi, "Power-Sharing in Comparative Perspective."

5. Mahaka, "The Soap," http://web.me.com/benmahaka/mahakamedia/Television.html.

6. "Newspaper Readership Surges"; Probe Market Research, *ZAMPS '99*.

7. Moyo, "ZBC Censors *Studio 263*"; Nunu, "Playwright Cont Breaks New Ground"; Muzari, "ZBC Dumps *Mai Chisamba Show.*"

8. Mhiripiri, "Thematic Concerns," 105.

9. Kumbuka, "Buffoons Masquerade as Comedians"; Moyo, "Trust Dead BC to Mess It Up!"

10. "Dangarembga Film Wins Milan Award."

11. Mhiripiri, "Thematic Concerns," 92.

12. Ibid.

13. Matema, qtd. in Mhiripiri, "Thematic Concerns"; Katedza, "Young Leaders Interview"; "The Axe and the Tree: Film Screening and Panel Discussion at NMF"; Mbanga, "We Need to Keep Telling Zimbabwe's Stories."

14. Bright, "Robert Mugabe, What Happened?"

15. Katedza, "Breaking Boundaries, Expanding Horizons," 13.

16. Guma, "Survey Reveals Increase in Internet Use"; "News Readership Up—ZAMPS"; "ZBC TV Viewership Hits Rock Bottom."

17. Pennycook, *Critical Applied Linguistics*, 2.

18. Katedza, "Young Leaders Interview."

19. "MultiChoice Zimbabwe."

20. Sundén, "I'm Still Not Sure She's a She," 291.

21. Connell, *Gender and Power*, 252.

BIBLIOGRAPHY

Abercrombie, Nicholas. *Television and Society.* Cambridge: Polity Press, 1996.

AIDS–Free World. *Electing to Rape: Sexual Terror in Mugabe's Zimbabwe.* New York: AIDS–Free World, 2009.

Allen, Robert C. "As the World Turns: Television Soap Operas and Global Media Culture." In *Mass Media and Free Trade: NAFTA and the Cultural Industries,* ed. Emile G. McAnany and Kenton T. Wilkinson, 110–27. Austin: University of Texas Press, 1996.

Andersen, Michael Bruun. "Television, Political Culture, and the Identity of Citizenship." *Critical Arts* 11, no. 1 (1997): 28–45.

———. "The Janus Face of Television in Small Countries: The Case of Zimbabwe." In *Perspectives on Media, Culture, and Democracy in Zimbabwe,* ed. Ragnar Waldahl, 45–68. Oslo: University of Oslo Department of Media and Communication, 1998.

Anderson, Benedict R. *Imagined Communities: Reflections on the Origin and Spread of Nationalism.* London: Verso, 1991.

Andersson, Jens A. "Reinterpreting the Rural-Urban Connection: Migration Practices and Socio-Cultural Dispositions of Buhera Workers in Harare." *Africa: Journal of the International African Institute* 71, no. 1 (2001): 82–112.

Ang, Ien. "Melodramatic Identifications: Television Fiction and Women's Fantasy." In *Television and Women's Culture: The Politics of the Popular,* ed. Mary Ellen Brown, 75–88. Newbury Park, CA: Sage, 1990.

———. *Watching Dallas: Soap Opera and the Melodramatic Imagination.* London: Methuen, 1985.

Appadurai, Arjun. "Disjuncture and Difference in the Global Cultural Economy." In *Planet TV: A Global Television Reader,* ed. Lisa Parks and Shanti Kumar, 40–52. New York: New York University Press, 2003.

Arnsten, Hilde. "'You've Come a Long Way, Baby?' Some Questions of Gender Representation in Zimbabwean Women's Magazines." In *Perspectives on Media, Culture, and Democracy in Zimbabwe,* ed. Ragnar Waldahl, 82–114. Oslo: University of Oslo Department of Media and Communication, 1998.

Auret, Mike, and Gerry Jackson. "Policies and Legalities Surrounding Capital Radio." *Afrol News,* 2000. http://www.afrol.com/html/Countries/Zimbabwe/backgr_capitol_radio.htm.

Barber, Karin. "Audiences in Africa." *Africa: Journal of the International African Institute* 67, no. 3 (1997): 347–64.

Barlet, Oliver. *African Cinemas: Decolonizing the Gaze.* New York: Zed Books, 2000.

Barnard, Ian. "The Language of Multiculturalism in South African Soaps and Sitcoms." *Journal of Multicultural Discourses* 1, no. 1 (2006): 39–59.

Barnes, Teresa. "*Days* and *Bold:* The Fascination of Soap Operas for Black Students at the University of the Western Cape, South Africa." In *Leisure in Urban Africa,* ed.

Tiyambe Zeleza and Cassandra Rachel Veney, 343–56. Trenton, NJ: Africa World Press, 2003.

Blommaert, Jan. *Discourse: A Critical Introduction*. Cambridge: Cambridge University Press, 2005.

Boni-Claverie, Isabelle. "When Gazelles Fly: An Inventory of Cinema." *Revue Noire* 28 (May 1998): 58–61.

Bright, Simon. "Robert Mugabe, What Happened?" Movie Page. *Facebook*, n.d. https://www.facebook.com/mugabemovie.

———."Video for Extension Workers in Zimbabwe." *Media in Education and Development* 18, no. 4 (December 1985): 171–74.

British Broadcasting Corporation. *Report by the Study Group on the Future of Broadcasting in Zimbabwe*. Harare: BBC, 1980.

Brown, Mary Ellen. *Soap Opera and Women's Talk: The Pleasure of Resistance*. Thousand Oaks, CA: Sage, 1994.

Brown, William J., and Arvind Singhal. "Ethical Considerations of Promoting Prosocial Messages through the Popular Media." *Journal of Popular Film and Television* 21, no. 3 (Fall 1993): 92–100.

Bruner, Jerome. "A Narrative Model of Self-Construction." *Annals of the New York Academy of Sciences* 818 (2006): 145–61.

———. "Self-Making and World-Making." *Journal of Aesthetic Education* 25, no. 1 (Spring 1991): 67–78.

Bruner, Jerome, and Susan Weisser. "The Invention of Self: Autobiography and Its Forms." In *Literacy and Orality*, ed. David R. Olson and Nancy Torrance. Cambridge: Cambridge University Press, 1991.

Burns, James. "A Source of Innocent Merriment: Cinema and Society in Colonial Zimbabwe." *South African Historical Journal* 48 (May 2003): 130–37.

———. *Flickering Shadows: Cinema and Identity in Colonial Zimbabwe*. Athens: Ohio University Press, 2002.

———. "John Wayne on the Zambezi: Cinema, Empire, and the American Western in British Central Africa." *International Journal of African Historical Studies* 35, no. 1 (2002): 103–17.

———. "Watching Africans Watch Films: Theories of Spectatorship in British Colonial Africa." *Historical Journal of Film, Radio, and Television* 20, no. 2 (2000): 197–211.

Bush, Ray, and Morris Szeftel. "Editorial: Sovereignty, Democracy, and Zimbabwe's Tragedy." *Review of African Political Economy* 29, no. 91 (March 2002): 5–20.

Campbell, Horace. *Reclaiming Zimbabwe: The Exhaustion of the Patriarchal Model of Liberation*. Claremont, South Africa: David Philip, 2003.

Canclini, Nestor García. *Hybrid Cultures: Strategies for Entering and Leaving Modernity*. Minneapolis: University of Minnesota Press, 1989.

———. "North Americans or Latin Americans? The Redefinition of Mexican Identity and the Free Trade Agreements." In *Mass Media and Free Trade: NAFTA and the Cultural Industries*, ed. Emile G. McAnany and Kenton T. Wilkinson, 142–56. Austin: University of Texas Press, 1996.

Capricorn Video Unit. *Directory of Film and Video Distribution Networks in Zimbabwe.* Harare, August 1993.

Cheeseman, Nic, and Blessing Miles Tendi. "Power-Sharing in Comparative Perspective: The Dynamics of 'Unity Government' in Kenya and Zimbabwe." *Journal of Modern African Studies* 48, no. 2 (2010): 203–29.

Chimhundu, Herbert. "Language Standardization without Policy or Planning: Zimbabwe as a Case Study." In *Language Contact and Language Conflict.* Volda: Volda College, 1997.

———. "The Status of African Languages in Zimbabwe." *Southern Africa Political and Economic Monthly* 7, no. 1 (October 1993): 57–59.

Chiumbu, Sarah. "Redefining the National Agenda: Media and Identity—Challenges of Building a New Zimbabwe." In *Media, Public Discourse, and Political Contestation in Zimbabwe,* ed. Henning Melber, 29–35. Uppsala: Nordiska Afrikainstitutet, 2004.

Chiwome, Emmanuel Mudhiwa. "The Interface of Orality and Literacy in the Zimbabwean Novel." *Research in African Literatures* 29, no. 2 (Summer 1998): 1–22.

Collins, Patricia Hill. "Mammies, Matriarchs, and Other Controlling Images." In *Feminist Philosophies,* ed. Janet A. Kourany, James P. Sterba, and Rosemarie Tong, 119. Englewood Cliffs: Prentice Hall, 1990.

Comaroff, Jean, and John L. Comaroff. "Naturing the Nation: Aliens, Apocalypse, and the Postcolonial State." *Journal of Southern African Studies* 27, no. 3 (2001): 627–51.

Connell, Raewyn W. *Gender and Power: Society, the Person, and Sexual Politics.* Cambridge: Polity Press in association with B. Blackwell, 1987.

Court, Elsbeth Joyce. "Dollar Falls, Transnational Dynamics, and Mediums of National Art." *African Arts* 42, no. 2 (June 1, 2009): 9–11.

Cowling, Lesley. "South Africa." In *Global Entertainment Media,* ed. Anne Cooper-Chen, 115–30. London: Routledge, 2005.

"Dangarembga Film Wins Milan Award." *Zimbabwe Standard,* April 10, 2005. http://docs.newsbank.com

Dangarembga, Tsitsi. "Film in Zimbabwe." Interview by Mai Palmberg, August 8, 2003. http://www.nai.uu.se/research/areas/cultural_images_in_and_of/zimbabwe/film/dangarembga/

———. *Nervous Conditions.* Harare: Zimbabwe Publishing House, 1988.

Derges, Anne. "Bringing Our Cinema Home." *Southern Africa Political and Economic Monthly* 6, nos. 3/4 (1992): 48–49.

Desai, Gaurav. "Theater as Praxis: Discursive Strategies in African Popular Theater." *African Studies Review* 33, no. 1 (April 1990): 65–92.

Diawara, Manthia. *African Cinema: Politics and Culture.* Bloomington: Indiana University Press, 1992.

Edmondson, Laura. "National Erotica: The Politics of 'Traditional' Dance in Tanzania." *Drama Review* 45, no. 1 (Spring 2001): 153–70.

Engelke, Matthew. "Text and Performance in an African Church: The Book, 'Live and Direct.'" *American Ethnologist* 31, no. 1 (2004): 76–91.

Epprecht, Marc. "The 'Unsaying' of Indigenous Homosexualities in Zimbabwe: Mapping a Blindspot in an African Masculinity." *Journal of Southern African Studies* 24, no. 4 (1998): 631–51.

Fairclough, Norman. "A Reply to Henry Widdowson's 'Discourse Analysis: A Critical View.'" *Language and Literature* 5, no. 1 (1996): 49–56.

———. "Critical and Descriptive Goals in Discourse Analysis." *Journal of Pragmatics* 9, no. 6 (1985): 739–63.

———. *Critical Discourse Analysis: The Critical Study of Language.* Harlow, UK: Longman, 1995.

———. *Discourse and Social Change.* Cambridge: Polity Press, 1992.

Fiske, John. *Reading the Popular.* London: Routledge, 1989.

Frederikse, Julie. *None but Ourselves: Masses vs. the Media in the Making of Zimbabwe.* Harare: Zimbabwe Publishing House, 1982.

Furusa, Munashe. "Television, Culture, and Development in Zimbabwe." In *Indigenous Knowledge and Technology in African and Diaspora Communities: Multi-Disciplinary Approaches,* ed. E. Chiwome, Z. Mguni, and Munashe Furusa, 73–87. Harare: Southern African Association for Culture and Development Studies, 2000.

Garlake, P. S. "Prehistory and Ideology in Zimbabwe." *Africa: Journal of the International African Institute* 52, no. 3 (1982): 1–19.

Gecau, Kimani. "Audience Responses to a Film in Rural Zimbabwe." *Journal of Social Development in Africa* 16, no. 1 (January 1, 2001): 45–83.

Gentile, Mary C. *Film Feminisms.* Westport: Greenwood Press, 1985.

Geraghty, Christine. *Women and Soap Opera: A Study of Prime Time Soaps.* Cambridge: Polity Press, 1991.

Gibbons, John. "Language and the Law." *Annual Review of Applied Linguistics* 19 (2003): 156–73.

Gikandi, Simon. *Maps of Englishness: Writing Identity in the Culture of Colonialism.* New York: Columbia University Press, 1996.

Government of Zimbabwe. Broadcasting Services Act, 2001. http://www.kubatana.net/html/archive/legisl/010404broa.asp

———. *The Democratization of the Media in Independent Zimbabwe.* Ministry of Information, Posts, and Telecommunications, November 1988.

———. "Why You Should Film in Zimbabwe!" Government of Zimbabwe, May 1985.

Guma, Lance. "Survey Reveals Increase in Internet Use in Zimbabwe." *SW Radio Africa News,* February 18, 2011. http://www.swradioafrica.com

Gwarinda, Shingai. "Development Theory and the Role of Film in Colonial and Post-colonial Zimbabwe." MA thesis, University of Zimbabwe, 2000.

Gwyn, Richard. "'Really Unreal': Narrative Evaluation and the Objectification of Experience." *Narrative Inquiry* 10, no. 2 (2000): 313–40.

Hadland, Adrian. *Re-visioning Television: Policy, Strategy, and Models for the Sustainable Development of Community Television in South Africa.* Cape Town: HSRC Press, 2006.

Hall, Stuart. "Cultural Identity and Diaspora." In *Theorizing Diaspora: A Reader,* ed. Jana Evans Braziel and Anita Mannur, 233–46. Malden, MA: Blackwell, 1990.

Hammar, Amanda. "The Making and Unma(s)king of Local Government in Zimbabwe." In *Zimbabwe's Unfinished Business: Rethinking Land, State, and Nation in the Context of Crisis,* ed. Amanda Hammar, Stig Jensen, and Brian Raftopoulos, 119–54. Harare, Zimbabwe: Weaver Press, 2003.

Harrow, Kenneth W. *African Cinema: Postcolonial and Feminist Readings.* Trenton, NJ: Africa World Press, 1999.

———. *Postcolonial African Cinema: From Political Engagement to Postmodernism.* Bloomington: Indiana University Press, 2007.

Hausmann, Christine. *Bending Tradition to the Changing Times: The Use of Video as an Empowerment Tool in Nonformal Adult Education in Zimbabwe.* Frankfurt am Main: IKO—Verlag für Interkulturelle Kommunikation, 2004.

Heidegger, Martin. *Being and Time.* Trans. John Macquarrie and Edward Robinson. New York: HarperPerennial/Modern Thought, 2008.

Higham, Bill. "Face from the Past a Real Jolt." *Out of Africa International* 1, no. 4 (April 2000): 35–36.

Hoad, Neville. "Between the White Man's Burden and the White Man's Disease: Tracking Lesbian and Gay Human Rights in Southern Africa." *GLQ: A Journal of Lesbian and Gay Studies* 5, no. 4 (1999): 559.

Honeyman, Russell. *1986 Audio Visual Zimbabwe: A Multimedia Production Directory.* Harare: Furco, 1986.

Horne, Gerald. *From the Barrel of a Gun: The United States and the War against Zimbabwe, 1965–1980.* Southern Africa Political Economy series. Chapel Hill: University of North Carolina Press, 2001.

Hoskins, Colin, Adam Finn, and Stuart McFadyen. "Television and Film in a Freer International Trade Environment: U.S. Dominance and Canadian Responses." In *Mass Media and Free Trade: NAFTA and the Cultural Industries,* ed. Emile G. McAnany and Kenton T. Wilkinson, 63–91. Austin: University of Texas Press, 1996.

Hove, Chenjerai, Chido Makunike, and Ish Mafundikwa. Comments presented at the Local Content Panel, Book Café, Harare, August 8, 2001.

Huckin, Thomas. "Critical Discourse Analysis." In *Functional Approaches to Written Text: Classroom Applications,* ed. Tom Miller, 78–101. Washington, DC: United States Information Agency (USIA), 1997. http://eric.ed.gov

Hungwe, Chipo. "Putting Them in Their Place: 'Respectable' and 'Unrespectable' Women in Zimbabwean Gender Struggles." *Feminist Africa* 6, Subaltern Sexualities (2006).

Hungwe, Kedmon. "Media in the Primary Schools of Zimbabwe: An Analysis with Special Reference to Children's Entertainment Films." PhD diss., University of Wisconsin, Madison, 1987.

———. "Narrative and Ideology: Fifty Years of Film-making in Zimbabwe." *Media, Culture, and Society* 27, no. 1 (2005): 83–99.

Jeater, Diana. *Law, Language, and Science: The Invention of the "Native Mind" in Southern Rhodesia, 1890–1930.* Portsmouth, NH: Heinemann, 2007.

Johnson, T. *Yellow Card: Preview Assessment of the John Riber Film in Five Countries of Sub-Saharan Africa.* Harare: Population Communication Africa, January 2000.

Kahari, G. P. *The Rise of the Shona Novel: A Study in Development, 1890–1984*. Gweru: Mambo Press, 1995.

Kangai, Tirivafi. "Radio and Television Expansion in Zimbabwe." *Combroad* 59 (April 1982): 10–12.

———. "Radio as a Medium of Mass Communication." In *ZBC radio 4 seminar*, 40–43. Harare: Zimbabwe Broadcasting Corporation, 1984.

Kapasula, Jessie Kabwila. "The African Public Space, Patriarchy, and Women's Dressing: Where Patriarchy Stumbles and Sometimes Falls Apart: Feminist Agency in the Public Space of Dangarembga's *Neria*." Presented at the CODESRIA 12th General Assembly, Yaounde, Cameroon: Council for the Development of Social Science Research in Africa, December 7, 2008.

Kark, Austen. "Broadcasting in Zimbabwe." *Combroad* 47 (June 1980): 10–14.

Katedza, Rumbi. "Breaking Boundaries, Expanding Horizons." *Vertigo* 2, no. 6 (Spring 2004): 13–14.

———. "Young Leaders Interview." Interview by BMW Foundation. Video recording, April 13, 2011. http://www.youtube.com/watch?v=HQPulNZb4uc

Kembo-Sure and Vic Webb. "Languages in Competition." In *African Voices: An Introduction to the Languages and Linguistics of Africa*, ed. Vic Webb and Kembo-Sure, 109–32. Oxford: Oxford University Press, 2000.

Kerr, David. "The Best of Both Worlds? Colonial Film Policy and Practice in Northern Rhodesia and Nyasaland." *Critical Arts* 7 (1993): 11–42.

Kim, Joohan, Robert O. Wyatt, and Elihu Katz. "News, Talk, Opinion, Participation: The Part Played by Conversation in Deliberative Democracy." *Political Communication* 16, no. 4 (1999): 361–85.

Kumbuka, Desmond. "Buffoons Masquerade as Comedians." *Zimbabwe Standard*, October 5, 2003. http://docs.newsbank.com

Lafon, Michael. "Shona Class 5 Revisited: A Case against *ri- as Class 5 Nominal Prefix." *Zambezia* 21, no. 1 (1994): 51–80.

Lamb, Christina. *House of Stone: The True Story of a Family Divided in War-Torn Zimbabwe*. Chicago: Lawrence Hill Books, 2007.

Larsen, Peter. *Import/Export: International Flow of Television Fiction*. Paris: UNESCO, 1990.

Lee, Christopher Joon-Hai. "Desperately Seeking Tsitsi: A Conversation with Tsitsi Dangarembga." *Transition* 96 (2006): 128–50.

Liebes, Tamar, and Elihu Katz. *The Export of Meaning: Cross-Cultural Readings of* Dallas. Hoboken, NJ: Wiley-Blackwell, 1993.

Livingstone, Sonia M., and Peter Kenneth Lunt. *Talk on Television: Audience Participation and Public Debate*. London: Routledge, 1994.

Lloyd, Fiona. "First Local Feature Film: *Jit* Is It—Zimbabwean All the Way." *Africa South* (August 1990): 38–39.

Loomba, Ania. *Colonialism–Postcolonialism*. London: Routledge, 1998.

Lund, Giuliana. "Harmonizing the Nation: Women's Voices and Development in Zimbabwean Cinema." *City & Society* 11, nos. 1–2 (1999): 213–35.

Lundby, Knut. "Going to Tsanzaguru; Communication and Identity: A Case Study." In *Perspectives on Media, Culture, and Democracy in Zimbabwe,* ed. Ragnar Waldahl, 24–35. Oslo: University of Oslo Department of Media and Communication, 1998.

Lunga, Violet Bridget. "An Examination of an African Postcolonial Experience of Language, Culture, and Identity: Amakhosi Theatre, Ako Bulawayo, Zimbabwe." PhD diss., Simon Fraser University, 1997.

Mabaso, Clemence. "Southern Africa's Film Makers Fight to Control Distribution." *Southern Africa Political and Economic Monthly* 6, no. 10 (July 1993): 29–30.

Mafundikwa, Saki. "About the Film." *Shungu—The Resilience of a People,* 2009. http://shungu.maumbile.com/synopsis.

Makoni, Busi, Sinfree Makoni, and Pedzisai Mashiri. "Naming Practices and Language Planning in Zimbabwe." *Current Issues in Language Planning* 8, no. 3 (2007): 437–67.

Makoni, Sinfree, Busi Dube, and Pedzisai Mashiri. "Zimbabwe Colonial and Post-Colonial Language Policy and Planning Practices." *Current Issues in Language Planning* 7, no. 4 (2006): 377–414.

Makoni, Sinfree, Janina Brutt-Griffler, and Pedzisai Mashiri. "The Use of 'Indigenous' and Urban Vernaculars in Zimbabwe." *Language in Society* 36, no. 1 (February 2007): 25–49.

Mandizvidza, Tazzen. "ZBC/Joy Junkyards of Outdated Western Movies." *Zimbabwe Mirror.* Harare, February 9, 2001.

Mangin, Geoffrey. *Filming Emerging Africa: A Pioneer Cinematographer's Scrapbook from the 1940s to the 1960s.* Cape Town: Het Ronde Doornbosjen, 1998.

Mano, Winston. "The Media and Politics in Zimbabwe: Turning Left While Indicating Right." *Harvard International Journal of Press/Politics* 13, no. 4 (2008): 507–14.

———. "Indigenising the African Film." *Southern Africa Political and Economic Monthly* 6, no. 6 (March 1993): 30.

Mashiri, Pedzisai. "Representations of Blacks and the City in the Zimbabwean Post-Independence Television Drama." In *Orality and Cultural Identities in Zimbabwe,* ed. Maurice Taonezvi Vambe, 105–16. Gweru, Harare, and Masvingo: Mambo Press, 2001.

———. "Shona-English Code-Mixing in the Speech of Students at the University of Zimbabwe." *Southern African Linguistics and Applied Language Studies* 20, no. 4 (2002): 245–61.

Matelski, Marilyn J. *Soap Operas Worldwide: Cultural and Serial Realities.* Jefferson, NC: McFarland, 1999.

Mawere, Mutumwa. "My Problem with Jonathan Moyo." *newzimbabwe.com,* 2006. http://www.newzimbabwe.com/pages/mawere20.14259.html

Mazango, Eric. *Broadcasting and Telecommunications Law in Zimbabwe.* Harare: Media Institute of Southern Africa–Zimbabwe Chapter, 2001.

Mbanga, Wilf. "We Need to Keep Telling Zimbabwe's Stories." *Business Day.* Johannesburg, March 2, 2011. http://docs.newsbank.com

McAnany, Emile G., and Kenton T. Wilkinson, eds. *Mass Media and Free Trade: NAFTA and the Cultural Industries.* Austin: University of Texas Press, 1996.

Media Institute of Southern Africa. "Draconian Media Bill Passed in Zimbabwe,"
    December 3, 2001. http://www.misa.org/oldsite/alerts/20011203.
    zimbabwe.1.html

———. "Draconian New Broadcasting Regulations in Zimbabwe." *Afrol News,*
    October 13, 2000. http://www.afrol.com/

———. "Minister Goes Back on Promise to Liberalise Broadcasting." *Afrol News,*
    September 20, 2000. http://www.afrol.com/html/News/zim035_broadcasting.htm

———. "Minister Makes Commitment on Liberalising the Airwaves." *MISAZIM,* June 15,
    2000. http://www.misa.org/

———. "Minister Orders the Resignation of Entire State-Broadcasting Board." *MISAZIM,*
    October 15, 1998. http://www.misazim.co.zw

———. "MISA Zimbabwe Statement on the Banning of the NDA Sponsored
    Programme," June 7, 2001. http://www.misa.org/oldsite/alerts/20010607
    .zimbabwe.1.html

———. "No Trace to Documentaries as Viewers Accuse Broadcasters," September 11,
    1997. http://www.misa.org/oldsite/alerts/19970911.zimbabwe.1.html

———. "Public Broadcaster and Information Minister Taken to Court over Ban of
    Television Program." November 13, 2001. http://www.misa.org/oldsite/
    alerts/20011113.zimbabwe.0.html

———. "Public Broadcaster Ordered to Bring Back Banned Programme," May 31, 2002.
    http://www.misa.org/oldsite/alerts/20020531.zimbabwe.1.html

———. "Supreme Court Rules against Monopoly of State Broadcaster." *Afrol News,*
    September 25, 2000. http://www.afrol.com/

———. "Television Programme Banned," June 6, 2001. http://www.misa.org/oldsite/
    alerts/20010606.zimbabwe.0.html

Media Monitoring Project Zimbabwe. *Election 2000: The Media War.* Harare: Media
    Monitoring Project Zimbabwe, 2000.

———. "Election 2002: ZBC a Tool for Zanu PF Propaganda." 2002. http://www.mmpz
    .org.zw/advocacy/elect.htm

Mhando, Martin. "Approaches to African Cinema Study." *Sense of Cinema* 8 (July 18,
    2000). http://www.sensesofcinema.com/2000/8/african/

Mhiripiri, Nhamo Anthony. "Thematic Concerns in the Emergent Zimbabwean Short
    Film Genre." *Journal of African Cinemas* 2, no. 2 (December 2010): 91–109.

Miller, Daniel. "*The Young and the Restless* in Trinidad." In *Consuming Technologies,*
    ed. Roger Silverstone and Eric Hirsch. London: Routledge, 1992.

Morkel, Keith. "You'll Love This Station." *Zimbabwe Review* (January 1998): 28–29.

Morley, David. *Television, Audiences, and Cultural Studies.* London: Routledge, 1992.

Morris, Meaghan. "Banality in Cultural Studies." *Discourse* 10, no. 2 (1988): 3–29.

Moyo, Dumisani. "From Rhodesia to Zimbabwe: Change without Change? Broadcasting
    Policy Reform and Political Control." In *Media, Public Discourse, and Political
    Contestation in Zimbabwe,* ed. Henning Melber, 12–28. Uppsala: Nordiska
    Afrikainstitutet, 2004.

Moyo, Mavis. "Development of Women in Broadcasting in Zimbabwe." *Combroad*, no. 77 (1987): 15–24.

Moyo, Peter. "Trust Dead BC to Mess It Up!" *Zimbabwe Standard*, February 16, 2003. http://docs.newsbank.com

———. "ZBC Censors Studio 263." *Zimbabwe Standard*, March 2, 2003. http://docs .newsbank.com

Moyo, Sam, and Paris Yeros. "Intervention: The Zimbabwe Question and the Two Lefts." *Historical Materialism* 15 (September 2007): 171–204.

Muchemwa, Kizito Z. "Galas, Biras, State Funerals, and the Necropolitan Imagination in Reconstructions of the Zimbabwean Nation, 1980–2008." *Social Dynamics* 36, no. 3 (2010): 504–14.

"MultiChoice Zimbabwe." *DStv Africa*, 2009. http://www.dstvafrica.com/dstvafrica/ content/en/zimbabwe/

Mumpande, Isaac. *Silent Voices: Indigenous Languages in Zimbabwe: A Report*. Avondale, Harare: Sable Press, 2006.

Munjoma, Leonisa. "A New Look: African Film Makers on Their Mettle." *Africa South* (June 1990): 38.

Muzari, Godwin. "ZBC Dumps Mai Chisamba Show." *Zimbabwe Standard*, June 20, 2009. http://docs.newsbank.com

Ndlela, Nkosi. "Broadcasting Reforms in Southern Africa: Continuity and Change in the Era of Globalisation." *Westminster Papers in Communication and Culture* 4 (2007): 3.

Ndumbu, Abel. "Africa." In *Import/Export: International Flow of Television Fiction*, ed. Peter Larsen. Paris: UNESCO, 1990.

Neill, Howard. "Re: [AlanB] Help—Need a Song or Two or Three," June 16, 2005. http://www.videouniversity.com/

Nell, Louis. *Images of Yesteryear: Film-making in Central Africa*. Harare: Harper Collins, 1998.

"News Readership Up—ZAMPS." *Zimbabwean*. Harare, February 16, 2011. http://www .thezimbabwean.co.uk

"Newspaper Readership Surges, TV Slumps in Q4 2010." *BizCommunity.com*, February 18, 2011. http://www.bizcommunity.com/Article/196/19/56907.html

Ngugi wa Mirii. "The State of Theatre in Zimbabwe." *Journal on Social Change and Development*, nos. 42/43 (August 1997): 19–20.

Nunu, Leslie. "Playwright Cont Breaks New Ground with Comedy DVD." *Zimbabwe Standard*, August 2, 2008. http://docs.newsbank.com

O'Grady, Vaughan. "Shows of Independence." *TV World* 11 (October 1988): 119–20.

Panafrican News Agency. "Government Sets Up Media Watch Dog." *allAfrica.com*, December 12, 2000. http://allafrica.com/

Partridge, Derek. "About Derek." *Derek Partridge*, n.d. http://www.derekpartridge.com/ aboutDerek.php

Pennycook, Alastair. *Critical Applied Linguistics: A Critical Introduction*. Mahwah, NJ: L. Erlbaum, 2001.

Philander, Frederick. "Hard Won Progress in Local Film Industry." *Namibian,*
    September 4, 1998, sec. Arts and Entertainment. http://www.namibian.com.na/
    Netstories/Arts8-98/scriptwriters.html

Pickard, Nicole. "Rhodesian Nostalgia," 2006. http://www.nicolepickard.com/rhodesia/
    rhodesians.html

Poblete, Juan. "New National Cinemas in a Transnational Age." *Discourse* 26 (2004):
    214–34.

Potter, Jonathan. *Representing Reality: Discourse, Rhetoric, and Social Construction.*
    Thousand Oaks, CA: Sage, 1996.

Press, Andrea. "Class, Gender, and the Female Viewer: Women's Responses to *Dynasty.*"
    In *Television and Women's Culture: The Politics of the Popular,* ed. M. E Brown, 158–80.
    Newbury Park; CA: Sage, 1990.

Probe Market Research. *2000 Zimbabwe All Media, Products and Services Survey.* Harare:
    Probe Market Research, July 2000.

———. *Combined Summary of Adult and Teen Zimbabwe All Media and Products and Services
    Survey 2000.* Harare: Probe Market Research, 2000.

———. *ZAMPS '99 Radio & TV Diary, Volume One.* Harare: Probe Market Research, 1999.

Raeburn, Michael. Interview by Kedmon Hungwe, 2001. http://www.ed.mtu.edu/
    ~khungwe/afrika/

"Rebel Radio." *Africa Film & TV,* January 2001: 11. http://www.africafilmtv.com/pages/
    archive/magazines/afm27e/broadcastnews.htm

Reuters. "Zimbabwe's Mugabe Urges Blacks to 'Strike Fear in Heart of the White Man.'"
    CNN, December 14, 2000.

Roberts, John. "RBC: Rhodesian Broadcasting Corporation: Memories." Interview by
    MaryAnne (a.k.a. The Pumamouse), January 2004. http://pumamouse.com/
    RBCessayJRmemories.html

Rønning, Helge. "Democratisation Processes in Southern Africa and the Role of the
    Media." In *Perspectives on Media, Culture, and Democracy in Zimbabwe,* ed. Ragnar
    Waldahl, 4–23. Oslo: University of Oslo Department of Media and Communication,
    1998.

Shepperson, A., and M. Tager. "Reviews: Generations." *Culture, Communication, and
    Media Studies,* 1998. http://ccms.ukzn.ac.za/index.php?option=com_content&task
    =view&id=214&Itemid=43

Siwela, Winston. "*Dallas, Dynasty,* and Michael Jackson Prevail: African Culture Not
    Given Enough Attention, Delegates at Conference Complain." *Africa South,* August
    1990, 39.

Smyth, Rosaleen. "The British Colonial Film Unit and Sub-Saharan Africa, 1939–1945."
    Historical Journal of Film, Radio, and Television 8, no. 3 (1988): 285–98.

———. "The Development of British Colonial Film Policy, 1927–1939, with Special
    Reference to East and Central Africa." *Journal of African History* 20, no. 3 (1979):
    437–50.

Stapleton, Chris, and Chris May. *African Rock: The Pop Music of a Continent.* New York:
    Dutton, 1990.

Summer Institute of Linguistics. "Ethnologue: Top 100 Languages by Population," February 1999. http://paginaspersonales.deusto.es/abaitua/konzeptu/nlp/top100.htm

Sundén, Jenny. "'I'm Still Not Sure She's a She': Textual Talk and Typed Bodies in Online Interaction." In *Talking Gender and Sexuality*, ed. Paul McIlvenny, 289–312. Philadelphia: John Benjamins, 2002.

Taylor, Ian, and Paul Williams. "The Limits of Engagement: British Foreign Policy and the Crisis in Zimbabwe." *International Affairs (Royal Institute of International Affairs 1944–)* 78, no. 3 (July 2002): 547–65.

"Telly Five Club." Facebook Group Forum. *Old Zim Memories*, March 13, 2009. http://sv.facebook.com/topic.php?uid=2314887761&topic=3072

"The Axe and the Tree: Film Screening and Panel Discussion at NMF." *International Center for Transitional Justice*, 2011. http://ictj.org/event/axe-and-tree-film-screening-and-panel-discussion-nmf

Thompson, Katrina Daly. "Imported Alternatives: Changing Shona Masculinities in *Flame* and *Yellow Card*." In *Men in African Film and Fiction*, ed. Lahoucine Ouzgane, 100–112. James Currey, 2011.

———. "Viewing the Foreign and the Local in Zimbabwe: Film, Television, and Shona Viewers." PhD diss., University of Wisconsin, Madison, 2004.

Tichatonga, Grey. "Contributions of Organisations and Ministries to Radio Programmes." In *ZBC Radio 4 Seminar: Radio and Community Development, 3rd & 4th December 1983*, 8–11. Harare: Zimbabwe Broadcasting Corporation Radio 4, 1984.

———. "Developing a Contemporary Television System in Zimbabwe." *Combroad 86* (March 1990): 21–22.

Turino, Thomas. "Are We Global Yet? Globalist Discourse, Cultural Formations, and the Study of Zimbabwean Popular Music." *British Journal of Ethnomusicology* 12, no. 2 (2003): 51–79.

———. *Nationalists, Cosmopolitans, and Popular Music in Zimbabwe*. Chicago: University of Chicago Press, 2000.

Ukadike, N. Frank. *Black African Cinema*. Berkeley: University of California Press, 1994.

———. *Questioning African Cinema: Conversations with Filmmakers*. Minneapolis: University of Minnesota Press, 2002.

"Union of National Radio & Television Orgs. of Africa (URTNA)," June 12, 1994. http://www.africa.upenn.edu/Audio_Visual/Union_19589.html

URTNA. "The Renaissance of a Continental Union." *Union of National Radio and Television Organizations of Africa*, n.d. http://urtna.org/EN/indexENG.html.

Veit-Wild, Flora. "'Zimbolicious'—The Creative Potential of Linguistic Innovation: The Case of Shona-English in Zimbabwe." *Journal of Southern African Studies 35*, no. 3 (2009): 683–97.

Velasco, Jovenal D. "Imitation and Indigenization in Filipino Melodramas of the 1950s." *Asia Culture Forum* (2006): 46–59.

Wagnleitner, Reinhold, and Elaine Tyler May, eds. *"Here, There, and Everywhere": The Foreign Politics of American Popular Culture*. Hanover, NH: University Press of New England, 2000.

Webb, Victor N. *Language in South Africa: The Role of Language in National Transformation, Reconstruction, and Development.* Philadelphia: John Benjamins, 2002.

Weedon, Chris. *Feminist Practice and Poststructuralist Theory.* Oxford: B. Blackwell, 1987.

White, Luise. *The Assassination of Herbert Chitepo: Texts and Politics in Zimbabwe.* Bloomington: Indiana University Press, 2003.

Windrich, Elaine. *The Mass Media in the Struggle for Zimbabwe: Censorship and Propaganda under Rhodesian Front Rule.* Gwelo [Gweru]: Mambo Press, 1981.

Worby, Eric. "The End of Modernity in Zimbabwe? Passages from Development to Sovereignty." In *Zimbabwe's Unfinished Business: Rethinking Land, State, and Nation in the Context of Crisis,* ed. Amanda Hammar, Stig Jensen, and Brian Raftopoulos, 49–81. Harare, Zimbabwe: Weaver Press, 2003.

Zaffiro, James J. *Media & Democracy in Zimbabwe, 1931–2002.* Colorado Springs, CO: International Academic Publishers, 2002.

"ZBC TV Viewership Hits Rock Bottom." *Zimbabwe Standard,* February 20, 2011. http://docs.newsbank.com

Zindi, Fred. "Should the Media Be Concerned about the Legacy of Cultural Imperialism?" *Southern Africa Political and Economic Monthly* 6 (November 1992): 52–53.

Zook, Kristal Brent. *Color by Fox: The Fox Network and the Revolution in Black Television.* New York: Oxford University Press, 1999.

Zulu, Ben. "African Movies and the Global Mainstream." Interview by Kedmon Hungwe, July 6, 2000. http://www.ed.mtu.edu/~khungwe/afrika/

Interviews with Culture Workers

Arsenault, Amelia. At the Zimbabwe International Film Festival offices, Harare, April 11, 2001.

Auret, Michael, Sr. At his home, Harare, April 10, 2001.

Bhagat, Heeten. At a café, Avondale, Harare, May 14, 2001.

Birdas, Ernie. At my home, Harare, January 23, 2001.

Bright, Simon. At the Zimmedia offices, Harare, April 25, 2001.

———. Via email, August 16, 2011.

Chidzawo, Dorothy. At ZBC, Harare, May 15, 2001.

Chikuhwa, Arthur. At the Capricorn Video Unit offices, Harare, April 6, 2001.

Chimedza, Albert. At the National Gallery of Zimbabwe, Harare, April 4, 2001.

Chisamba, Rebecca. At her home, Harare, March 27, 2001.

Dangarembga, Tsitsi. Via telephone, June 21, 2011.

Dore, Geven. At Mighty Movies offices, Harare, January 16, 2001.

Dorn, Karl. At ATA Home Video, Harare, January 18, 2001.

Gondo, Nancy. At Joy TV offices, Harare, May 10, 2001.

Gunda, Tawanda. At a café, Harare, July 29, 2001.

Kanengoni, Alexander. At ZBC offices, Harare, March 21, 2001.

Kilalea, Rory. Via email, May 5 and 8, 2001.

Langeveldt, Edgar. Via Facebook messages, June 7–9, 2011.

Mahaka, Ben. Via email, June 12 and 28, 2011.

Maruma, Olley. At his home, Harare, April 5, 2001.

Maruta, Charity. At the International Video Fair offices, Harare, April 26, 2001.

Memper, Willy. At the Video Productions offices, Harare, January 31, 2001.

Msasa, Remias. At the ZBC offices, Harare, April 3, 2001.

Ndoro, Ogo S., and Tafataona Mahoso. At Harare Polytechnic, Department of Mass Communications, Harare, February 1, 2001.

Phiri, Leo. At a café, Avondale, Harare, May 13, 2001.

Riber, John. At the MFD offices, Harare, March 22, 2001.

Shoko, Arnold. At ZBC, Harare, April 19, 2001.

Sinclair, Ingrid. At her home office, Harare, April 25, 2001.

Spicer, Edwina. At her home office, Harare, February 7, 2001.

Tsodzo, Thompson. At his government office in the Mukwati Building, Harare, August 1, 2001.

Viriri, Itayi. At the offices of the *Standard,* Harare, March 6, 2011.

Zulu, Ben. At the African Script Development Fund offices, Harare, March 19, 2001.

Zvoma, Francis. At UNESCO Film and Video Training School, Harare, January 16, 2001.

News Sources

Agence France-Presse (Paris)

BBC News (London)

Business Day (Johannesburg)

CBC News (Toronto)

CNN.com (Atlanta)

Daily Nation (Nairobi)

Daily News (Harare)

Deutsche Press-Agentur (Hamburg)

Financial Gazette (Harare)

Herald (Harare)

Independent (London)

Inter Press Service Africa (Johannesburg)

Mail and Guardian (South Africa)

Miami Times (Miami)

Namibian (Windhoek)

New York Amsterdam News (New York)

New York Times (New York)

Panafrican News Agency (Dakar)

SAPA News Agency (Johannesburg)

Scotsman (Edinburgh)

Sunday Mail (Harare)

SW Radio Africa News (London)

Times Live (Johannesburg)

Washington Post (Washington, DC)

Washington Times (Washington, DC)

Zimbabwe Independent (Harare)

Zimbabwe Mail (London)

Zimbabwe Mirror (Harare)

Zimbabwe Standard (Harare)

Zimbo Jam (Harare)

This list has been compiled using a number of sources. It is not, I am sure, a complete list. In some cases I have had to make an educated guess as to whether the film was made after 1980. For example, if a film refers to Zimbabwe in its title, I assume it was made post-independence unless there is evidence to suggest otherwise. I have organized the list by genre, including feature films, shorts, docudramas, documentaries, television, and unknown genre. I have also included a list of films made by Zimbabweans outside of Zimbabwe and international productions made in Zimbabwe.

In addition to information regarding writer, producer, and director of each film, I have included references to filmmakers who were involved as cast or crew, if they are well known in Zimbabwe's film industry or if they participated in my research. Where I knew of the language or languages used in the film, I have included that information as well.

Feature Films

Big Time. Film. 2003. Olley Maruma, writer, producer and director. Stephen Chigorimbo, line producer. Moonlight Films. In English.

Bitter Pill. 2007. Ben Mahaka, director, editor, and actor. High definition. 75 mins.

Choice. 2008. Lawrence Mutasa, director and producer. Michael Zuze and Trevor Chidzodzo, writers. 120 mins.

Everyone's Child. 1996. Tsitsi Dangarembga, director. John Riber, Ben Zulu, and Jonny Persey, producers. Patrick Lindsell, cinematography. Media for Development Trust. In English; available in Shona dub. 90 mins. 35mm.

Evil in our Midst. 2006. Anopa Makaka, director. Assegai Promotions, Global Arts Trust and FIFFT. 84 mins.

Flame. 1996. Ingrid Sinclair, writer and director. Simon Bright and Joel Phiri, producers. Black and White Productions. In English. 90 mins. 35mm.

I Am the Future. 1993. Godwin Mawuru, director. Kubi Indi, producer. In English. 110 mins. 35mm.

I Want a Wedding Dress. 2008. Tsitsi Dangarembga, director. In Shona with English subtitles. 27 mins. Beta.

Jit. 92 mins. 1990. Michael Raeburn, director. Rory Kilalea, producer. John Riber, cameraman. Cast includes Dominic Mukavachuma and Oliver Mtukudzi. In English. 35mm and 16mm.

The Legend of the Sky Kingdom. 2002. Roger Hawkins, director. Phil Cunningham, writer. Sunrise. In English. 74 mins.

Matters of the Spirit. 2003. Norbert Fero, director. Ruth Nyilika, producer. Chameleon Films. Video.

More Time. 1993. Isaac Mabhikwa, director. John and Louise Riber, producers. Ben Zulu, executive producer. Media for Development Trust. In English. 90 mins. 35mm.

Neria. 1992. Godwin Mawuru, director. John Riber, producer. Tsitsi Dangarembga, story. Isaac Mabhikwa, first assistant director. Cast includes Jesesi Mungoshi and Oliver Mtukudzi. Media for Development Trust. In English.

Secrets. 2003. Ngugi wa Mirii, director. Visions of Africa.

Tanyaradzwa. 2005. Tawanda Gunda, writer and director. Dorothy Meck, producer. In Shona and English with English subtitles. 70 mins.

Yellow Card. 2000. John Riber, director. John Riber and Louise Riber, producers. John Riber and Andrew Whaley, screenplay. Heeten Bhagat, wardrobe. Charity Maruta, production manager. Cast includes Walter Muparutsa. Media for Development Trust. In English. 90 mins. 35mm.

Shorts (Short Fiction)

After the Wax. Chaz Mavinyane-Davis, director. 17 mins.

Ah! Footsek! 2000. Beta. Carine Tredgold and Heeten Bhagat, producers and directors. Masala Media. 17 mins.

Akakodzera Ndiani? 2008. Yeukai Ndarimani, director. Musha Langton Chari, writer. Short Film Project. In English and Shona, with English subtitles.

Another Day, Another Life. 6 mins.

The Assegai. 1982. Olley Maruma, director.

Bad Acting. 2000. Carine Tredgold and Heeten Bhagat, producers and directors. Masala Media. 15 mins. VHS.

Bero the Bad. Louis Nell, writer and producer. Production Services.

Big Balls. 2001. Heeten Bhagat, director. Carine Tredgold, producer. Cast includes Dominic Kanaventi. Masala Media. 4 mins.

Black Market. 1994. Tsitsi Dangarembga, director.

Blood Stones. 2004. Michele Mathison, director. Nakai Matema, producer. Engelbert Phiri and Tapiwa Kapuya, writers. Short Film Project. 8 mins.

Bloodshed—Ngozi. 1995. Amazement Mupotyo, producer and director. 70 mins. TV.

Bloodshed—Ngozi—Part One. 1994. Amazement Mupotyo, producer and director. In Shona. 90 mins. TV.

Checkmate. 2006. Itai Kakuwe, director. Patric Mahlasera, producer. Short Film Project. 23 mins.

Chinoziva Ivhu—Painting a Scene. 2000. Tawanda Gunda, writer and director. UNESCO-FVTP. In Shona with English subtitles. 14 mins.

Chocolate and Cheese. 2000. Carine Tredgold and Heeten Bhagat, producers and directors. Masala Media. Video.

Consequences. 1988. Olley Maruma, writer and director. John Riber, producer. Media for Development Trust, 1988. In English; available in Shona and Ndebele dub. 54 mins.

Cousin Brother. 2005. Comfort Mbofana, writer. Ben Mahaka, director. Nakai Matema, producer. Zimbabwe International Film Festival. 15 mins.

Danai. 2002. Rumbi Katedza, writer and director. Nakai Materma, producer. Zimbabwe International Film Festival and Ice Films. In English.

Dr. Juju. 2000. Roger Hawkins, director. Liam Forde, producer. 52 mins. VHS.

Dropout Hero. Trevor Mataruka, director. 101 mins. TV.

Eva Adaptor. 2007. Allan Muwani, director. Gerald Banda, writer. Nakai Matema, producer.

Face to Face. 2002. Godwin Mawuru, director. Davis Guzha, producer. Stephen Chifunyise, writer. Creative Native. 62 mins.

Greener Pastures. 2004. Mary Ann Mandishona, director. Nakai Matema, producer. Bongani Ngungama, writer. Zimbabwe. Short Film Project. 13 mins.

Grind Your Mind. Trevor Chidzodzo, director. Theressa Muchemwa, writer. Trevor Chidzodzo, Judy Stewart, and Theressa Muchemwa, producers. 8 mins.

Ha! . . . Inga. 2003. Cyrus Nhara, director. Nakai Matema, producer. Cast includes Marian Kunonga. Short Film Project. In Shona and English with English subtitles. 8 mins.

Heart of Hearts. 2008. Nakai Matema, director. Gerald Banda, writer. Joint Animators of Africa Group.

In the Upper Room. 1999. Celine Gilbert, producer and director. 34 mins. Beta.

Infantalia. 2 mins.

Insecurity Guard. 2007. Rumbi Katedza, director. Fides Fortuna Films, 2007. Super 16mm.

Kare Kare Zvako—Mother's Day. 2005. Tsitsi Dangarembga, director and writer. Rumbi Katedza, first assistant director. Nyerai Films, Pangolin Films, Mama Meida, and Women Filmmakers of Zimbabwe. In Shona with English and French subtitles. 30 mins.

Kukura Kuremerwa. 2005. Samuel Ziso Mudiwa, writer. Brighton Taziwa, director. Nakai Matema, producer. Short Film Project. 16 mins.

Kuzvipira. 2004. Ruvimbo Musariri, director. Nakai Matema, producer. Short Film Project. 14 mins.

The Last Picture. Farai Sevenzo, director. In Shona with English subtitles. 26 mins.

Mangwana. 1997. Manu Kurewa, director. In Shona with English subtitles. 26 mins.

Mbavha Gororo. 2008. Garikai Chawasarira, director and writer. Nakai Matema, producer.

Moon Creatures. 1999. Carine Tredgold and Heeten Bhagat, producers and directors. Masala Media. Video.

Musikana Wangu. 2004. Ashwin Sikireta, director. Nakai Matema, producer. Tafadzwa Njovana, writer. Short Film Project. 16 mins.

Musinsimuke. Elizabeth Markham, director and producer. In Tonga with English subtitles. 60 mins.

Mwanasikana. Ben Zulu, director. John Riber, producer. In Shona with English subtitles. 40 mins. 16mm.

Naka Yedu. 2006. Marion Kunonga, director. Nakai Matema, producer. 20 mins.

Ndaifara. 2006. Mercy Mafudze and Craig Kim, directors. Runyararo Katsande, writer. Rumbi Katedza, producer. 2006. Shona with English subtitles. 6 mins.

Ndodii? 2001. Farai Matambidzanwa, director. King Dube and Don Edkins, producers. Video Audio Network and Steps for the Future. In Shona with English subtitles. 13 mins.

Nhasi Tava neHama. 1993. Capricorn Video Unit, distributor. In Shona; available in English and Ndebele dubs. 45 mins. Video.

Nyaminyami. 2005. Blessing Magombo and Carl Joshua Ncube, writers. Carl Joshua Ncube, director. Nakai Matema, producer. Short Film Project. In English. Available online at http://www.youtube.com/watch?v=1MdUcIDsarY

Olu Olu—Water from the Well. 1999. Carine Tredgold and Heeten Bhagat, producers and directors. Masala Media. Video.

Oh Mama. 2006. Thelma Maduma, director. Rumbi Katedza, producer. In Ndebele with English subtitles. 7 mins.

On Death Bed. 2001. Norman Madavo, director. Nakai Matema, producer. Short Film Project. In English and Shona. 5 mins.

Pamvura (At the Water). 2005. Tsitsi Dangarembga, producer. Women Filmmakers of Zimbabwe and Nyerai Films. In Shona with English subtitles. 14 mins.

Passport to Kill. 1993. Tsitsi Dangarembga, director.

Peretera Maneta—Spell My Name. 2006. Tawanda Gunda Mupengo, director. Women Filmmakers of Zimbabwe and Nyerai Films. In Shona with English subtitles. 24 mins. Beta.

Phoenix Rising. 2006. Patience Tawengwa, director. 20 mins.

Portraits from Southern Africa. Capricorn Video Unit. In English. 12 mins.

Positive? 1999. Dylan Wilson-Max, director. Walter Maparutsa, writer. Godwin Mawuru, camera. Rooftop Promotions. 40 mins. Beta.

Positive Parenting. Tim Dehn and Roger Hawkins, directors and producers. In English. 35 mins.×8 episodes.

Pumpkin Graduate. 2008. Trevor Chidzodzo, director. Michael Zuze, writer. Trevor Chidzodzo and David Muponda, producers. 65 mins. Digital video.

The Return. 2007. Patience Tawengwa, director. Ruth Bingepinge, writer. Nakai Matema, producer. In English.

Revenge. 2004. Boarding Dzinotizei, director. 10 mins.

Riches. 2001. Ingrid Sinclair, director. Simon Bright, producer. Ernest Birdas, second assistant director. Heeten Bhagat, wardrobe. Zimmedia. In English. 26 mins. TV.

Rwendo. 1993. Farai Sevenzo, director. In Shona. 49 mins. 16mm.

Sara Saves Her Friend. Neil Mckee, director. In English. 15 mins.

Sara—The Special Gift. Neil Mckee, director. In English. 15 mins.

The Search. 2006. Brighton Tazarurwa, director. Nakai Matema, producer. 12 mins.

Shamwari. 1980. Clive Harding, director and producer. Cast includes John Indi, Steve Chigorimbo, Dominic Kanaventi, and Jane Kilalea. Released in the USA as *The Chain Gang Killings*. 93 mins.

Shungu. 2007. Brighton Tazarurwa, director. Tawanda Mutero Kanengoni, writer. Nakai Matema, producer. 17 mins.

Special Delivery. 2001. Tawanda Gunda Mupengo, director. Short Film Project.

Strange Bedfellows. Helge Skoog, director. Stephen Chifunyise, writer. 48 mins.

Super Patriots and Morons. Tawanda Gunda Mupengo, director. Raisdon Baya and Leonard Mutsa, writers. 52 mins.

Tamara's Diary. 2005. Musekiwa Samuriwo, writer. Nyaradzo Muchena, director. Short Film Project. 10 mins.

Tick Tock. Louis Nell, writer and producer. Production Services.

Tiraburu. 2004. Knox Chatiza, story. Elton Mjanana, writer. Marian Kunonga, director. Nakai Matema, producer. Short Film Project. In Shona with English subtitles. 15 mins.

Trapped. 2007. Rumbi Katedza, co-writer and co-director. Super 16mm.

The Truck Driver. 2007. Garikai Chawasarira, director and writer. Nakai Matema, producer.

Update. Edgar Langeveldt, director and writer.

Vengeance Is Mine. 2001. Tawanda Gunda Mupengo, director. UNESCO-ZFVTP.

Who's in Charge? 2003. Beautie Masvaure, director. Nakai Matema, producer. In English. 11 mins.

Zimbabwe, the Best Country. 2008. Patience Gamu Tawengwa, director. Nakai Matema, producer. 2008. In English. 16 mins.

Zvinhu Zvacho Izvi. 2003. Nocks Chatiza, writer. Marian Kunonga, director. Short Film Project. In Shona. 10 mins.

Docudramas

The Bin. 2007. Carlos Chima, director and writer. Nakai Matema, producer.

Burning Spears. Capricorn Video Productions. 7 mins.

Chickenfeed. 1988. Edwina Spicer, producer. 10 mins. Video.

Choose Freedom. Tim Dehn, director. Roger Hawkins, producer. 68 mins.

Domestic Violence. 1998. Edwina Spicer, producer. 17 mins. Video.

Fragile Riches. In English. 34 mins.

Hot Pursuit. 1995. Esko Metsola, producer and director. In English; available in Shona and Ndebele dubs. 13 mins. 16mm.

The Husband. 2006. Allan Muwani, director. Nakai Matema, producer. 10 mins.

The Money Grows in Trees. 1995. Esko Metsola, producer and director. In English; available in Shona and Ndebele dubs. 19 mins. 16mm.

Returning Takes Time. 1991. Rebecca Garrett, producer. Capricorn Video Unit. 19 mins. Video.

The Rope and Washer Pump. 1988. Edwina Spicer, producer. 20 mins. Video.

Where Have All the Trees Gone? 1995. Esko Metsola, producer and director. 13 mins. 16mm.

Your Child Too. 1991. Mark Kaplan and Farai Sevenzo, directors. Intermedia and Capricorn Video Unit. In English; available in Shona and Ndebele dubs. 34 mins. Educational drama.

Documentaries

Adventure Unlimited. Scripture Union Africa. 7×14 mins.

Africa's Publishing Shop Window: The 1992 Zimbabwe International Book Fair. 1992. Capricorn Video Unit.

After the Hunger and Drought. 1985. Olley Maruma, director and producer.

After War. Pre-1993. Chaz Maviyane-Davies, director.

AIDS in Industry. Pre-1993. In English; available in Shona dub.

AIDS—What Shall We Do? 1999. Ben Mahaka, writer and director. Simon Bright, producer. Zimmedia. 15 mins.

All Africa Council of Churches. 1992. Capricorn Video Unit. 41 mins.

Anna, Part One. 2001. Masala Media. 4 mins.

Arcadia. 2000. Mufadzi Nkomo, producer and director. 15 mins. Beta.

The Axe and the Tree: Zimbabwe's Legacy of Political Violence. 2004. Rumbi Katedza, director. International Center for Transitional Justice, Curious Pictures, and Pivot Pictures. In English and Shona with English subtitles.

Bernard Takawira: Negotiating with Stone. 1994. Olley Maruma, camera and commentary.

The Best of Their Ability. 1990. Edwina Spicer, producer. 20 mins. Video.

Beyond the Kitchen. 1995. Prudence Uriri, producer and director. ILO and Ministry of Public Service, Labour and Social Welfare.

Big House, Small House. 2010. Rumbi Katedza, co-writer/director. Action Institute for Environment, Health, and Development Communication, Theory X, and Soul City Institute for Health and Development Communication of South Africa. 24 mins.

The Bikita Experience. 2000. Ben Mahaka, writer and director. Simon Bright, producer. Zimmedia. 38 mins. Video.

Biko: Breaking the Silence. 1986. Edwina Spicer, director. Olley Maruma, scriptwriter, executive producer, and co-director. 50 mins. 16mm.

Bio-piracy: Who Owns Life? 2002. Ingrid Sinclair, director. Simon Bright, producer. Ben Mahaka, researcher and production manager. Zimmedia. 30 mins.

Bird from Another World. 1992. Ingrid Sinclair, producer. Zimmedia. 28 mins.

Blue Sky. 2000. Patrick Meunier, director. Pangolin Films, producer. 52 mins. Beta.

Bound to Strike Back. 1986. Capricorn Video Unit. 50 mins. Video.

Breaking the Barriers. 1993. Tsitsi Dangarembga, director.

Caught in the Crossfire. 1991. Edwina Spicer, producer. 90 mins. Video.

Census '92. 1992. Production Services.

Challenges in AIDS Counseling. 1991. Media for Development Trust.

Cherish Our Land. Louis Nell and Chaipachii Gwishiri, writers and producers.

Children's Parliament. 1992. Production Services.

Cholera. 18 mins. 1993. Conrad Gombakomba, producer and director. In English; available in Shona and Ndebele dubs. 16mm.

Continental Drift. 25 mins.

Corridors of Freedom. 1987. Simon Bright, director. Ingrid Sinclair, producer. 52 mins.

Cultural Heritage. 1990. Production Services.

Dance of Peace. 1994. Simon Bright, producer. Zimmedia. 52 mins. Video.

Dancing out of Tune. 1999. Video. Edwina Spicer, producer. 63 mins.

Danger Mines! End of an Era. 2000. Tsitsi Dangarembga, director. 40 mins.

Early Childhood Education. 1989. Production Services.

Education with Production / Musami School. 1985. New Directions. In English; available in Shona. 16mm.

ESAP. 1991. Lintas Advertising. In English; available in Shona dub. 16mm.

Facilitation—Techniques in Training. 1988. Godwin Mawuru, director. Media for Development Trust. Available in English, Shona, and Ndebele. 55 mins.

Farming Good Health. 1985. Talent Consortium.

Fatima Family Investments. 1992. Capricorn Video Unit. In English; available in Shona and Ndebele dubs. 28 mins.

Fifty Years On. Pre-1982. 16mm.

Fight against Poverty. 2006. Tinashe Maravanyika, director. Rumbi Katedza, producer. 7 mins.

Fraud and Corruption. Ben Zulu, director and producer. Media for Development Trust. 30 mins.

From Rhodesia to Zimbabwe. 1981. United Nations. 19 mins.

Fuel Diaries: Pushing Tin. 2000. Farai Mpfunya, director. UNESCO-FVTP. 12 mins.

The Future Is Green. 2010. Ben Mahaka, director. International Committee of the Red Cross.

Gender and Good Governance Conference—Harare, May 1998. 1998. Edwina Spicer, producer. 26 mins. Video.

Give Us Peace. 2002. Ingrid Sinclair, director. Simon Bright, producer.

A Golden Opportunity. 2001. Ben Mahaka, writer and director. Simon Bright, producer. Zimmedia. 25 mins. Video.

Growing Stronger. 2006. Tsitsi Dangarembga, director. Nyerai Films. In English and Shona. 30 mins. Beta.

Hama Ndedzedu: The Terminally Ill Are Our Family. 1992. Capricorn Video Unit. In Shona. 15 mins. Video.

Hard Earth: Land Rights in Zimbabwe. Mukundwa Francis Zvoma, director. Tsitsi Dangarembga and Olaf Koschke, producers. Nyerai Films. In Shona and English. 54 mins.

Harurwa. Cloud Marechera, director.

Heads and Tales. 7×1 minute. Video. Masala Media and SAfAIDS, 2002.

High Hopes. Tsitsi Dangarembga, director. Nyerai Films. In Shona, English, and German. 30 mins. Beta.

Home-Based Care at Murambinda Hospital. Pre-1996.

How to Vote. 1990. Production Services.

Hungry Minds. 2000. Ben Mahaka, producer, writer, and director. British Council. 8 mins.

Hupenyu Hwedu. Lata Murugan, director. Unifem Zimbabwe and Unesco Zimbabwe Film and Television Production Unit. In Shona and English. 25 mins.

Independence Day, 1986. 1986. Production Services. In English; available in Shona dub.

Ingwazi Jive. 2006. Abigail Mlotshwa, director. Rumbi Katedza, producer. Ndebele with English subtitles. 7 mins.

It's Not Easy. Pre-1993. In English; available in Shona dub.

Jazz Tales. 1997. Albert Chimedza, director.

Journey to the Ocean. 1999. Mosco Kamwendo, director. Jesesi Mungoshi, producer. In English. 52 mins. Beta.

Keep on Knocking. 1999. ZCTU, directors. Simon Bright, producer. Zimmedia. 2×30 mins.

Keeping a Live Voice. 1995. Video. Edwina Spicer, producer. 84 mins.

Know Your Snakes. 1982. Production Services. In English; available in Ndebele dub. 16mm.

Landscape of Memory: Soul in Torment. 1999. Prudence Uriri, director. Prudence Uriri and Don Edkins, producers. Capricorn Video Unit. 26 mins. Beta.

Learning Together. John Riber, producer and director. Media for Development Trust. 50 mins.

Life. Prudence Uriri, director. 26 mins.

The Life You Save. 1990. Edwina Spicer, producer. 20 mins. Video.

Lightning. Pre-1990. Production Services. In English; available in Shona dub. 16mm.

Limpopo Line. 1989. Ingrid Sinclair, director. Simon Bright, producer. Zimmedia. 40 mins. Video.

Lion in the Stones. 1993. Edwin Angless, director. ICE Media. 30 mins.

Listening for an Echo. 1994. Edwina Spicer, producer. 35 mins. Video.

Makoni Farm Worker Development Project. 1999. Ben Mahaka, producer, writer, and director. Simon Bright, producer. Zimmedia.

Makwaya—Dancing with Hope. 1993. Simon Bright, producer. Zimmedia. 15 mins. Video.

Male Motivation. 1987. In English; available in Shona and Ndebele dubs. Talent Consortium. Video.

Mashambanzou. 1993. Edwina Spicer, producer. In Shona. 20 mins. Video.

Mashonaland Central. 1991. Production Services.

Masiiwa: A Love for Life. 2005. Tawanda Gunda Mupengo, director and writer. Daves Guzha, producer. Creative Native. 55 mins.

Mazvikadei Dam. 1992. Production Services.

Mmabana: The Orphans and Vulnerable Children's Programme. 2002. Ben Mahaka, writer, director, and editor. W. K. Kellogg Foundation.

Mbira Music: Spirit of the People. 1990. Ingrid Sinclair and Kristina Tuura, directors. Simon Bright, producer. Zimmedia. 52 mins. Video.

Memory Work. 2006. Ben Mahaka, director and cameraman. Family AIDS Caring Trust.

Microscale Irrigation. 1988. Edwina Spicer, producer. 10 mins. Video.

More Freedom. Aaron Karnel and Kathryn Miles, directors. John Riber, producer. In English. 27 mins.

Moving On: The Hunger for Land in Zimbabwe. 1982. Peter Entell, producer, director, and editor. Belgium-Zimbabwe Friendship Association. 52 mins. TV.

Mubundu Muthihi Bhiko Llithithi: One Community, One Sweat. 1992. Rebecca Garrett, director. Capricorn Video Unit. 30 mins.

Mukai. 2000. Kenneth Ruchaka, director. UNESCO-FVTP. 24 mins.

Mukaka muMaruwa. 1988. Edwina Spicer, producer. In Shona; available in Ndebele dub. 15 mins. Video.

My Home Is the Street: Harare's Streetkids. Shuvai Chikombah, director and scriptwriter. C. Cyden Film Production. Shona with English subtitles. 30 mins.

My Land, My Life. 2002. Rehad Desai, director. Tendeka Matatu, producer. Ice Media / Uhuru Pictures. 52 mins.

Never the Same Again. 2000. Video. Edwina Spicer, producer. 90 mins.

The New Zimbabwe. Pre-1983. Mary Knoll. 28 mins.

Newspaper—Africa. 1984. Edwina Spicer, producer. 40 mins. Video.

Newsreel 1985. 1985. Production Services. In English; available in Shona dub. 16mm.

Night of the Orange Moon. Elizabeth Markham, director. In English. 45 mins.

No Need to Blame. 1993. Edwina Spicer, producer. In English; available in Shona dub. 35 mins. Video.

Oliver Mtukudzi. Pre-1985. Production Services. 16mm.

On the Border. 2000. Tsitsi Dangarembga, director. Olaf Koschke, producer. Nyerai Films. In Shona and English. 45 mins. Beta.

Only the Beginning: The Rise of Worker Cooperatives in Southern Africa. 1990. Capricorn Video Unit. 1:23 mins. and 2:20 mins. Video.

Opening of Parliament. 1989. Production Services.

Operation Nyaminyami. Louis Nell, writer and producer. Video.

Partnership against Poverty. 1991. Capricorn Video Unit. 22 mins. Video.

The Past Speaks. 1991. Production Services.

A Place for Everybody. 1992. Edwina Spicer, producer. Video.

Postcards from Zimbabwe. 2006. Rumbi Katedza, producer. 4×digital video shorts.

Power for Zimbabwe. Pre-1982. 16mm.

Prime Minister's Visit to Moteli Secondary School. Pre-1985. Production Services. In English; available in Shona dub. 16mm.

PTA at Five. 1990. Talent Consortium. Video.

PTA Trade Fair. 1990. Talent Consortium. Video.

Rambisai: Voices of the Ancestors. Pre-1993. Capricorn Video Unit.

Reading for Grade One. 2002. Ben Mahaka, co-writer, director, and editor. UNESCO International Institute for Capacity.

Reclaiming Our Heritage. 1992. Production Services.

Recollecting the African Identity. 2001. Prudence Uriri, director. Capricorn Video Unit. 3 episodes. 26 mins.

Reconciliation in Zimbabwe: The First Ten Years. 1990. Mark Kaplan, director. Capricorn Video Unit. 34 mins.

Robert Mugabe . . . What Happened? 2011. Simon Bright, director and co-writer. Ingrid Sinclair, co-writer. Michael Auret, producer. Zimmedia and Spier Films. 80 mins.

Ronald's Story. Pre-1993. In English; available in Ndebele dub.

Rural Library Projects: Matabeleland North Donkey Cart Library and Nyajezi Community Library, Nyanga. 2002. Ben Mahaka, cameraman. World Libraries Association.

Ruvheneko 2006. 2006. Ben Mahaka, writer, director, and editor. 20 mins.

SADCC: The First Decade. 1990. Edwina Spicer, producer. 50 mins. Video.

Sadza with Curry. 2001. Lata Murugan, director. Heeten Bhagat, camera. 60 mins. Video.

The Sanctions Debate. 1990. Simon Bright, producer. Zimmedia. 40 mins. Video.

Seeds of Choice. Pre-1993. Capricorn Video Unit.

Sex in the City: Harare. 2009. Ben Mahaka, director. Charity Maruta, producer. International Video Fair Trust. 58 mins.

Shanda. 2002. John and Louise Riber, directors. Features Oliver Mtukudzi. Cross Cultures. 70 mins.

Sharing Day. Tsitsi Dangarembga, director. Nyerai Films. In Shona with English subtitles. 17 mins. Beta.

Shungu. 2009. Saki Mafundikwa, director. Gandanga Media.

Sitting on a Fence. 2001. Tjenesani Ntungakwa, director. 21 mins.

The Smoke That Thunders. Pre-1993. Capricorn Video Unit.

Solar Cooker Project. 2000. Ben Mahaka, director. Rotary International.

Some Zimbabwe Birds. 16mm.

Sounds from the South. 1995. Simon Bright, producer. Zimmedia. 52 mins. Video.

Southern Africa—The Challenge Ahead. Louis Nell, writer and producer. Video.

Soviet Implosion. 2001. Martin Chiketa, director. 2 parts. Betacam SP/VHS.

Soya Bean Production. 1989. Talent Consortium. In English; available in Shona and Ndebele dubs. Video.

Spirit of Music. Tonderai Makaniwa, director and producer. 25 mins.

Take Care. Capricorn Video Unit. In English. 30 mins.

Take Charge. 1999. Ben Mahaka, producer, writer, and director. Simon Bright, producer. Zimmedia. 15 mins.

Talking with Stones. Mango Productions. 30 mins.

Talking Back. Capricorn Video Unit. 26 mins.

Tariro. 2009. Rumbi Katedza, co-director. 10 mins. Digital video.

Tariro—A Piece of Africa. 2008. Simbirirai Solomon Maramba, director. 3 mins.

The Test. 2004. Ben Mahaka, co-producer, director, and editor. International Video Fair.

That's Me. 2001. Sasha Wales-Smith, director. Jackie Cahi, producer. Patrick Lindsell, cinematographer. Pedro Pimenta, professional support. Pangolin Films. 7 mins.

Thicker than Water. 2001. Leo Phiri, director. Nakai Matema, producer. Short Film Project. 8 mins.

Tides of Gold. 1998. Ingrid Sinclair, director. Simon Bright, producer. Zimmedia. 52 mins. TV.

Together as One. 1991. Fiona Lloyd, director. Capricorn Video Unit and Kopinor, producers. 20 mins. Video.

Trade Fair Highlights. Pre-1988. Production Services. In English; available in Shona dub. 16mm.

Traditional Dancing. Pre-1985. Production Services. In English; available in Shona dub. 16mm.

Traditional Dancing and Music. 1987. In English; available in Shona dub. FilmCom. 16mm.

Traditional Midwives. 1988. Talent Consortium. Video.

Ungochani. 2010. Porcia Mudavanhu, director. 43 mins.

Voices of Change: Women of Zimbabwe. Joanna Burke, director and producer. English and Shona. 27 mins.

Vukani Mukai Awaken. 1990. Doe Myer, director. Ranche House College. In English. 27 mins. Video.

Water Harvesting. 15 mins.

What Is IYB? Improve Your Business—Practical Management for Small Business. 1995. John Riber, producer. 18 mins. Video.

When the Cows Come Home. Elizabeth Markham, director. 35 mins.

The Whisper: Gender and Development in Zimbabwe. Prudence Uriri, producer and director. Capricorn Video Unit. 57 mins. Video.

Wildlife, Relic of the Past or Resource of the Future? 1992. Simon Bright, producer. Zimmedia. 40 mins. Video.

Wither Zimbabwe? 1995. Tula Dhlamini, director, producer, and writer. ZBC. 20 mins. Broadcast.

Woman Cry. 1985. Talent Consortium. Video.

A Woman's Place. 2000. Ben Mahaka, director. Simon Bright, producer. Zimmedia. 30 mins. Video.

Women in Theatre: Discussion and Performance from Southern Africa. 1990. Mark Kaplan, director. 17 mins. Video.

Yellow Fever. 2000. Leo Phiri, director. In English. 30 mins.

Youth Brigades. Pre-1988. In English; available in Shona dub. 16mm.

Z.I.T.F. 1992. Production Services.

Zimbabwe AIDS Programme. Pre-1993.

Zimbabwe and the E.C. Co-operation in Action. Louis Nell, writer and producer.

Zimbabwe Arts in Action. Afro Eye Films. In English. 23 mins.

Zimbabwe at 10. 1990. Talent Consortium. Video.

Zimbabwe Countdown. 2003. Michael Raeburn, director. TACT productions and ARTE France. 52 mins.

Zimbabwe Township Music. 1992. Joyce Makwenda, producer and director. 55 mins.

Zimbabwe. Pre-1982. Ministry of Information. 35 mins. 16mm.

Zimbabwe: Our Heritage. Pre-1982. 20 mins. 16mm.

Zimbabwe: Something to Sing About. 1989. Mark Kaplan, director. Capricorn Video Unit. 25 mins. Video.

Zimbabwe's Precious Weed. Pre-1982. 16mm.

Zimbabwe's Wild Heritage. Pre-1982. 16mm.

ZNA/Deadliest. 1989. Production Services.

Zviripo Maererano neAIDS. 1994. Prudence Uriri, director. Capricorn Video Unit. In Shona. Video.

Zvitambo. 1999. Ben Mahaka, writer and director. Simon Bright, producer. Zimmedia. 20 mins.

Television

Studio 263. 2002–2009. Ben Mahaka, director of about three hundred episodes from February 2003 to January 2005, and actor from October 2002 to June 2005. ZBC and PSI.

Tsitsi. Thomas Danielsson, director. Sweriges Television. In Shona with English subtitles. 5×10 mins.

Waiters. 1999–2000. Marion Kunonga, Stephen Chigorimbo, Manu Kurewa, and Roy Barber, directors. Daves Guzha, producer. Creative Native. 26 mins.×26 episodes.

Who Is Next? Garikai Chawasarira, director. Arthur Chikuhwa, producer. 8 mins.×14 episodes.

Unknown Genre

Aweppa. 1989. Production Services.

Baby. 2003. Heeten Bhagat, director. Zimbabwe International Film Festival Trust. 10 mins.

Castle of Cards. 2008. Patience Tawengwa and Yeukai Ndarimani, directors. Paolo Genovesi and ZIFFT, producers. Zimbabwe International Film Festival Trust. In English and Shona with English subtitles. 20 mins.

Devera Ngwena. 1983. ZBC. In Shona. 16mm.

Faith in the Accordion. 2007. Patience Tawengwa, director. 7 mins.

I Am the Rape. 2007. Heeten Bhagat, producer, director, and editor.

Pfuma Yedu (Our Heritage). Pre-1993. African Sun.

The Tree Is Mine. 1987. Godwin Mawuru, director. Short film. [Short Film Project?]

Tormented Soul. 1990. Olley Maruma, producer and director.

The Value of the Beast. 1995. In English; available in Shona and Ndebele dubs. 26 mins.

Cinematic Texts Made by Zimbabweans outside of Zimbabwe

Asylum. 2007. Rumbi Katedza, writer and director. Made in the UK. 5 mins. Super 16mm.

Bana ba rona. 2004. Ben Mahaka, producer, director, and editor. W. K. Kellogg Foundation. Made in Zimbabwe, Botswana, and South Africa. Documentary.

Fools. 1997. Ramedan Suleman, director. Pedro Pimenta, executive producer. Ray Phiri, music. JBA Production. Made in South Africa. Feature.

From Subsistence to Success. 2003. Ben Mahaka, writer, director, and editor. W. K. Kellogg Foundation. Made in Swaziland, South Africa, Mozambique, Zimbabwe, and Zambia. Documentary.

High Density Solutions: Child Aid Doornkop. 2005. Ben Mahaka, co-cameraman, director, and editor. Made in South Africa. Documentary.

Home, Sweet Home. 1999. Michael Raeburn and Heidi Draper, directors. Mukuvisi Films. Made in France, USA, and Zimbabwe. In English. Documentary feature.

Jewels. 2008. Ben Mahaka, director, cameraman, and editor. Made in Mozambique. Documentary.

Leadership Development Program. 2008. Ben Mahaka, producer and director. W. K. Kellogg Foundation. Made in six countries. Documentary.

Love Abstract. 2008. Allan Muwani, director. Michael Banda, writer. Nakai Matema, producer.

A Matrix of Hope. 2003. Ben Mahaka, writer, director, and editor. W. K. Kellogg Foundation. Made in South Africa.

Police Beat. 2006. Charles Mudede, writer. Northwest Film Forum / WigglyWorld Studios. Made in the USA. In Wolof and English. 80 mins. Feature.

The Puppeteer. 1996. Tsitsi Dangarembga, writer and director. Nyerai Films.

Respect the Rules. 1998. Ben Mahaka, director. International Committee of the Red Cross. Made in Liberia. Video.

The Silent Fall. 2006. Roger Hawkins, director and writer. Eternal Pictures. Made in South Africa. 94 mins.

Surrender. 2001. Celine Gilbert, director. Richard Green and Associates and Zenj Films. Made in Zanzibar, Tanzania. In Swahili with English subtitles. Short fiction.

The Team. 2011. Rumbi Katedza, producer and director. Made in Kenya. In English and Sheng. TV series.

The Thuthuzela Care Centers. 2003. Ben Mahaka, writer, director, and editor. W. K. Kellogg Foundation. Made in South Africa. Documentary.

Victoria. 2005. Ben Mahaka, director, editor, and co-producer. International Video Fair. Made in Mozambique.

Women's Land Rights in Africa. 2008. Ben Mahaka, technical advisor, director, and editor. Action Aid International. Made in Kenya, Ethiopia, Zimbabwe, and the Democratic Republic of the Congo. Documentary.

International Productions Made in Zimbabwe

250: Zimbabwe's Remaining Rhinos. USA, 1995.

African Journey. Canada, 1990. Cast includes Jesesi Mungoshi. TV.

Alien from L.A. USA / South Africa, 1988.

Allan Quatermain and the City of Lost Gold. USA, 1987. Olley Maruma, assistant director. Rory Kilalea, production manager. Cast includes Rory Kilalea.

Aristotle's Plot. France / UK, 1996. Carine Tredgold, production design.

Bopha! USA, 1993.

Cry Freedom. USA, 1987. Olley Maruma, assistant director. Rory Kilalea, location man-
· ager. Steve Chigorimbo, co–first assistant director. Cast includes Andrew Whaley, Dominic Kanaventi, and Walter Muparutsa.

Dark River. USA, 1990. Isaac Mabhikwa, assistant director. TV.

Don't Forget Your Passport. USA, 1999. TV series.

A Dry White Season. USA, 1989. Olley Maruma, assistant director. Rory Kilalea, produc-tion manager. Isaac Mabhikwa, third assistant director. Cast includes Andrew Whaley.

A Far-off Place. USA, 1993. Carine Tredgold, art direction. Cast includes Isaac Mabhikwa and Andrew Whaley.

Forbidden Fruit. Germany, 2000.

A Fountain for Susan. Slovakia, 1999. Carine Tredgold, production design. Heeten Bhagat, costume design.

Going Bananas (aka *My African Adventure*). USA, 1988.

Heat of the Sun. UK / USA, 1999. TV miniseries.

High Explosive. USA, 2000. Norman Madawo, second assistant director. Karl Dorn, cast-ing. Cast includes Ernie Birdas and Edgar Langeveldt.

I Can Hear Zimbabwe Calling. Canada, 1981.

Itinéraire d'un enfant gâté. France / West Germany, 1988.

Jake Speed. USA, 1986.

King Solomon's Mines. USA, 1985. Rory Kilalea, production manager. Cast includes Isaac Mabhikwa and Andrew Whaley.

Kini and Adams. France / Burkina Faso, 1997. Leo Phiri, second assistant director. Heeten Bhagat, costumes.

Kongo. Belgium/Netherlands/Sweden, 1997. Leo Phiri, assistant director. Carine Tredgold, production design. TV miniseries.

The Lost World. Canada, 1992.

Lumumba. France/Belgium/Germany/Haiti, 2000. Charity Maruta, production manager. Carine Tredgold, art direction. Andrew Whaley, casting.

Le Maître des éléphants. France, 1995. Joel Phiri, executive producer.

Mal d'Africa. Italy, 1990. Steve Chigorimbo, unit production manager. Joel Phiri, production secretary. Patrick Lindsell, cinematography.

Mandela. UK/USA, 1987. Cast includes Andrew Whaley. TV.

The Midday Sun. Canada, 1989. Cast includes Godwin Mawuru and Dominic Kanaventi.

Mugabe and the White Man. 2009.

Music of the Spirits. Canada, 1989.

Mysterier fra fortiden. Norway, 2001. TV series.

Ngoma Buntibe, Music of the Valley Tonga. Canada, 2000.

Nicholas Mukomberanwa. Denmark, 2000. Mango Productions. Carola and Torben Rasmussen, directors and producers. In English. 29 mins.

Nkululeko Means Freedom. 1982.

Pamberi neZimbabwe. Mozambique/Angola, 1981.

Paul Simon, Graceland: The African Concert. USA, 1987. TV.

The Power of One. France/USA/Australia, 1992. Rory Kilalea, production supervisor. Cast includes Andrew Whaley, Dominic Kanaventi, Dominic Mukavachuma, and Joel Phiri.

Return to the Lost World. Canada, 1992.

Safari Hunter's Journal. USA, 2002. TV series.

Side by Side: Women against AIDS in Zimbabwe. 1994. Peter Davis, director. Harvey McKinnon, producer. In English; available in Shona and Ndebele dubs. 47 mins. 16mm.

Soldier, Soldier. UK, 1997. TV series (season 7).

Den Store fisketuren. Norway, 2002. TV series.

Tengenenge. Denmark, 1998. Carola and Torben Rasmussen, directors. Mango Productions. In English. 29 mins. Documentary.

Thinking about Africa. Germany/Italy, 1999. TV miniseries.

Transformation. Canada, 1984.

Tusks. USA, 1990.

Tuxedo Warrior. UK, 1982.

United Trash. Germany, 1996.

Victoria Falls. USA, 1999. Video.

Voting for Change. 7 min. 30 sec. 21 February 2005.

White Hunter, Black Heart. USA, 1990. Isaac Mabhikwa, third assistant director. Andrew
   Whaley, casting. Cast includes Andrew Whaley.

A World Apart. New Zealand / Great Britain/Zimbabwe, 1988. Isaac Mabhikwa, third
   assistant director. Rory Kilalea, location manager. Andrew Whaley, casting. Godwin
   Mawuru, camera trainee. Cast includes Andrew Whaley and Cont Mhlanga.

Zimbabwe—Respect for Africa. Austria, 1994. Music by Oliver Mtukudzi.

The Zimbabwean Marimba of Alport Mhlanga. Canada, 2000.

INDEX

KATRINA DALY THOMPSON is Associate Professor in the Department of Applied Linguistics at UCLA and an affiliated faculty member in African Studies, the Center for the Study of Women, and Islamic Studies. She specializes in critical approaches to African languages and identities with a focus on Zimbabwean and Tanzanian discourse.

Printed and bound by CPI Group (UK) Ltd, Croydon, CR0 4YY

13/04/2025

14656548-0001